THE CHANGING FAMILY

BETTY YORBURG

A Columbia Paperback $2.95

THE CHANGING
FAMILY

THE CHANGING FAMILY

FAMILY

BETTY YORBURG

COLUMBIA UNIVERSITY PRESS

NEW YORK AND LONDON

LIBRARY OF CONGRESS CATALOGING IN PUBLICATION DATA
Yorburg, Betty.
  The changing family.
  Includes bibliographical references.
  1. Family.   I.   Title.
HQ728.Y65   301.42   72-7284
ISBN 0-231-08317-3 Paperback
ISBN 0-231-03461-x Clothbound

To my mother

PREFACE

It has become very difficult, as scientific knowledge accumulates, to select, organize within a theoretical framework, and present to students and general readers a comprehensive, carefully documented synthesis of a specialized field of study. A short, general source that brings together the basic ideas of a sociological perspective on the family is rare in an age of specialization.

Introductory textbooks on this topic are usually massive and encyclopedic. They lack the integration of a unified theoretical perspective and they burden the student with summaries of countless numbers of discrete and fragmented studies whose relevance to major issues and problems in contemporary American family life is often lost. The statistics that are dutifully reported in such sources are soon outdated and even sooner forgotten.

Popularized accounts of topics such as divorce, marital infidelity, adolescence, and the so-called sexual revolution are interesting and relevant but may contain generalizations that are oversimplified or untrue. I feel it is an important obligation of social scientists to make available to others their information and their understanding of the nature of our society, carefully and in a language that communicates and does not alienate or frustrate the reader. Because my goal is a broad synthesis of accumulated social scientific knowledge about family life, rather than a detailed analysis, many subtleties and qualifications of the accumulated evidence will necessarily be omitted. I feel this is legitimate as long as the standard of accuracy is respected and pursued.

Whatever the variations in the structure and functioning of the family at different times and in different places, it is the basic group in human societies. It provides newborn members with their initial experiences of other human beings and with their earliest definitions of themselves and the world in which they are destined to live.

Knowledge of the roles people have played in family dramas through time and in different societies, the new roles and values that are emerging or becoming more widespread, and the societal sources and consequences of these changes in roles and values is a first step for individuals who want a basis for making choices in family life. We live in an era of unprecedented searching for meaning and guidance. Never before in Western societies has there been so much freedom for so many people to choose varying solutions to the problems of living.

Students in my classes at the City College of New York have been actively engaged in this search and in making these choices. Their refusal, at times, to accept the traditional wisdom has taught me, through the years, to avoid oversimplification, to go back, search the literature, reexamine the evidence on family life, and to come up with new answers—and new questions.

BETTY YORBURG

PELHAM MANOR, NEW YORK
OCTOBER, 1972

CONTENTS

THE CHANGING
FAMILY

1

THE SOCIOLOGICAL
MANDATE

We live in a time when traditional definitions of basic institutions are being challenged on the basis of new values or an insistence that old values be more effectively promoted. In family life, the formerly dominant values of loyalty, obligation, deference, and self-sacrifice are slowly being displaced by the standards of happiness, companionship, erotic gratification for both sexes, equalitarianism, and compatibility, at least among the upper strata in advanced industrial countries.

Critical questioning of social institutions arises whenever there is mobility: geographic (within and between countries), social (up and down the class structure), and psychological (in aspirations and expectations). In modern societies, these kinds of mobility are commonplace. Social change in the material and nonmaterial spheres is accelerated by developments in mass transportation and mass communication. Few men can avoid contact with innovations in thought and technology. The remotest village is subject to the step-by-step invasion of modernity: first a road and a bus, then an electric power line, then a radio and, finally, television and the world.

Human expectations not only rise, they change or they become confused and uncertain. Modern man has far greater possibilities of choice and an unprecedented availability of alternatives. He tends to feel, increasingly, that these choices should be made rationally, although he may have grave doubts that this is possible.

In the past, during periods of rapid change and the breakdown of tradition, philosophers and religious and political leaders have arisen to provide alternatives and solutions. In modern times, social scientists are drawn into this arena, willingly or not. They are the new and the latest men of knowledge. In the history of science, objects farthest removed from man (the stars and the planets) were the first to be withdrawn from the realm of the sacred and deemed proper subjects for study by the experimental method. The social sciences were the last to achieve the status of sciences, as man himself came to be viewed as a legitimate object of empirical study and rational direction. The social scientist's first task is to provide accurate and reliable information about social life—information based on observation rather than on impression or speculation. The existence of social science is a logical outgrowth of trends toward secularism and rationalism in urban, industrial societies.

Religion declines in its influence over mens' minds as the realm of the uncertain, the unknown, and the uncontrollable is narrowed by developments in science and technology. The belief in supernatural intervention in the affairs of man is supplanted, increasingly, by rational techniques for influencing these affairs. Ancient man prayed to the gods for safe passage across the seas; modern man invents radar. Faith and fatalism decline together—often to be replaced by pessimism, however, in recent times.

Rationalism implies a means-ends orientation in action: a choice of the most efficient, logically and empirically effective means for realizing one's goals. Values determine goals. They are the intervening variables that may deflect behavior from the most rational course. Force, for example, or violence, may apparently be the most effective means for obtaining or maintaining power in a particular situation. Yet it is rejected as a possible means where humanistic values prevail.

Rationalism and secularism proceed together to change the quality of human life. To give an example from contemporary social life, traditional prescriptions and proscriptions regarding sexual behavior are losing their hold on the populace. Empirical investigations such as those by William Masters and Virginia Johnson seek new prescriptions for sexual behavior on the basis of the scientific study of the sexual act.[1] For these scientists, the criteria for determining sexual norms are rational rather than traditional or religious. The new value underlying their investigations is sexual gratification, a value that is consistent with the general decline in self-denial that is characteristic of economies of abundance.

This is only one example of the widespread tendency in modern societies to seek guidance for personal behavior from experts and from scientific knowledge. The psychotherapist, the doctor, and the social worker replace the priest, faithhealer, and extended family as a source of advice, support, and designs for living as individuals become increasingly aware of the possibility of scrutinizing and directing their personal destinies.

THE ROLE OF SOCIOLOGY

August Comte, the French social philosopher who gave sociology its name in the 1830s, defined the field as the scientific study of society. Its purpose, as in all science, was "to know in order to predict, to predict in order to control." When it is human beings, groups, or societies that one is studying, questions of control become problematic, however. Control involves a conception of desired goals. These goals depend, ultimately, on the values in a society and, in complex, heterogeneous societies, many values are not shared by all. The implementation of goals will depend on the allocation of societal resources by national decision-makers, based on priorities as they define them. Sociologists have been involved in these decisions only as consultants. They can, however, provide the raw material of rational choices. Their work can provide new awareness, understanding, implications, and guidelines for action.

Knowledge and understanding of human needs and how they are met or not met in various social settings can provide a basis for action in social affairs, just as basic research in medicine guides the clinician's work and research in physics is applied by engineers. Inequalities in the distribution of power, privilege, and prestige and the existence of values and emotions in human beings preclude the possibility of unbridled human engineering, but the analogy is not entirely false.

Sociological knowledge cannot directly help people in making choices. Sociology is an academic discipline, not a helping profession. It can, however, help individuals understand that what they may regard as unique and idiosyncratic frustrations or dissatisfactions are a common response to common life conditions. Men and women are rarely alone in their suffering. Accurate information about society may reveal this fact to them in a way that is more convincing, if not more dramatic, than the novel or play.

Human beings, particularly in individualistic America, dislike being pegged and classified. Nevertheless, there are certain regularities, recurrences, and typicalities in social life, and while there are few unvarying laws, generalizations can be made. Individuals can make choices more critically if they are more aware of the constraints, the necessities, and the accidents of human existence.

Sociological knowledge can also dispel common-sense notions that are untrue. Impressions are often a poor guide to what is actually going on in large, complex, rapidly changing societies. In the area of family study, for example, sociologists have found that the majority of women who are poor and who are the mothers of large families do not and have not wanted more children than do middle-class mothers; [2] that parents with large numbers of children (more than three) report themselves as less happily married than those with small families; [3] that children of middle-class working mothers are not more apt to be delinquent and do not have a higher incidence of neurotic symptoms than children of the same class whose mothers are available full-time at home. [4]

Contradictory adages such as "absence makes the heart grow fonder" and "out of sight, out of mind" are both part of the folk wisdom of our society. Which is true? Only the painstaking, careful accumulation of evidence on the effects of separation on marriage can answer this question. The answer is that both are true. Short separations make the heart grow fonder; prolonged separations wreck marriages. Societal myths, whatever their reason for being, crumble in the face of hard evidence and an open mind.

THEORETICAL MODELS

Philosophers, theologians, and literary observers have speculated about the family, its problems, and its destiny since the beginning of written history. Empirical study of the family, however, did not begin until the last half of the nineteenth century, in Europe. The incentive was the need for reform that followed the confusion and disorganization of the Industrial Revolution: the increase in poverty, prostitution, illegitimacy and divorce and the rise of movements to emancipate serfs, slaves, workers, and women.

The methods used in these early studies were 1) historical: the collection and interpretation of data about the family from surviving firsthand accounts; 2) survey research: the use of questionnaires and interviews to obtain contemporary information about the family; and 3) case study and participant observation: the intensive study of families in nonliterate societies by anthropologists who lived in the community or with the families they studied, and by others who collected and wrote down life histories of members of families.

These methods, increasingly refined to eliminate sources of bias and error, are still the most popular in family study. Modern technology, the use of the tape recorder and video type for data collecting and computers for data processing, for example, has improved the accuracy and the efficiency of both qualitative and quantitative social scientific research on the family.

The experimental method, in which the family is observed in interaction for a limited period of time, under controlled conditions and for the purpose of measuring one or more variables (dominance of one member over others, communication patterns or decision-making processes, for example), is an additional method that has become popular, particularly since World War II.[5]

Science requires not only the accumulation of facts but the interpretation and explanation of these facts. This is what sociological theory is: statements of association or cause and effect that attempt to answer the question "Why?" These statements are formulated with the help of concepts and models. All sciences have models, or frames of reference, that define their particular windows on the world. These models consist of concepts that sensitize and guide observation, although they may also distort it. Concepts are useful for summarizing complex aspects of reality in shorthand words or phrases, or for pointing to aspects not readily apparent to the casual observer.

In the Marxian economic model of society, for example, class struggle, exploitation, and alienation (currently) are central concepts. The concept of class is a succinct way of referring to a large category of people who possess similar amounts of prestige, power, and wealth. Given this concept of class, one can investigate the relationship between class and values, class and childrearing practices, and class and personality. Without this concept, a possible source of explanation of similarities or typical differences that exist in a society would be unavailable.

Fads in the use of specific concepts in the social sciences reflect the changing salience of one or another aspect of social or personal reality during any particular historical era. Currently, the concepts of alienation, identity, power structure, charisma, counterculture, and life style have moved out of the realm of social science analysis and become adopted as part of the popular culture.

For interpreting patterns in social life, models that have been influential in the social sciences are Social Darwinism,[6] Marxism,[7] and functionalism.[8] Other models that have been employed particularly in studying the family have been useful primarily as frameworks for organizing descriptive information about the family.[9] The family life-cycle model, for example, helps organize research data about the family on a time perspective from the beginning of a marriage to its usual end, with the death of one of the marital partners. The concepts in this model, concepts such as development or developmental tasks, are descriptive rather than explanatory. They provide rubrics under which can be placed descriptions of role changes that occur in typical family groups through time, as children are born, or leave after growing up, and as parents age. The model has little usefulness in explaining long-range historical changes in family functioning, however.

Social Darwinism, Marxism, and functionalism, on the other hand, contain concepts that embody built-in explanatory assumptions. In the Marxist model of society, for example, class struggle is a concept that has intrinsic explanatory implications. It is a principle that is used to explain the course of world history. Class, on the other hand, is a descriptive concept.

One model may include both types of concepts. In the psychoanalytic model, the concept of psychosexual stages is descriptive and helps organize data on personality development. The concepts of the unconscious and oedipal conflict, however, are more closely linked to the problem of interpreting and explaining the particular course that personality development takes in an individual's life history.

SOCIAL DARWINISM

Social Darwinism is an evolutionary model of societies and social change that had its greatest vogue at the end of the nineteenth century. Darwin's theory of organic evolution, in which the human species was the ultimate product of a unilinear and progressive selective breeding process, was applied to different populations and to the evolution of their technologies and cultures. The principles of struggle for survival, natural selection, and survival of the fittest (fittest in terms of intellectual superiority) were used to explain the inequality of nations, races, classes, and men and women. The assumption was that those at the top belong there by virtue of better biological endowment—opportunity and other factors having always been equal.

Historically, the model served to legitimate colonialism and as an argument against social reform, since helping the poor was regarded as preserving the unfit. The white, upper-class, nineteenth-century Englishman and his culture were believed to be the ultimate among men, the final and perfected products of selective evolution. Proponents of Social Darwinism chose from history examples that supported their thesis of biological determinism and ignored contradictory evidence. Institutions such as the family were believed to have evolved to monogamy as the highest and most perfect form. The many examples of monogamy within nonliterate, tribal societies, among the African Bushmen, for example, were ignored. The notion of white supremacy prevailed despite the fact that the founders of

Western civilization, the ancient Egyptians, were a mixture of Negro and Semitic stocks and the Dark Ages in Europe coexisted with a period of high technological development in China.

Social Darwinism still persists in some quarters to explain or justify differences in the power and privileges of human beings. A recent example of this kind of thinking is the assertion by Arthur Jensen that American Negroes have different, genetically determined, "patterns of ability" than do whites.[10] Specifically, he refers to a lesser, hereditary capacity for problem-solving behavior and abstract reasoning. He argues, further, that while "the full range of human talents is represented in all the major races of man, Negroes brought here as slaves were selected for docility and strength rather than mental ability and that through selective mating the mental qualities never had a chance to flourish." [11] He raises the spectre, once again, of the "dysgenic effects" on the total population (the lowering of the general I.Q. level) of current welfare practices, which presumably preserve the genetically unfit.[12]

Few would argue that there is a hereditary component in the intelligence of individuals. Studies of identical twins reared apart and numerous other kinds of studies support this argument. But there is no evidence to support the claim of genetically determined intellectual abilities specific to particular classes, nations, races, or sexes.

In Jensen's argument about the American Negro, a major untested and questionable assumption is that docility and strength (traits which presumably characterized the initial slave population) are negatively associated with hereditary intelligence. Furthermore, despite the tendency in human societies for intraracial selective mating, the initial gene pool of blacks in this country has not been preserved in pristine state. Physical anthropologists estimate that at least 70 percent of American blacks have some degree of white ancestry in their biological makeup at this point in history.

Social Darwinism and biological determinism are generally discredited now as explanatory principles. Divorced of these aspects, the evolutionary model, however, does have explanatory value when applied to technological development and the accumulation of scientific knowledge in human societies. This particular application of the model, in fact, has become quite popular recently in sociology and anthropology in interpreting the course of world history.[13]

In the realm of technological change, there has been a trend toward the selecting out of more efficient and effective techniques in controlling the material environment. Historically, there has been a progressive harnessing of energy (from animal power, to steam power, to electric power, to atomic power) and a progressive accumulation of scientific knowledge. Some societies have remained stationary, in this respect, for thousands of years, while others have regressed technologically, usually after a defeat in war. Ancient Rome is an example; its defeat ushered in the technologically impoverished Dark Ages in Europe. Still others have skipped stages, sometimes quite dramatically, by borrowing techniques, skills, and knowledge from more technologically advanced societies (cultural diffusion). The rapid industrialization of the Soviet Union and China are examples.

While the claim that differential technological development is related to different genetic endowments of human population cannot be supported, the theory of a progressive and cumulative trend in technological development as a basic factor in the course of world history does seem to be generally valid, despite some fluctuations.

We cannot claim, however, that there has been a concomitant evolutionary pattern in other institutional spheres and in the realm of attitudes and values and in the nonmaterial quality of human life. It would be very difficult to support the argument that there has been a progressive trend toward greater happiness, justice, morality, and freedom in human societies.

Patterns of killing and maiming have changed: cannibalism, scalping, and human sacrifice have been supplanted by more efficient techniques such as atomic and germ warfare, gas chambers, and napalm. But hatred and cruelty persist. We no longer hang people for stealing a loaf of bread, but justice tends to favor the rich and the powerful. To my knowledge, no upper-class person has ever been executed for murder in this country, despite convictions of murder in this class.

Of human happiness we have no measure. The sources and reasons for unhappiness have changed, but discontent, hopelessness, and despair persist. The misery that results from actual material deprivation has declined in industrial societies, but the misery that results from rising but unfulfilled expectations has increased. The mass media, particularly television, have whetted appetites in a way that far surpasses the unaided imagination of isolated man in traditional societies.

Freedom has increased in the sense that a greater number of people have more choice in determining their individual or collective destinies, but again this is largely a matter of class. The poor have few choices. And involuntary servitude persists in prisons, mental hospitals and in other, less obviously restrictive, groups and organizations.

Technological change, however, up to the point of achieving the possibility of destroying the world by contamination, nuclear warfare, or overpopulation (science and technology keep people alive) has been progressively adaptive—if we use the standards of the sources of energy available and the accumulation of empirical knowledge about the world.

It is this aspect of the evolutionary model, the progressive development of science and technology, that I will use as a criterion for constructing a typology of human societies in chapter 3. On the basis of this typology, it is possible to understand and explain many of the patterns and the changes in family functioning and family values that have taken place during the span of human history.

THE MARXIAN MODEL

A second model of society that has been influential in the social sciences, particularly in Europe, is the Marxian model. This model is commonly referred to as "economic determinism" by American social scientists. The Marxian model is one in which the basic conflicts, the distribution of power, and the nature and course of social change in societies are believed to be a product of the economic organization of the society: the way in which goods and services are produced and distributed. Conflict, between societies, classes, and men and women, based on differences in the control of productive property and in economic interests, is seen as the motive force in human history. The means of production in this model refers to technology and economic resources; the relations of production refers to the class system. Social change rests, ultimately, on technological development and the conflicts that derive from differences in property and power.

This explanatory model, relabeled the conflict theory model and modified to give weight to other, noneconomic factors in determining social order and social change, has grown more popular in America, now that protest movements, the rediscovery of poverty, and economic and political crisis are prominent features of the American scene. The emphasis on conflict (class struggle in the original model, plus race and generational conflict currently) now seems more appropriate to an explanation of American social reality than it did during the period of enforced consensus in the silent 1950s. There are fads in models as well as in concepts that reflect societal needs for explanation at any particular time.

The Marxian model, particularly as it promotes sensitivity to the relationship between economic resources and power, can be very helpful in interpreting changes in family life historically. Authority relations within the family, between husband and wife, and parent and child, are and have been strongly influenced by economic factors. The changing status of women during the course of world history has been closely tied to their changing economic roles in various types of societies, as we will see. And, at any particular time in history, including the present, the economic class location of families in a society is a very important factor in understanding typical differences in family values and family relationships in that society.

FUNCTIONALISM

Functionalism is a model of society that derives its name from the fact that the existence of any phenomenon in a society (the family, social inequality, the incest taboo, for example) is explained in terms of the function it performs for the maintenance or preservation of the society. The primary focus is on the needs of society rather than on the needs of man: "The basic function fulfilled by the family in all societies is the replacement of dying members." [14] The function of social stratification, the system of unequal rewards and privileges in a society, is to "insure that the most important positions are conscientiously filled by the most qualified persons," and the occupations that are most highly rewarded in terms of income, status, and power are those that "(a) have the greatest importance for society, and (b) require the greatest amount of training or talent." [15] The poor have

higher rates of illegitimacy because: "The society will be less concerned with illegitimacy when it occurs in the lower social ranks,
since their position is less significant for the larger social structure." [16]
Incest taboos are found in every society known to man because:
"They force the young in each generation to leave the nuclear family
in order to find mates. Therefore the society is made more cohesive,
for many links are forged between families that might otherwise turn
inward on themselves." [17] Individual needs are subordinated to social
needs as explanatory principles in the functionalist model.

Functionalists view society as a system of interrelated parts. Change
in one part of the system reverberates throughout the system and
reacts back on the original source of change. Change may occur independently in any major institutional sector: the family, the economy,
religion, or government. Causation, therefore, is multiple and recipro-
cal. This is a major difference in the model from that of the biological and economic determinisms of Social Darwinism and Marxian
economics.

Social integration, according to the functionalist model, is based on
consensus within the society, particularly about values. Economic interdependence as a source of integration is deemphasized,[18] as is the
integration forced by political repression. The role of technological and
economic factors in social change is minimized. Ideological factors
(attitudes, values, and beliefs) are given greater weight relatively.[19]
The concepts of power and conflict are usually omitted from the
model.[20] In this respect functionalism is antithetical to the Marxian
model of society. Functionalists, guided by their model, see order and
consensus wherever they look; Marxists, surveying the same social ter-
rain, see disorder and conflict.

Some functionalists posit a state of equilibrium as the natural tendency of society, corresponding to the tendency toward homeostasis in
the human body. They interpret permanence and change in a society
in terms of this standard. They believe that social phenomena that are
dysfunctional for the equilibrium of the system are cast out or modified and absorbed into the system, just as antibodies engulf and absorb
invading microbes in the human body. Thus, revolution leads to
counterrevolution and back again to a new stability in the interrelationships between the major institutions in a society. Attitudes and

values tend to catch up with changes in the economy, for example, that disrupt social order. The dislocations, disorganization, and suffering caused by the Industrial Revolution are eventually balanced by changes in attitudes and values that lead to a redefinition of the role of government. The government, in socialist or welfare state form, takes over the functions that the lord of the manor or the extended family no longer performs. Equilibrium is thus restored by virtue of society's inherent self-regulating propensity and, in the process, all major interdependent institutions in the society are transformed.

An objection that has been leveled against the equilibrium aspect of the model is that the assumption of an inherent tendency for societies to restore themselves can be used as an argument against deliberate reform and planned social change. Furthermore, when societies are in constant change, how does one determine disequilibrium or restored equilibrium?

Probably most contemporary American sociologists, including ones who would not identify themselves as functionalists, would accept the multiple causation aspect of the model.[21] They view the major institutions in society as interdependent and interrelated. They accept the importance of consensus in society but feel that conflict, dissent, and disequilibrium are equally intrinsic to social life. They feel that both aspects of social reality must be accounted for in an adequate general description or model of society.[22]

Many sociologists also feel that both individual and social needs must be taken into account in analyzing social phenomena. The family does function to replace dying members of society, but this is not necessarily a more basic function than that of providing for the needs of newborn members of the society. Both are equally valid reasons for the universal existence of family groups.

The incest taboo controls envy, conflict, and hostility within the family, thus facilitating the fulfillment of family members' needs for love and security. These needs are as important as the need of society for links between family groups. Actually, marriage in urban, industrial society no longer fulfills the function of forging links between families and promoting social cohesiveness. Marriages based on personal preference and relatively free choice and resulting in independent, mobile, increasingly isolated nuclear families are not the alliances between families that they once were when families, particularly in the upper strata, arranged the marriages of their offspring.

THE CONFLICT THEORY MODEL

Sociologists who do not accept the consensus and equilibrium aspects of the functionalist model, but who are not traditional Marxists are usually identified as conflict theorists. For them conflict and instability is the natural state of society. Many conflict theorists, unlike orthodox Marxists, however, give independent weight to ideological factors in explaining social change and historical trends and, as I pointed out earlier, they focus on other sources of societal conflict in addition to economic differences.

Traditional China provides an excellent example of the role of ideology in the history of a particular society. This country possessed many of the technological preconditions of industrialization. China was the first country to invent paper, printing, gunpowder, and the compass. While learning was valued, however, the memorizing of the Confucian classics and the mastery of over 2,000 elaborate ideographs was not the kind of learning that promoted technological development. On the other hand, the ideology of the socialist revolution in China has inspired rapid and far-reaching technological change in that country in recent times.

It is now generally accepted that attitudes, beliefs, and values in a society can have a powerful inhibiting or accelerating effect on technological and economic change. In this country the American Dream (the belief that success is open to everyone and failure is a matter of individual responsibility) has probably been a very important factor in the slow pace of economic reform in America relative to certain other, European, democracies.

Ideologies affect the rate of technological development and the content of technological innovation. A country that values power very highly is more likely to develop rockets and atomic bombs, assuming it has the necessary technological base, than a country that values peace at almost any price. But other factors such as cultural diffusion, climate and geography, war and conquest are also significant in determining the direction and pace of technological development.

Ideological factors become more important in affecting social change in industrial societies. The concentration of power at the top levels of government (whether these governments are democratic, oligarchic, or totalitarian), the existence of mass communication and mass transportation (which makes it easier to reach and control all citizens in a society), and the fact of far greater economic and technological resources at the command of political leaders, all combine to enhance the role of ideology in social change. It is much easier now for rulers to implement decisions based on ideological principles than it has been in the past.

The conflict model has become more popular in American sociology recently, while functionalism is declining in influence. This reflects the greater prominence of overt conflict in American society in the last few years. Either model used alone can distort the observation of social reality, and yet both have a handle on the truth. The distortion in the functionalist model lies in its overemphasis on consensus in societies. This stems, in part, from the fact that the model was originally formulated on the basis of data from nonliterate tribal societies, where overt conflict is usually repressed and where consensus regarding values *is* almost universal: class, ethnic, racial, or religious minorities are rare in these societies; there is little contact with widely differing societies and alternative values, and the rate of social change is slow. In this type of society, one can speak of a social phenomenon as being functional (advantageous) for the entire society because interests within different segments of the society are not that dissimilar.

In complex heterogeneous societies, however, one has to ask, functional for whom? The social stratification system of these societies is not equally functional for all segments of the society, for example. There are stumbling blocks to perfectly free social mobility: parents pave the way for their children, if they can. Unequal rewards of power and privilege may be functional for the society in that it motivates people to train for more difficult occupations, but stratification systems are, nevertheless, most functional for those at the top, and their children, regardless of their occupations.

Social inequality also has dysfunctional as well as functional consequences for the preservation and the maintenance of the entire society. The anthropological evidence points quite clearly to the fact that there was much less conflict, envy, and hostility within simple

hunting and gathering societies, where differences in economic rewards and privileges were minimal. The sharing of the catch and the
kill was common; it was essential for survival. Warfare and pronounced intragroup hostility arose with the development of technology and the accumulation of an economic surplus in societies that was
not shared equally by all.

Of course there are other factors involved in the close association
between warfare and more advanced technological development.
When hunting declines and other animals are no longer the object of
the kill, man's aggressive impulses, everpresent because frustration is
everpresent, become directed toward his fellow man, stranger and
friend, particularly if the culture does not prohibit this or if social
control mechanisms are ineffective.

The conflict theory model may also distort the perception of its
users so that the actual or potential conflict in a society is overesti-
mated. Affluence diminishes the intensity of intra- and intergroup
conflict. This is the rationale behind reforms from above instituted by
the ruling strata in industrial societies. Cooptation usually works. And
conflict between groups also has positive functions in that it promotes
solidarity within groups. The civil rights movement has enhanced
feelings of a common identity and a common heritage among American blacks, as revealed in the concept of "soul" and in the borrowing
of family appelations such as "brother" and "sister" to refer to fellow
blacks.

MODELS AND INTERPRETATIONS

Proponents of any one of the three original models—Social
Darwinism, Marxism, and functionalism—have interpreted the
same social fact differently. An illustration will make clear how models shape scientific investigation and explanation.

Male superiority within the family, in prestige, authority, and privilege, is a fact of life in almost all known societies. No valid instances
of true matriarchal societies have been known to exist. Even in societies where descent is calculated through the female line (matrilineal

descent) and where newly married couples reside with the wife's relatives (matrilocal residence) authority in the family is usually invested with the wife's male relatives. How can this be explained?

Herbert Spencer, probably the most prominent of the late nineteenth-century Social Darwinists, attributed male superiority to the biological fact that women experience "a somewhat earlier arrest of individual evolution . . . necessitated by the reservation of vital power to meet the cost of reproduction." The "mental manifestations" of the earlier biological maturation of women are a "perceptible falling-short in those two faculties, intellectual and emotional, which are the latest products of human evolution—the power of abstract reasoning and that most abstract of the emotions, the sentiment of justice—the sentiment that regulates conduct irrespective of personal attachments and the likes or dislikes felt for individuals." [23]

Functionalists would interpret male superiority in terms of the more significant roles males play in the fulfillment of certain societal needs: their greater role in war, in government, in the economy, and in ceremonials that promote social solidarity and cohesiveness, particularly in nonliterate tribal societies and in preindustrial societies. "The higher the skill and responsibility of the man in extrafamilial roles, the greater is the effective superiority of the husband in family decision-making." [24] Notice that this explanation rests on the male's level of skill and responsibility within the society and not necessarily on his relationship to the economic means of production.

According to the Marxian model, male superiority arises and is related to the control of private property by males. Frederick Engels traced an evolutionary pattern in husband-wife relationships within the family that corresponded to stages of economic development. The earliest stages, where property was communal, were characterized by the relatively unstable matings of group marriage or temporary "pairings." Women's status was not only high, it was "supreme" because the natural fathers of offspring could not be identified and because in the communistic household "the administration of the household entrusted to women was just as much a public function, a socially necessary industry, as the procuring of food by men." [25] We see here, incidentally, in the relating of the performance of "socially necessary" functions to the status of women, that this model overlaps with the functionalist model. The reverse is also true. Functionalists find it difficult to avoid economic interpretations in their analyses.

Engels claimed that women lost their high status after the domestication of animals took place. This led to the accumulation of wealth and the concept, as well as the fact, of private property. Men, who commanded the herds, took command in the home also: "women were stripped of their dignity, enslaved, [and became] the tools of men's lust and mere machines for the generation of children." Monogamy arose, not as the "fruit" of individual "sex love" but to guarantee the transmission of the patriarch's property to his legitimate heirs.[26] Monogamy [fidelity], however, applied, in fact, only to the female. The double standard, prostitution, and hetaerism coexisted with monogamy as a consequence of the male's superior power and privilege. The class struggle and oppression in the wider society were paralleled by the struggle between man and wife in the home.

Engels' solution was the abolishment of private productive property and the employment of women in public industry. The necessity of women to surrender themselves for money would then disappear, prostitution would be abolished, and effective monogamy for both sexes would become a reality. Economic considerations would become irrelevant to the choice of a marriage partner, since both mates would be economically independent. There would be no motive for marriage except mutual inclination and women would not tolerate infidelity because they would no longer be dependent upon their husbands for the support of themselves and their children.[27]

Ample support can be mustered for Engels' thesis of a relationship between economic factors and free choice in courtship and marriage. Historically, the higher the class, the more likely that marriages were arranged by the two families involved, with or without the consent of the prospective married pair. On the other hand, in traditional rural China, marriage was decided and arranged by family elders even among the poorest peasants. In this kind of situation, where there was strong emphasis on family lineage and filial piety (respect and deference for elders) and where the young couple lived with the husband's parents, the personality of the prospective bride and likelihood that she would be compatible with her new relatives (particularly her mother-in-law) was an important reason for the control of marriage by parents. Economic factors were not absent, however, since likely prospects were also evaluated in terms of qualities such as physical strength, good health, and ability to work hard.

In contemporary American society, while romantic love is the culturally prescribed basis for marriage, economic factors are obviously not irrelevant since the great majority of marriages take place between people of the same class. The effect of economic factors on marital choices may be indirect, however, since class is associated with attitudes, values, education, and other factors that affect feelings of mutual attraction.

While male superiority is a pattern in all societies, the degree of difference between men and women in power and privilege tends to decline considerably in urban, industrial society. How would the three models be used to explain the rising status of women in highly industrialized societies?

Social Darwinism cannot explain this fact since genetic endowment does not change rapidly enough to account for a change that has occurred largely within the past fifty years.

An explanation in terms of economic factors seems to be more valid. While women have always contributed to the economic resources of the family, converting raw materials brought in by males into prepared food, clothing, and household necessities, they did not have an independent source of income until they went out of the home to work in factories, offices, stores, and schools. The patriarch thereby lost exclusive control over the distribution of goods and services within the family and at least one important source of his authority.

Functionalists would explain the rising status of women in terms of their greater participation in nonfamilial activities that are important to the maintenance of society in modern times, particularly in the economy, but also in recreation (entertainment) and, to a much lesser extent, in government and the military. This, in turn, has to be explained (and, in fact, it has been explained) by functionalists largely in terms of changes in the economy and technology since the Industrial Revolution that have propelled women into gainful employment outside of the home to a greater extent in modern times.[28]

Assuming complete interchangeability in work roles, the male unemployment rate does not begin to approach the number of women in the work force. If all women were removed from the economy, the vast, interdependent network of exchange of goods and services that characterizes industrialized economies would collapse.

The proposition that control over economic resources has an important relationship to authority within the home is supported by recent American survey research evidence. Married women who work have more authority in decision-making processes within the family; the longer thay have worked the greater is their authority; and, the higher the prestige and income of their occupation, relative to their husband's, the greater is their authority in the home.[29]

Studies in less highly industrialized societies, however, such as Greece, Yugoslavia, and France, indicate that where strong patriarchal values persist, they diminish the effects of gainful employment of the wife on family authority patterns. The cultural context has to be taken into account in making this kind of generalization. The trend, nevertheless, is clearly in the direction of greater female participation in the work force, particularly during certain periods of the life cycle, and concomitantly greater legal, political, personal, and marital autonomy in modern societies.[30]

Further evidence on this point is provided by anthropological accounts of horticultural societies. These societies have the technique of plant cultivation, but they do not have the plough and they do not have the knowledge of irrigation, fertilization, and crop rotation techniques. In horticultural societies, women are more apt to do the planting and harvesting, since the gardens and small fields are close enough to the hearth so that this kind of work does not interfere with the childbearing and childrearing obligations of women.

Matrilineal and matrilocal types of family organization, in which women have somewhat higher status and authority, are most likely to be found in this type of society. In advanced agricultural societies and in industrial societies, where men make the most significant direct contribution to the subsistence needs of the family, these patterns of family organization are rare.

The responsibility in providing for the economic resources of the family is not the only basis for authority in the family, however.

Other resources, such as intelligence, education, good health, and physical strength that may be differently distributed between husband and wife also affect authority patterns within the home. In the working class, for example, in all countries for which there is evidence, including the United States, male authority may take the form of dominance based on greater physical strength. Wife beating may maintain the husband's authority even where the wife works and has an independent source of income.

A SOCIOLOGICAL PERSPECTIVE

An analysis of family life through time and across cultures that claims to present an adequate sociological perspective should attempt to integrate the valid aspects of the evolutionary, functionalist, and the Marxist or conflict theory models. These models are useful to an understanding of the problems of order and change in total societies—the macrosocial level of analysis. They can help answer questions such as why some societies have developed along certain economic, political, and cultural directions while others have had very different histories.

THE ROLE THEORY MODEL

A sociological perspective should also provide a framework that joins the individual in the family group to the larger society and the culture. The role theory model provides this missing link. This model applies to the microsocial level of analysis—interpretations of interactional processes within social groups.

I pointed out earlier that theory is concerned with explanations, with answering questions of *why* certain phenomena exist or occur. At a more concrete and more readily observable level, theory is also concerned with explaining *how* certain events unfold and take place. The role theory model is useful in answering these kinds of questions. The focus is on the socialization process, the learning of roles or scripts that establish the guidelines for behavior in various kinds of group situations, including the family.

This model contains fewer untested or untestable assumptions than

Social Darwinism, Marxism, or functionalism. It falls within the realm of what Robert Merton called "theories of the middle range." [31] Sociologists and social psychologists who employ role theory in their research do not answer ultimate questions about social life and social change, but they tread on less controversial ground because their propositions are more closely tied to the collection of data.

It is easier to be convincing when one is explaining how and why the process of socialization leads to typical values that underlie behavior, obedience to authority in the working class, for example, than to support the thesis that there is a tendency toward equilibrium in societies.

The basic assumptions of the role theory model are that human beings are not born with hereditary instincts that determine complex, goal-oriented behavior and that they behave in patterned and more or less predictable ways because they learn roles that define mutual expectations in typical and recurring social relationships.

While few social scientists would quarrel with the first assumption, there are some who would claim that there are very few specific and widely agreed upon roles or scripts associated with any particular status, that most individuals improvise behavior from cues in actual interactional settings and that they establish patterns in succeeding interactions on the basis of trial and error rather than preconceived expectations. The other extreme allows for very little deviation from what is believed to be rather rigid and unmanipulable role prescriptions for most social relationships. Reality, in urban, industrial societies, lies somewhere in between.

Role is a central concept in sociology, comparable to the concept of personality in psychology. Humans are social animals. In most of their relationships with other human beings they act from the vantage point of a widely recognized position or status, such as mother, doctor, president, or priest and they tend to abide by internalized roles, or guides to behavior that are defined as appropriate to these statuses by the groups with whom they identify or who control them. These scripts or roles specify the rights and obligations of individuals occupying a particular status. They consist of prescriptions for behavior, thought, and emotion that are normatively regulated.

College students, for example, entering a classroom for the first time at the beginning of a semester, follow certain general guidelines and fulfill generally agreed upon expectations in their behavior. They take a seat. They listen and take notes. They raise their hands if they wish to speak. They use formal and polite rather than personal or intimate language. And they leave usually after a prescribed period of time. Variations of ritual are permissable, but usually within explicitly defined and permitted limits.

Professors also fulfill mutual expectations in their role performance. If they stood on their heads instead of lecturing, the situation would become unstructured, unpredictable, and even ludicrous. Much humor, incidentally, stems from the unexpected stepping out of the role by participants in a familiar and recurring social situation. Laughter is often the response to incongruous role behavior which startles, confuses, or embarrasses partners in typical social interactions.

The culture, the basic heritage of knowledge, skills, attitudes, values, and behavioral norms, that is transmitted to almost all members of a society defines the limits, the extremes of variation in role prescriptions. No infant in American society is weaned at the age of six or swaddled from head to toe at birth, although these patterns have been typical in other societies. Most Americans speak English, learn to read and write, and value achievement.

Within the broad limits set by the culture, subcultures contain typical variations in role definitions and specify somewhat different intellectual, emotional, and behavioral requirements for playing the same roles. The major subcultures in urban, industrial societies are those associated with class, national origin, race, religion, sex, and age. Subcultural variations in role prescriptions reflect differences in life circumstances of various segments of the society. As these life circumstances change, and they change very rapidly in highly industrialized societies, roles change. The lag between traditional role conceptions and changed social conditions accounts for much confusion and suffering in society today, particularly in family life.

In addition to subcultural differences in role definitions, the ultimate source of variation in role performance, and a very important one, lies in individual differences in intelligence, constitution, and temperament, and in unique life experiences. For this reason, no two individuals occupying the same status will play the prescribed role exactly the same way, although certain similarities based on cultural and subcultural dictates and common life experiences will be obvious. In any stable group such as a particular family, furthermore, the adaptive process consists of a selective screening of cultural role prescriptions modified by individual proclivity which results in a special variant of the cultural or subcultural ideal.[32] Any single family, in other words, has a collective life of its own, typical and yet not quite typical, especially in rapidly changing, complex societies. Here we will be concerned with the typical, as culturally prescribed, but the uniqueness of individuals and families is important to acknowledge and to bear in mind.

Role conceptions, embodied in the culture and subculture, are transmitted by socializing agents, authority figures, and peers, who use positive and negative sanctions to ensure conformity to their norms. Negative sanctions range from teasing, ridicule, and gossip, to expression of disapproval, withdrawal of love, physical punishment, imprisonment, expulsion, and death. Positive sanctions are rewards such as friendship, affection, love, promotions, honors, fame, and fortune that reinforce the pursuit of goals by socially prescribed means.

Conformity, which reflects the effectiveness of social control, varies with the strength and nature of group ties. Where group ties are weak, individuals are less bound by group norms, a condition characterized by Emile Durkheim as "anomie." [33] Juvenile delinquency and crime are practically unknown in nonliterate societies because group ties are strong and all encompassing. Social control in these societies is highly effective, and most people play their roles willingly and with commitment.

The degree of commitment to the role or conflict about the role will be affected not only by the unique experiences of socialization that the individual has undergone but by social, structural and cultural factors such as rates of social change, ambiguities, contradictions, modifications, and alternatives in prevailing role definitions, the availability of facilities for adequate role performance (class factors, for example), and the strength of group integration, solidarity, and social control.

In highly industrialized societies, these factors associated with role performance become increasingly problematic, adversely affecting the commitment to prescribed roles and, also, the achievement of identity. Role and feelings of identity are closely related, but not necessarily congruent. At deeper psychological levels, confusion and doubt about identity may coexist with apparent certainty and confidence at the behavioral level. The two tend to coincide, however, and the prevailing social context affects the degree to which they do coincide. Widespread problems of identity in society are a modern phenomenon related to inconsistent, confused, and outmoded role definitions.

Not all role learning takes place within groups, although much of it does. Individuals may pick up attitudes, values, and behavior patterns in anticipation of a status that they hope to achieve. An example is the deliberate adoption of ways of dressing, speaking, and acting that are customary in the middle class by members of the working class who are hoping to rise in the class structure. This kind of socialization may not occur as a result of group interaction since the individual's group memberships are usually limited to his own class. He will use models that are not in his immediate environment, such as those in the mass media, to learn the appropriate norms of the middle-class status that he wants to achieve. In traditional societies, the learning of role behavior from individuals outside of the primary group is rare, as is mobility, for that matter.

Not all roles are subculturally defined. Within group situations informal roles arise during the process of interaction: the role of joker, opinion leader, scapegoat, or taskmaster, for example. These roles fall within the broader limits of cultural role prescriptions. Personality factors determine who will adopt them.

Another point that should be stressed, because it is often overlooked, is that the role theory model is concerned with normatively regulated thought and emotion as well as behavior. The knowledge and skills appropriate to the role of the professional, for example, are sanctioned by degree and licensing requirements established by authorities in the field of specialization. In addition, however, professional associations sanction attitudes and emotions insofar as these are embodied in conceptions of professional ethics.

At the level of the emotions, psychological traits, the use of particular mechanisms of defense such as repression, projection, or displacement, for example, may be characteristic of large numbers of people who are similarly located in the society and who undergo certain common socializing experiences. In the lower working class particularly, to give an example, subcultural definitions of the masculine role prescribe toughness, stoicism, and denial and avoidance of introspection in the face of anxiety and threat. Confiding and the communication of intimate inner feelings is regarded as effeminate and sissified. It is for this reason that working-class men experience great difficulty in responding successfully to the conventional insight therapy relationship: mutual trust, emotional openness, and empathy are curbed in their relationships with other important figures in their lives.

Emotional defenses are psychological traits, but they are sociological facts if they are a result of socialization into subcultural values and norms—in this case, those defining the masculine role and male identity.

A few examples, at this point, of how the status of class, race, sex, or age is associated with varying role definitions and how these definitions are related to past, current, or changing life circumstances will be helpful.

CLASS. Class has very significant implications for role conceptions and performance. Class will determine, to a large extent, the amount of autonomy the individual has, in all areas of life—particularly on the job. The factory worker has much less control over his work conditions than the professional. It is understandable, then, that working-class parents in bringing up their children are more apt to emphasize obedience to authority and conformity to externally imposed rules than middle-class parents.[34] In the middle class, parents stress general principles rather than obedience to discrete rules in their disciplinary efforts. The child is allowed and encouraged to make more independent decisions. This finding holds true cross-nationally, wherever studies on childrearing practices have been conducted, despite differences in history, culture, or stage of economic development in different societies.

RACE. Race, particularly when combined with class, is another very significant determinant of role expectations and behavior. The lower working-class Negro male, for example, in the face of discrimination and constraints on occupational achievement, tends to define his male status in terms of his sexual rather than his economic behavior. For many working-class black males, sexual conquest rather than occupational success confirms masculinity.[35] This is a common response to common class- and race-determined life experiences of economic deprivation. It is also a product of socialization into subcultural expectations and definitions of black maleness that have been passed on from generation to generation among the black poor in this country since the days of slavery.

The two sets of factors, economic and subcultural, reinforce each other. Spurred by the civil rights movement, current efforts to break the cycle, starting with changes in economic opportunity, have not yet had a widespread impact on prevailing subcultural definitions of black maleness within the poorest stratum of blacks in this country.

SEX. Sex is a locating factor in society that also has typical consequences for role behavior regardless of class or race. Research on children in America and cross-culturally (including nonliterate tribal societies) indicates that females in almost all societies are more nurturing, passive, and affiliative and less self-reliant, independent, and achievement-oriented than males.[36] The difference in role expectations for females are clearly related to the traditional domestic and childrearing obligations of women.

Changes in these obligations, primarily reflecting changing needs of the economy, are resulting in changing role definitions. The upper strata in highly industrialized societies are beginning to deemphasize differences between male and female children in expectations for achievement, aggressiveness, and self-reliance, although significant differences still persist.

The women's liberation movement, calling for a redefinition of women's roles in which there would be a minimum of difference in role prescriptions for males and females, is a reflection of changing conditions that have called into question certain traditional definitions of the female role. Women are being equally educated with men, up to the level of higher education, and are expected to compete equally in the school situation. The percentage of women in the labor force is growing constantly, although the percentage in the top professions is declining, for the moment.

In industrialized countries, women must work outside of the home in order to make a direct economic contribution to the family's finances. This conflicts with homemaking and childrearing obligations. Grandparents and other relatives are not as available as they once were to take over these functions. The failure of government to provide day care services for children of working mothers may be viewed as a cultural lag, comparable to previous government delays, historically, to provide the services that the extended family is no longer able to provide for its geographically, socially, and psychologically mobile members.

In this country today, class determines certain typical variations in the way the role of wife and mother is conceived and played out. The traditional role is played by a majority of married women. Basic variations in the role, however, are found in the subcultures of the very rich and the very poor, and a newly emerging variation is becoming more frequent in the college educated, urban upper middle class.[37]

The traditional obligations of married women in Western society have been to bear and raise children, to perform household chores, to subordinate self-interests to the needs of other family members, to accept the authority of the husband in decision-making, particularly that having to do with finances, and to stay close to home, at least while the children are young. They have had the right to support, security, alimony in the event of divorce, loyalty and fidelity of the husband, and gratitude from the husband and children for nurturing services performed.

This picture is obviously an idealized one, but it represents the conception of their role that guides the behavior of a majority of wives and mothers in the middle economic levels of American society today. Companionship between husband and wife is not a crucial requirement of the role, although it is becoming more important as affluence, leisure, and the life-span increase.

Among the very rich, the companionship aspect of the role is most highly valued and is vital to the relationship between husband and wife. Empty shell marriages may persist for the sake of preserving family alliances and fortunes but no longer is this a generally accepted duty in this particular stratum of society. Divorces are becoming more frequent.

The wife is not obliged to perform domestic service in the home other than as manager of paid surrogates who do the actual cooking, cleaning, marketing, errand running, and childrearing. She has a great deal of freedom, travels widely, and is provided with ample funds for dress, recreatiónal, and educational activities. She shares recreational and other pleasures with her husband. Her obligations are to maintain her beauty and intellectual alertness and to provide stimulating companionship and erotic gratification for her husband. The rights to fidelity and marital security rest on these obligations rather than on domestic services or childrearing.

Among the very poor in our society, married women have few rights and, often, both domestic and economic obligations. Security, support, or alimony in the event of divorce are not expected, primarily because they are not economically possible. Illegitimacy and common law marriages are a reflection of this fact. Companionship is almost nonexistent, as this is a luxury of time and economics. Contrary to stereotyped notions of impulsiveness and abandon among the poor, the wife is less apt than her middle- and upper-class counterparts to enjoy sex and tends to regard it as a duty and a chore.[38] Survival is the crucial value in these family relationships.

Among urban professionals, particularly, a new role is emerging in which the wife is employed full time and contributes as a partner, according to her ability, to the economic assets of the family. She may not perform homemaking or childrearing services, which are sometimes delegated to others. She shares authority more equally with the husband. Companionship is highly valued but is limited by time-consuming career obligations. In the event of divorce, the wife receives partial child support but not alimony. The marital tie rests on mutual compatibility rather than the symbiotic nurturing functions of the wife and economic functions of the husband.

Reality is, of course, more complex than the foregoing descriptions. Many women combine several aspects of the major kinds of roles, shift from one type of role to another in different stages of their life cycle, or experience conflict between their role conceptions and their husbands' expectations.

AGE AND GENERATION. Age and generation are also associated with typical role definitions ("Act your age!") which, in turn, are a reflection of life circumstances and the biology of the life cycle.

Among the elderly and retired, differences in economic and family functions of men and women are minimal. Males tend to become more nurturing, passive, and affiliative and women more assertive and less self-sacrificing.[39] Both exhibit a turning inward, a greater introspection, and a greater preoccupation with naricissistic needs, which reflects the decreased social interaction and failing bodily functions of old age.

The disengagement that the elderly experience is "functional" for the society; [40] it permits the younger generation to take over with a minimum amount of disruption in ongoing societal activities. It is culturally defined as appropriate in industrialized societies, as indicated by compulsory retirement laws. On the other hand, disengagement on the part of the aged is usually not voluntary, except in the case of physical disability. The wealthy and the powerful, who have more choice in these matters, do not willingly withdraw from the arenas of power and action. This is a prime source of conflict between the generations and, as recent evidence indicates, has apparently always been so.[41]

THE SOCIALIZATION PROCESS

We are now in a position to understand how role theory provides the bridge between the individual, the culture, and the society. Cultural and subcultural role prescriptions are transmitted to the individual through the process of socialization.

The socialization process begins at birth and continues until death, or as long as the individual takes on new statuses. Newborn infants must learn the role that is defined by their family and their society as appropriate to their status. They learn a series of obligations: to sleep at night and through the night, to prefer certain kinds and quantities of food and to eat them at specified times and, eventually, to eliminate in places set aside for this purpose. They also learn to express emotions in certain ways, or to repress them, typically, that is, and depending ultimately on cultural and subcultural definitions. The basic right that is granted to them, at least ideally, is to receive help from their families in the task of achieving physical, emotional, and intellectual maturity.

The final status that individuals occupy is that of a dying member of the society. Even this role is normatively regulated, more or less explicitly. Individuals learn the role that is defined as appropriate by their culture and subculture, and they usually play it out that way, whatever their feelings of estrangement or doubt.[42]

The role theory model is applicable to an understanding of group interaction and individual personality development and change, particularly as this is typical in certain segments of the society. It is not adequate for understanding overall social change in the total society. It is at this level that the evolutionary, functionalist, and conflict theory models, corrected for distortions, can be helpful with the never-ending challenges of explanation in social life. One hundred years from now these models will probably be obsolete in certain respects. One hundred years ago, Social Darwinism was ascendant in the budding social sciences. We work with what we have.

AN INTEGRATED APPROACH

The four current models in contemporary sociology—evolutionary, functionalist, conflict, and role theory—can be integrated hierarchically in terms of the time and space perspectives that they encompass. The technological evolution model is basic and subsumes the other models in that it applies to total societies and change through time in these societies.

The functionalist model is subsumed by the evolutionary model in that it is cross-sectional and provides a view of society at a particular time, the emphasis being on ideology, consensus, and institutional interrelationships. The conflict model parallels the functionalist model but the focus is on conflict, dissent, and the sources of social change (largely economic and political) within societies.

Like the evolutionary model, the conflict model has a longitudinal dimension, but technological development underlies and limits, if it does not determine forms of economic and other institutions in societies. In societies where science and technology are rudimentary, the accumulation of an economic surplus is impossible, as are large populations, permanent settlements, highly developed occupational specialization, an economic class structure, a leisure class, literacy, a money

economy, government, military, religious, and educational bureaucracies, and innumerable other preconditions of the complex and complicated life.

The conflict model is a valuable interpretative tool in that it focuses attention on the effects of heterogeneity, stratification and
differences in interests, values, and life circumstances on family roles
and relationships. The current interest in poverty and its effects on
minority group family life is an example of an important area of
study where this model is frequently employed.

The role theory model has the most limited scope of the four, since
it is restricted to the group and group interaction. Changes in the
content of roles, particularly in values and attitudes, are usually related to changes in social conditions, primarily in the technological
and economic spheres. It is important to remember, however, that
processes of change are multidirectional. The individual, furthermore,
is the ultimate source of social change, particularly in industrial societies, where social constraints are more tenuous and alternatives are
more readily available. Individuals are not blank tablets; they act
back on the group and the society. Acting singly, or with others, they
innovate, discover, and dissent; they accept or reject the accumulated
heritage of their culture and other cultures.

Most sociologists have used one or another of the four explanatory
models in attempting to answer the basic questions of order and
change within the family and within the wider society. They have
added or dropped concepts according to the accumulated state of
knowledge in the field and changing explanatory needs. The concept
of adolescence, for example, was not to be found in the nineteenth
century in most societies. Adolescence was not a problem at that time
and there was no word to refer to this particular social status.

At the present time, American sociologists have become more interested in macrosocial analysis, after decades of being the vanguard
in international sociology in the analysis of small group processes and
quantitative survey research. This shift probably reflects the increasing
concern among intellectuals for the overall fate of American society.
America has lost its privileged status of splendid geographic isolation
now that atomic weapons and rockets are a part of the arsenal of war.
In the past, European sociologists, whose countries have been less pro-

tected by the accident of geography, have been more concerned with questions of the fate of total societies through time.

Sociologists, in their study of family structure and functioning, have viewed the family as the prototype of all social groups, its members functioning according to culturally prescribed roles that have varied with time and place. They have studied the process of internalization of roles, which results in the kind of order and predictable family relationships that is based on consensus and complementarity of expectations between family members. They have also studied the societal sources and consequences of conflict and change in family roles that results in new expectations and new definitions of mutual rights and obligations in family life.

In employing the concepts of the role theory model, my emphasis here will be on the content of family roles—on culturally and subculturally defined values, attitudes, beliefs, and norms that have guided and prescribed family relationships—and how and why these have changed. Lack of space and lack of adequate historical data preclude an analysis of the interactional processes of socialization at the microsocial level—the actual learning of roles in family groups, historically and at present.

In the realm of values, the major change in family roles, historically, has been the shift from the traditional values of familism, fatalism, ethnocentrism, religiosity, and authoritarianism to the modern, urban values of individualism, achievement motivation, tolerance, rationalism and secularism, and equalitarianism in family role conceptions and relationships. This will become clear as my story of the family unfolds.

The family has usually been viewed by social scientists as an object of social change, or as a facilitator or inhibiter of certain kinds of change. It has rarely been viewed as a source of social change. Changes in other areas, in technology and the economy, particularly, usually impinge on the family. The family is the preserver of tradition. In revolutionary situations, the family is attacked by new regimes that attempt to remove the young as much as possible from its influence. Cultural innovators, whether they be criminals, scientific or artistic geniuses, or leaders of social movements, usually have weak family ties.

After approximately one hundred years of social scientific study of the family, certain basic sociological generalizations about family life have been accumulated. I would like to bring together some of these ideas and interpretations, beginning with the distant past, concentrating on the complex and constantly changing present, particularly in America, and venturing into the future, guardedly, but with some confidence that certain current trends are likely to continue, given the continuation of human societies.

Human biology underlies and sets certain limits to the possible range of variation in family roles. The question, even, of the continued existence of a family group in human societies is tied to the basic biological needs and characteristics of the human animal. We begin, then, with a discussion of these biological traits as they affect family functioning and as they bear on the question of the necessity of the family as a human group and as a social institution.

2

THE BIOLOGICAL
BASE

Family life has not been characterized by an infinite diversity in human societies. Certain patterns are universal and while certain other patterns appear to be arbitrary, they are rarely unique. Before we can go on to a discussion of the range of variation in culturally defined family roles, it is important to try to determine to what extent these definitions have been arbitrary and to what extent particular patterns in family life are inevitable by virtue of the imperatives of human biology.

A discussion of the biological traits of man, as distinct from other animals, is a logical preliminary to an analysis of past and present family functioning. We can then have some idea of the possible limits to variation in family roles and the essences and accidents in the role of wife and mother, husband and father, daughter and sister, and son and brother.

THE PROBLEM OF DEFINITION

We begin by defining the family. To do this is not easy if we include all types of families that have existed in all societies. If we define the family according to specific functions it performs, economic functions for example, we can define away the family in certain societies where the family does not have the responsibility of providing for the economic needs of its offspring, at least not directly. The Israeli kibbutz is an example of this kind of community.

If we define the family as a group that fulfills certain needs of the society, to replace dying members, for example, it is possible to argue that other kinds of groups could perform these functions just as well, perhaps even better. One would then be unable to explain why the family, in terms of the definitions of the people involved, is universal.[1] If we focus on the universal biologically based needs of human beings, however, I think we have a sounder basis for describing what families do and have done, and incidentally for predicting whether they will continue to exist, regardless of how they may change.

The family is a group that engages in socially sanctioned, enduring, and exclusive relationships that are based on marriage, descent, adoption, or mutual definition (as in common law marriages). I include common law relationships in this definition because participants define themselves as families, because the phenomenon is relatively frequent among the poor in certain industrializing and industrialized countries, and because these relationships are socially sanctioned within some subcultures of poverty: they are recognized and defined as acceptable, although not preferable.

The family group has functioned everywhere and at all times, more or less adequately and more or less completely, to fulfill the emotional, physical, and intellectual needs of its members. These responsibilities may be shared with other nonfamily members of a society to a varying extent at different times and in different places. The family, however, has the initial responsibility because it is usually there first. Different cultures may emphasize one or another of the basic human needs in prescribing family roles as, for example, in the Israeli kibbutz where the satisfaction of emotional needs is the paramount value underlying family relationships. No society, however, has ever assigned the satisfaction of the basic emotional needs of all of its members to nonfamily groups.

The basic family group is the nuclear family, which consists of husband, wife, and unmarried children. In most, if not all societies, this unit is recognized, but it has greater or less autonomy in different societies. It has less autonomy if it is part of an extended or consanguineal structure, such as a clan or tribe. The extended structure, actually, is any form in which members of several nuclear families defer to the same authority, exchange essential services, and either live together in the same household or close enough to be in daily contact. Polygamous forms are extended families in which the husband has several wives at one time (polygyny) or, and this is rare but not unheard of, the wife has several husbands (polyandry).

THE HUMAN ANIMAL

Why have all societies recognized family groups and regulated the behavior of family members? The ultimate answers lie in the biological characteristics of the human animal.

Man has the longest life-span of any animal, with the exception of the tortoise. He requires more intensive care and a longer period of nurturing than other animals. Full physical growth and sexual maturity may take anywhere from fourteen to twenty years; most other animals achieve maturity in a few weeks or months. Man also has the most complex physiological and neurological endowment and is far more dependent upon learning than his nearest ancestors. He is born with only a few adaptive reflexes. The behavior of lower animal forms, on the other hand, is guided largely by instinct, although recent evidence indicates that these instincts are not fully developed at birth and depend on environmental experiences for normal development and expression.[2]

Because of his complex neurological structure, man is capable of language, the use of symbols that have shared meanings within the group or the society. Language enables man to instruct his young, to transmit the accumulated wisdom and folly of his culture, and to spare his offspring much trial and error behavior. Subhumans cannot be told that fire burns. They learn this fact after they have been burned. They learn by gesture and imitation, but they cannot be warned in advance, however, of threats that are not immediate. They cannot be controlled by promises of future reward or punishment or prepared for future statuses in life by verbal instruction. While many species are superior to man in speed, strength, and sensory perception, only man has the ability to use abstract concepts in adapting to his environment.

One other biological feature that is unique to human beings and their closest relatives is the fact that the female does not have to be in heat before mating can take place. Man has no mating season, at least not one that is physiologically determined. Uncontrolled sexual behavior in societies could be an important source of conflict, jealousy, and destructiveness that would undermine the human need for prolonged and stable care from birth to maturity. It might prevent even a minimal degree of the cooperation that is necessary for human survival at any age. The incest taboo and marriage are human inventions that set limits to human sexual behavior.

The incest taboo is a universal means of controlling the continuous sex drive of men and women. It is found in all societies, although it may be extended quite arbitrarily to include nonblood relatives or individuals who share varying degrees of common biological ancestry. In the United States for example, some states define marriages between uncles and nieces as incestuous; others similarly define marriages between second cousins. And this varies for no obvious reason.

The taboo is apparently not based on instinct, since it has often been broken, and sometimes by subcultural prescription. Among the ruling strata in ancient Egypt, Peru, and Hawaii, for example, brother and sister marriages were customary and obligatory. We don't know why this custom arose. We can often explain the persistence of social norms: in this case the custom operated to preserve family fortunes. But other means of accomplishing this have been adopted elsewhere. The origins of this practice, however, as with many other cultural norms will very likely always be a mystery. Probably the custom originated as an idiosyncratic act by an individual of high status and a strong psychological need that was too powerful for the cultural taboo to contain. It was then adopted by others of similar psychological bent and the prestige and power to get away with it. With time it became a norm in the subculture of these particular ruling groups, shared by others in the group, and transmitted from generation to generation through the process of socialization.

The practice of brother-sister marriage was never sanctioned for the masses in these societies, however. The justification that the ruling groups put forth to legitimize their practice—that it kept the family fortune intact and that it protected aristocratic families from defilement by the blood of commoners—seems unsophisticated from the vantage point of twentieth-century depth psychology. It could explain the persistence but not the origin of the custom. But it is in the nature of ideologies that they are convincing to the people who hold them—a fact that is often not recognized by individuals who have different ideological persuasions.

Another major way of controlling sexual relationships in societies is by assigning some degree of sexual exclusiveness and permanence to the marital relationship. What outsiders have labeled adultery or promiscuity in other societies has often occurred under normatively controlled conditions of time, place, and circumstance. This applies to practices such as wife-lending and the right of the first night—in which the king, lord of the manor, chieftain, or medicine man was given the right of initial sexual access to newlywed virgins. Fidelity has been differently valued and enforced in different societies, but some degree of sexual exclusiveness and permanence is always implied in marital contracts.

The personnel even in the very rare and not fully authenticated cases of group marriage did not vary. Exclusive and enduring sexual relationships were bounded by the family group, even if they did not take place, apparently, on a permanent pairing basis. In communal experimental groups sexual behavior has almost never been completely random or uncontrolled by group norms. The mega-family groups in Denmark, for example, consist of a number of unrelated adults and their children who live together. They hold group sex sessions several times a week, involving all adult members. Nevertheless they recognize nuclear family units and proscribe private sexual liaisons between members who are not "steady partners." This is defined as "infidelity." [3]

Permanent mating relationships are rare among other animals. Nonhuman animals are usually promiscuous, mating with parents and siblings and rarely maintaining a durable lifetime relationship with a single mate. The care of the young is guaranteed, however, by the existence of a maternal instinct, which is controlled by female sex hormones. Maternal behavior can be induced in animals by injecting these hormones. In males, a hormonally based paternal instinct does not seem to exist. The male, as a matter of fact, is often a threat to his young or, at best, is uninvolved or indifferent to their needs, although there are, for example, species among fish where the male takes over the care of the fertilized ova completely.

Humans, unfortunately, cannot depend on their hormones to provide them with the appropriate sentiments for rearing their children. No one has been able to demonstrate the existence of a hormonally based maternal instinct or drive in human females, although much evidence has been accumulating recently on the effects of changing hormone levels on mood states in women during premenstral and postpartum periods and during menopause.[4]

If a maternal instinct does exist in the human female, it is easily overlayed by life experiences and cultural role dictates. Anthropologists have reported on societies where women experience little maternal warmth, view pregnancy with dread, and strongly reject and unwillingly perform the obligations of childbearing and childrearing.[5] Daily newspaper accounts of brutality toward children are a further indication that life experiences can overshadow any hormonally based propensities to nurture their young that are present in human females.

Family responsibilities, incidentally, are not necessarily based on blood relationships. In some societies, the contribution of the father to conception was unknown, since pregnancies were believed to occur as the result of the bounty and good will of the gods. In other societies, the identity of the biological father could not be determined because the marital contract did not specify an exclusive pairing relationship between one male and one female. Among the Todas of southern India, for example, where polyandry was practiced, the wife was shared by the brothers in a particular family. In these situations, where the fact of biological paternity was unknown or could not be established, a sociological father was assigned to each newborn child. He fulfilled the role of father, as defined by his culture and as sanctioned by his society.

While not all societies have emphasized the fact of biological paternity, all have attempted to define and regulate male as well as female responsibilities in family relationships. The universal existence of family groups with socially recognized statuses, such as mother and father, and socially sanctioned roles prescribing sexual behavior and childrearing responsibilities, serves the need of controlling sexual conflict in human societies and providing for the prolonged care of the human young.

The intellectual and physical needs of young children could be fulfilled by outside agencies but the gratification of emotional needs cannot be delegated completely. At the outer limits, culturally defined family roles must contain provision for the gratification of the biologically grounded emotional needs of the human young. Slaves, servants, and professionals have not and do not have the narcissistic investment in the young that parents have. Children, after all, are parents' odes to immortality.

Substitute groups who would have complete care of the young in populous modern societies would have to be bureaucratically structured in order to coordinate so vast an undertaking. Bureaucratic structures are, by definition, impersonal. For this reason, also, the task of providing for the emotional needs of infants and children (as well as adults) is not likely to be taken over completely by nonfamily groups. I will take up this question again when we look into the probable future of the American family.

All that is recognizably human in men and women is a product of social interaction with other human beings. Children who have been reared under conditions of extreme isolation and emotional deprivation are unable to walk, talk, express a wide range of emotions, or use their hands to manipulate their physical environment. The amount of impairment in physical and intellectual functioning, furthermore, is directly related to the amount of emotional deprivation these children have experienced.

Two illegitimate children discovered at the age of six after each had been isolated in attics for years responded quite differently to attempts to teach them to function at a human level. While the kind and quality of teaching varied in each case, it is significant that one child, who had been imprisoned with her deaf-mute mother, responded well and eventually attained what was reported as normal

speech and intellectual development. The other child, who had no
sustained contact with another human being, responded poorly to attempts to train her and died at the age of ten. Her speech never developed beyond the two-year level. While she learned to dress herself,
she was never able to fasten buttons or eat with a knife and fork.[6]
The extreme deprivation of human contact that she experienced had
consequences that were largely irreparable.

OTHER BIOLOGICAL UNDERPINNINGS

Cultural definitions of family roles are also affected by particular biological needs and changes in the human life cycle of family members
—especially during infancy and childhood, adolescence, and middle
and old age—and by the biological differences between the sexes.[7]
The question here, as in my discussion of basic human biological
needs, is to what extent culturally prescribed family roles are bound
by biology and to what extent these definitions are, or have been, arbitrary. And here too, while we need much more evidence, we can at
least point to possible limits to variations in family roles as determined by the biology of age and gender. We can also point to current
patterns in family life that are incompatible with the typical biological
characteristics of particular age groups and of the two sexes, as these
inconsistencies and irrationalities are played out in contemporary family life.

THE HUMAN LIFE CYCLE

The major milestones of growth and aging in the individual life cycle
are infancy and childhood, adolescence, and middle age and old age.
These three stages of life are characterized by rather clear-cut physiological, anatomical, and endocrinological changes, although the pace
and degree of change will vary for individuals.

Societies respond to these stages in the life cycle quite differently.
In a society in which the average citizen has a life expectancy at birth
of less than thirty years (and this has been the case, historically, in
the vast majority of societies, large and small) a woman of twenty-
eight may be an old woman, by social definition. Biologically, how-

ever, she has not passed through the changes that we associate with advancing or old age.

Societies will also vary in the extent to which they emphasize or deemphasize one or another of these stages and prescribe clearly defined roles for occupants of these statuses. For example, adolescence, which begins at puberty and ends with the assumption of full adult status in all spheres of life—marital, economic, political, and recreational—is not a clearly delineated status in nonindustrial society. It is of short duration, if it can be said to exist at all as a recognized social status.

Philippe Aries, in his account of the history of childhood during the medieval era in Western Europe, argues on the basis of an analysis of paintings, diaries, games, and schools and their curricula, that children were regarded as miniature adults in the Middle Ages almost from the time they were weaned (at about the age of seven). They dressed like adults and worked and played with adults, suffering little from invidious age distinctions and the pressures of youth subcultures.[8]

The aged are another category that is more distinctly recognized in urban, industrial society. There are more of them and they are no longer as locked into extended family groups as they once were. They are increasingly separate and segregated in rural counties, older urban and suburban neighborhoods and, recently, in retirement villages. In these retirement communities, a new territorially-based subculture is arising, based on common values of leisure, tranquillity, security, physical comfort, and convenience, which affects family role conceptions in a significant way.

INFANCY AND CHILDHOOD

Infancy and childhood, the first major stage in the human life cycle, has dramatic implications for family functioning. The introduction of a new child into the family group is more crucial for the rearrangement and redefinition of family roles than the gradual changes that occur with puberty and middle and old age.

Culture and social conditions begin to operate on the infant from the moment of conception. The quality, quantity, and type of food that the mother eats, the amount of rest and exercise she gets, the physical labor she performs, and the knowledge she has of prenatal care and the kind and availability of this care will depend to a large extent on cultural and social factors.

At birth, the infant requires basic emotional and physical care. The family group responds to these needs according to cultural prescriptions of the responsibilities and obligations of family members, varying life conditions (particularly economic and technological), and the individual personality factors of parents, siblings, and whatever other relatives or surrogates are assigned the responsibility for fulfilling the infant's needs by the society or subculture.

The distinctive personality traits of responsible figures in the infant's life, those that are not directly attributable to effects of culture, stem from differences in intelligence, temperament, and unique life experiences. These idiosyncratic factors become more significant in industrial societies, where the press of culture and subculture is less uniform, due to the greater mobility and greater contact of individuals with differing and rapidly changing culture patterns. Probably individual psychological factors will become even more significant in infant and child care in the future than they are now, as gross differences in childrearing practices are increasingly eliminated by the homogenizing and equalizing effects of mass culture and economic reform.

The gratification of the basic biological need for physical survival and growth involves, also and indirectly, provision for the emotional and intellectual problem-solving needs and capacities of the young. Without a dependable source of warm emotional response, physical growth, intellectual functioning, and survival are impaired in young children. These needs are interrelated and interdependent. Problem-solving capacity is adaptive and is also, ultimately, tied to physical survival, whatever the environmental circumstances. How have families functioned, historically, to fulfill these needs, and what are the possible limits to their role in meeting these responsibilities?

THE PROVISION OF PHYSICAL CARE. The gratification of the physical needs of the child, so that normal growth processes can take place and biological maturity is reached in good health, is and has been the most difficult responsibility of the family in nonindustrialized societies. Rational control over the physical environment, including disease-producing agents, is minimal. Childbearing and childrearing are highly inefficient, since the child's chances of survival are low. Women bear far greater numbers of children and often spend their entire lives, and in fact die, giving birth to children. High death rates balance high birth rates in nonliterate and preindustrial societies and the family requires a constantly renewed supply of hunters, herders, field hands, or gardeners to sustain itself in a labor-intensive economy.

In these societies, two hands can produce more than one mouth can eat because almost all hands work. This includes the young, from the time they can toddle out into the fields and sow seeds or carry small tools. The major problem in these societies is to keep the young alive.

In highly industrialized societies, providing for the physical needs and survival of children is not a major existential problem for most families. Science and technology, applied by legions of trained experts, supplement family responsibility in this respect. Compulsory health examinations for the young, welfare programs, family allowances, and other devices are elaborated to this end. The problem shifts from keeping children alive to keeping the birth rate down because so many stay alive.

While poverty, economic deprivation, and high infant mortality rates persist, they do not characterize a majority of the population in technologically advanced societies. Most individuals who are born reach maturity in more or less good health, the degree of health depending upon constitutional factors and, even more importantly, upon class factors. The higher the class, the better the nutrition and medical care that is available to the child and the adult, the fewer the environmental hazards he encounters, and the longer he can expect to live, on an average. Race is also relevant here. Blacks in the United States have a lower average life expectancy than do whites, although the average tends to be pulled down largely by much higher infant mortality rates.

THE SATISFACTION OF EMOTIONAL NEEDS. As for the task of providing for the emotional needs of children, here the historical record is much less clear with regard to the adequacy and limits to family responsibilities in this respect. The extent of mental illness in a society is a good index of the adequacy of family functioning in this area, although other factors must also be taken into account. What are the standards for making a judgment about the actual prevalence of mental illness in a society? Definitions vary. In complex societies the actual prevalence of psychological illness is almost impossible to determine because investigations are usually limited to data on hospital admission rates and official statistics are almost always biased in certain systematic ways. Class factors, for example, affect the likelihood of hospitalization. The poor are more likely than the rich to be hospitalized for mental illness, just as they are more likely to be imprisoned for crime.

Nevertheless, mental illness is universal. In all societies, some individuals exhibit gross disturbances in their perception of reality and experience degrees of anxiety and guilt that interferes, to a greater or less extent, with their ability to work, love, and play. Typical forms of mental illness vary in different cultures and in the same society at different times. In our own society, for example, conversion neuroses, such as hysteria, stemming from repression of sexual and aggressive impulses, apparently are declining, while character disorders seem to be on the increase. But we cannot answer the question whether actual rates of overall mental illness are more frequent now than in the past.

One study by Herbert Goldhamer and Albert Marshall, that attempted to shed light on this problem, found no increase in hospital admission rates for most types of psychosis in the state of Massachusetts in the mid-twentieth century as compared with the mid-nineteenth century.[9] Rates for age categories of fifty and under remained approximately the same, despite a trend toward hospitalization of patients with less extreme forms of mental illness in this century up to 1955. Thus, the amount of severe mental illness does not seem to be higher in modern civilizations than in newly industrializing societies. If this is so, it probably has to do with the fact of the extreme brutality of the material environment for the masses of the population in earlier stages of urbanization and industrialization. Whatever the potential for the outbreak of mental illness in a population, precipitating factors, particularly stressful economic conditions, appear to have been more potent during the period of early industrialization and unregulated capitalism in the West.

A possible analogy and further support for this thesis lies in the fact that rates of severe mental illness are highly correlated with social class in contemporary industrial societies. Class is a major determinant of differential environmental stress that families encounter. A massive study carried out in midtown Manhattan in the mid-1950s was unique in that an attempt was made to obtain information about the actual prevalence of psychological illness on the basis of door-to-door interviews in a heterogeneous (white) metropolitan community.[10] Previous studies had been limited to information about the relationship between social class and rates of hospitalized mental illness.[11] The midtown study revealed quite dramatically that in successively lower class levels there is a progressively greater likelihood that children will reach maturity with some degree of psychological damage.[12]

The adequacy of family functioning in rearing the young to a healthy emotional maturity is, and apparently has been, closely tied to economic factors in some societies. It is not possible to answer, unequivocally, the question whether the family functioned better in this respect in the past. Anthropologists, particularly, have tended to make invidious comparisons, with the contemporary family often coming out badly in these contrasts. I think the answer has to depend ultimately on the values of the observer. Judgments of relative weaknesses or strengths of family functioning depend on the standards one is using and the adequacy of historical data.

To take just one example, if family structure, culture, and social conditions promote stable, secure, and enduring affectional relationships for infants and young children, we can assume that the emotional needs of these children would be better gratified. Using this standard, families in nonliterate and nonurban areas of preindustrial societies would have the advantage. Family structure is usually extended where agriculture exists and the family group is tied to the land. Whether the extended family occupies a common household or not, there are more available familial members in the immediate environment to provide the emotional gratification and the socializing experiences that the child needs to mature and reach adulthood as a competent, functioning member of the society.

The experience of loss of a parent is not as traumatic when it occurs in the extended family setting. Ready substitutes, familiar and stable, are usually available to take over the role of mother or father.

In urban, industrial societies, orphanages, foster homes, or legally appointed guardians are hardly the equivalent in providing continuity in emotional gratification for the orphaned child.

On the other hand, from the records of anthropologists and historians we know that family conflict, rivalry, and envy are as old as man himself. The intensity of these conflicts at the psychological level seems to be more severe in independent, nuclear family groups, since there are fewer mediators and substitute family personnel to allay or mitigate negative feelings.

Social conditions such as rapid social change and large scale movement up and down the class structure are also factors that increase family conflict. The economic fate of the father is not necessarily the fate of the son where there is a relatively open class structure. Envy and guilt are more likely to characterize the same-sex parent-child relationship if the child can achieve a higher social status than his parents. This adds a sociological dimension to the other reasons for parental envy of their maturing offspring, such as their greater virility, energy, freedom, and youth. But it is at least possible now to escape these conflicts, if not to resolve them. The young can escape the battle arena and take up residence in another city or town.

In nonliterate or preindustrial societies, there is usually no place to go. The individual is bound to the family group since it is almost impossible to survive outside of it. There are no laundries, supermarkets, or restaurants to provide for the needs of unattached individuals.

We see then that in making historical and cross-cultural comparisons it is very difficult to make absolute judgments of the relative adequacy of family functioning in providing for basic emotional needs. It is necessary to be specific about what one is comparing and about what one thinks is more or less desirable. In the above illustration, the two conflicting values are emotional security versus individualism and freedom. They can go together, but often they do not. Which is preferable? It depends, as I said before, on the observer's hierarchy of values.

The related question of the possible limits to family responsibility in providing for the basic emotional needs of children also cannot be answered definitively, given our present state of knowledge. For lack of a better substitute group, this function, unlike many others, is not likely to be taken away completely from the family.

But what, then, is the best amount and kind of emotional support that is necessary for optimum physical, emotional, and intellectual growth and development? The answer to this question is the goal and has been the goal of a vast amount of research in the social sciences over the past hundred years.

Currently, the belief is growing that it is the quality of parent-child contact rather than the quantity, in terms of the amount of time spent together and the actual number and extent of services performed for the child, that is the significant factor in the emotional health of the child. This is the implication of the recent, more refined and more carefully controlled studies of the effects of maternal employment on children. Gross differences in the number and kind of neurotic symptoms between the children of working and nonworking mothers have not been found. Other factors such as class and the availability of continuous warm and accepting care by a mother substitute have been found to be more important than the fact of maternal employment per se. The mother who stays at home out of a sense of duty and obligation is, furthermore, not likely to provide this kind of care.

THE KIBBUTZ EXPERIENCE. The Israeli kibbutz settlements are natural experiments that could shed some light on the problem of the quantity and quality of parental contact necessary for healthy emotional development. Infants and children in most kibbutz communes are reared by nurses and teachers in separate residences. Children visit with their parents for two hours a day, usually. Parents are not responsible for their children's physical care and for a large part of their children's learning experiences. The parent-child relationship is limited to companionship and the sharing of recreational activities.

Studies of these settlements, particularly those aimed at evaluating the personality development of kibbutz-reared children, are inconsistent in the details of their findings. This reflects, in part, problems of definition and problems of validity in measuring personality traits and emotional disturbance.[13] The disagreements also reflect the bias of the investigators' values and the lack of data from a representative sample of all kibbutz communities.

Nevertheless, and despite disagreements, the conclusion that children reared in kibbutz settlements "fall well within the range of normal emotional adjustment" is not questioned by any observers.[14] Children and their parents have emotional ties, even though contact is limited and parents have very little responsibility for the daily custodial care of their children.

In thinking about the possible implications of the kibbutz experiments for family functioning in other societies, however, certain exceptional features of the kibbutz have to be borne in mind. Aside from the obvious difference in the communal ownership of property, kibbutz settlements in the past have been characterized by stability and a slow rate of change. They are child-centered, small in size, relatively homogeneous, and basically rural in their economic organization. Bureaucracy is not a characteristic feature of this type of community, viewed as an autonomous unit, and has not been a problem in structuring substitute groups that carry out functions previously performed by the family.

Kibbutz communities have been changing, particularly since Israel became an independent nation. The existence of a rapidly developing national state and the necessity to maintain relationships with this political entity has led to the proliferation of bureaucracy at the intermediate level, between kibbutz and state. Associations of kibbutzim, and national political parties, labor federations, settlement agencies, and ministries have diminished the autonomy of individual kibbutz settlements. More traditional patterns of family life are becoming reestablished to some extent. Sex role differentiation is becoming more pronounced—wives are more likely to perform domestic service tasks in communal structures and husbands are more likely to work in the fields. The autonomy and privacy of individual family units is also becoming more highly valued.[15]

Large-scale studies of Israeli kibbutzim that are now being undertaken should eventually result in more clear-cut and less controversial evidence about the relative effectiveness of this particular type of family and societal organization in producing emotionally mature adults. One thing seems clear, however, even at this point: traditional family patterns can be varied in very marked ways and still provide adequately for the emotional as well as the physical and intellectual needs of family members.

Here, again, the question of comparative judgments is a matter of values. The basic values of the kibbutz subculture have been collectivism, work, and equality for all members of the society. Family role conceptions have been consistent with these dominant values, conceptions that have been shared, furthermore, by entire kibbutz communities, at least in the past.

THE DEVELOPMENT OF INTELLECTUAL POTENTIAL. Up to now, I have discussed the adequacy and possible limits to family responsibility in providing for the physical and emotional needs of infants and children. The other major responsibility of the family is to develop intellectual competence in its young members. This requires the development of skills and the imparting of knowledge that will enable the child to function adequately in adult roles, particularly in the occupational sphere.

I will avoid the question of what are the genetic limits to intellectual functioning in human beings. This is a matter of definition and the problem lies in establishing standards. Then, there is the problem of measuring this potential accurately, a problem that I don't think we have yet conquered.

A related question is: How successfully have various types of societal institutions, the family in particular since this is our concern here, functioned to tap the maximum limits of this potential? Here again the problem lies in the lack of absolute standards.

We can only discuss the question in terms of how adequately mature human beings in a society are able to function in the roles that require intellectual competence of some kind. If there are shortages in some adult occupations for lack of skilled people and if large numbers of individuals in a society are ill prepared to function at the necessary level of skill and training required by the technology of the society, we can then make at least a relative kind of judgment about the adequacy of family functioning in this respect. This approach also has its problems since I will have to try to isolate the responsibility of the family from that of other socializing agencies concerned with the intellectual development of young children—the schools, for example, and indirectly, the government in modern societies.

One component of intelligence is the capacity to solve problems. In societies with highly developed technologies, skill levels are far more complex and problem solving challenges are constant. In this type of society the family is much less able to carry out the responsibility of developing the intellectual potential of the young. This is yet another function that the family once monopolized but now shares with trained experts. The degree of encroachment on the family's role in this respect has paralleled the development of technology in societies and the proliferation of specialized occupations.

In nonliterate, tribal societies the extended family had the sole responsibility for educating the young. Not until puberty, and even then not in all nonliterate societies, were children separated from the family and instructed by specialized nonfamily personnel. These individuals were not usually full-time instructors, however and, after initiation rites were over, they returned to their daily chores.[16] The curriculum, furthermore, was not vocational. Arts and crafts were somtimes taught to the initiates, but not gardening, hunting, or fishing skills. The emphasis was on myth, lore, religious, and magical knowledge rather than on necessary economic skills, which were easily transmitted and taught by family members.

Since social mobility was unknown (children usually performed the same occupational roles as their parents) and the rate of social change was slow (skills rarely became obsolete), the development of intellectual skills necessary for adult functioning was handled quite effectively by the extended family. Teaching was oral, based on the principles of apprenticeship and learning by doing and example. Because there was no economic class structure in the less developed nonliterate societies, almost all children of the same sex were educated equally, with few disparities in the amount and kind of training available to the young.

In preindustrial societies, the extended family continued in its role as prime educator for the masses of the population. Mobility was rare and social change continued to be relatively slow. Only the elite were literate; the common people did not have to know how to read or write in order to till the fields and harvest the crops. The instruction of the elite, usually by religious functionaries, was nonvocational, however, emphasizing character training, service, and the development of the poised and well-rounded, cultivated man.

In urban centers, which contained only a small proportion of the population, children were often apprenticed outside of the family for instruction in trades and crafts. In rural areas, priests occasionally took on the instruction of a few promising peasant children, but teaching was limited to the imparting of a simple literacy and the virtues of piety and docility. For the vast majority of the population in these societies, however, the family functioned relatively adequately and unaided in preparing its young to anticipate and cope with the intellectual challenges of adult life—as adequately as the general level of knowledge and technology permitted.

In highly industrialized societies, the family loses its monopoly over the development of intellectual skills in the young. The scope of this loss, in terms of the number of families who experience it and the lowering of the age when children are removed from its exclusive province in this respect, is greatly expanded. Not only literacy, but far more than that is required for intellectual functioning in automating societies.

The family's responsibility and adequacy in developing the intellectual potential of its children becomes, at the same time, contracted but crucial. It is crucial because the family, at least at present, still has the initial contact with its children and the earliest responsibility in preparing them for the formal educational experiences they will have in school and elsewhere.

The family loads the dice by its childrearing practices and by the fact that it places the child initially, and by the event of birth, within a particular location in the class structure. Both factors, and they are closely related, are very significant influences that will affect the nature and the amount of formal education the child will have and his receptivity to this experience.

Class overrides ethnic origin and race as a factor effecting the preschool preparation of children. The great divide, in this respect, is between the childrearing practices of the working class, particularly at the lowest levels, and the middle and upper classes. Lower working-class mothers, overwhelmed by numerous, closely spaced children to care for and by unremitting problems of physical survival, spend less time talking, smiling, and playing with their infants.[17] Later, they spend less time reading to their children. They are more apt to issue orders without explanations. They use concrete language. Their sentences are short, with little use of qualifying phrases. Their spoken language is less like written language, grammatically and syntactically, than in the middle class. They extinguish curiosity and question-asking behavior in their children because they are often too distracted to respond to questions. They tend to ignore the crying of their infants —which some psychologists feel is the origin of feelings of impotence and helplessness that the children of the poor often display in later life. In testing situations, for example, these children tend to give up and are less persistent at difficult tasks than are middle-class children.

Actually, the feelings of fatalism and helplessness that impoverished children often display are characteristic of adults as well as children in the subculture of the very poor. Daily experiences reinforce these feelings in almost all areas of life. Mothers have no reason to encourage optimism in their children and their children have no reason to feel it in test situations, real or artificial.

The list of the ways in which the material circumstances and child-rearing patterns of poor families do not prepare children for optimum intellectual functioning in school and thereafter is extensive. And the differences between poor and middle-class children in this respect show up very early. One study reported class-based differences in ability to distinguish between varying stimuli as early as twelve months in male infants and eight months in female infants.[18] The psychologist who conducted this study attributes the differences he found to more intensive mother-child contact, more deliberate teaching, and a generally more stimulating environment in the middle-class families studied. The value of constructive use of leisure time is applied by middle-class mothers in their expectations from their children practically at birth, with objects and toys that teach perceptual discrimination, grasping, and dexterity. Idle hands and minds are disapproved in this class.

How important are these early class-based environmental differences for the intellectual future of the child? A large body of evidence has been accumulating that points to the existence of "critical periods" in infant and early childhood histological (tissue), neurological, and biochemical development that are of the greatest significance for learning and behavior.[19] In toilet training, for example, there is an optimum time for teaching this behavior in terms of the child's neurological development.

In the development of intelligence, the research evidence seems to indicate that the child's future intellectual competence is strongly and critically affected by experiences that he encounters in the first three or four years of life, the period when the central nervous system develops most rapidly.[20] The human brain at birth is only about one quarter of the size it will reach at maturity—at about twenty years of age. It grows very rapidly during the first few years of life and reaches 90 percent of its final weight by the age of six.

This does not mean that change cannot occur in the child's relative intellectual functioning after this period; it means, simply, that environmental influences, attention and teaching by the mother and other figures who are significant in the child's life, for example, have a maximum impact on developing intelligence at this time. After this critical period, more effort is required to produce a change in the level of intellectual functioning.

This emphasis on the first three years of life, incidentally, parallels Sigmund Freud's belief that the first five years of life are crucial for personality development. The difference lies in the fact that Freud's interest was in the effect of experience on the emotions and drives. The new group of investigators is more interested in the relationship between early environmental experiences and intellectual growth.

Given this new emphasis on the importance of the first few years of life and the accumulating evidence that points to the need for additional help within poor families in providing for the intellectual as well as the physical needs of their children, we can predict that the role of the family in this respect, at least for those who are at the bottom of the class structure, will be curtailed further, eventually. But probably this will not come about on a widespread scale for some time yet, in America. A really serious concern with developing human resources in this country is not an overriding consideration in allocating the national income at present. Countries that are poorer in natural resources, the Scandinavian nations, for example, invest in human resources instead. America has not had this kind of pressure, although it is now moving in that direction.

ADOLESCENCE

BIOLOGICAL CHANGES. Adolescence is the next major stage in the human life cycle that affects family roles, rather dramatically, in modern societies. It is a status that has a physiological onset: puberty, and a sociological ending; full adult status, as defined by the society.[21] The biological changes that occur in adolescence are triggered by hormonal secretions which depend, in turn, on developmental changes in the central nervous system. The adolescent experiences a spurt in growth and in the development of primary sexual characteristics. The penis and scrotum become enlarged and ejaculatory capacity develops in males. Females begin to menstruate and their analogous sexual organs, the clitoris and labia majora, grow in size.

Secondary sexual characteristics also appear at this time: the enlargement of the breasts and pelvis and the growth of pubic and axillary hair in females, and voice and skeletal changes and the growth of pubic, axillary, and facial hair in males. Both sexes experience and enlargement of the sweat glands without a proportionate growth of the secretory ducts of these glands. This often results in skin disorders—a common and normal affliction of adolescence.[22]

These are the basic biological changes of adolescence. The sex drive becomes pronounced after a period of relative latency, depending on the society, and sexual and growth changes are accompanied by an increase in energy and emotional tumult, again, depending on the society. It is these latter phenomena that have the most direct effect on the family and are most directly affected by cultural role prescriptions and family behavior.

THE SOCIAL STATUS OF ADOLESCENTS. Societies very markedly in the criteria they lay down for the achievement of adulthood— criteria that may or may not coincide with the physiological ending of puberty. The steps to adulthood can be many or few, clear-cut or vague, achieved by some adolescents under certain culturally prescribed conditions, and never achieved by others in the society under any conditions—slaves, for example.

Most nonliterate societies provided for a dramatic, ritualized ordeal or initiation ceremony (*rite de passage*) to symbolize the attainment of adult status. While this usually involved damage to the skin, teeth, or genitals, individuals had the assurance of achieving a socially recognized maturity after a definite and circumscribed period of time. Their scars were visible symbols of an adulthood that was achieved early, rapidly, and unqualifiedly. And adulthood coincided with puberty.

In both nonliterate and preindustrial societies the individual was usually engaged in his adult occupational activities from early childhood. Marriage represented the final attainment of full adult status. And this, too, tended to coincide with puberty, since physiological maturity occurred much later in nonindustrialized societies. Developments in technology, medicine, and public health practices improve the food supply and the general health of the population in industrialized societies. Growth is enhanced and speeded up and the attainment of sexual maturity also occurs much earlier.

In industrial societies, adolescence as a status with a disparate biological and social termination becomes recognized, protracted, and defined as a social problem. Developments in science and technology make necessary an increasingly lengthened period of formal training for the young. The increased energy characteristic of this biological stage of the life cycle is, furthermore, not usually channeled into productive work until after, and sometimes long after, the attainment of puberty.

The marginal status that adolescence represents is extended at both ends. It not only ends later, it begins earlier. Norway, which has long-term records on the onset of menstruation in its female population, reported a decline in the average age of menstruation during the past one hundred years, from seventeen to thirteen years. Other countries, including the United States, have reported similar trends. The theory that this is related to the adequacy of diet and medical care is supported by the fact that puberty occurs somewhat later in the working class and is also delayed during periods of war and depression, when food supplies are less adequate.[23]

The interim period between childhood and socially recognized adulthood is not a time of unrestrained freedom. Behavior is regulated, and often very stringently, by peer groups. Collective behavior —proneness for fads, fashions, and social movements—is characteristic of individuals who occupy an insecure or marginal status. Since they are less locked into established patterns, they are more available to what is new. Adolescents are particularly prone to this type of behavior.

Adolescence is not a paradise of nonresponsibility, as it has often been depicted, particularly in the past. In mobile, class societies it is a time of preparation and competition for eventual jobs and marital partners. The family can guarantee neither in industrial society, although it plays a role in limiting possible choices. In traditional societies, the family not only limited but often determined both the occupation and the mate. The child did not have to ask: "Who am I?" or "What will I be when I grow up?" The family, rather than the vocation or profession, established the individual's adult identity in these societies.

In industrial societies the attainment of full adult status is piecemeal, arbitrary, and inconsistent. In the United States, for example, the adolescent pays adult fare at age twelve, may drive an automobile and is no longer subject to child labor laws at sixteen, serves in the military at eighteen, achieves legal maturity at twenty-one, and may achieve adult marital status without, however, having achieved adult economic status. Student marriages, relying on parental support, or the earnings of the wife, are an example of a pattern that is becoming increasingly widespread, particularly in the American middle class.

Adolescents, like the aged in technologically developed society, are outside of the productive process. They are, at the same time, a source of profit to business and a costly burden to the nuclear family, particularly in countries where higher education is not free to all students and where students do not receive government stipends. If they attempt to find work, they are usually restricted to marginal, low-paying jobs. Work-study programs and volunteer programs such as the Peace Corps and Vista, while also low-paying, represent attempts at partial rescue of at least a handful of adolescents from their preparatory status and their state of economic suspended animation and dependency.

THE GRATIFICATION OF SEXUAL DRIVES. A major source of frustration among adolescents stems from the difficulty they experience in gratifying their heightened sexual drives. Societies that are economically and politically stratified usually proscribe premarital sexual relationships for their young, at least ideally. Courtship and marriage are less easily regulated by the family when premarital liaisons are uncontrolled. Historically and cross-culturally, the higher strata have always been more concerned with controlling the marriages of their children in order to protect or enhance family lineage, power, and wealth. No society, however, has succeeded completely in preventing sexual liaisons that are proscribed, and some have been notoriously unsuccessful in this respect. The mother-son incest taboo is the only sexual taboo that seems rarely to have been broken in human societies.

While extramarital relationships have been prohibited except under normatively regulated conditions in almost all, if not all, societies, premarital sexual relationships have been permitted in a majority of nonliterate societies. This was particularly true in hunting and gathering societies where differences in wealth and power between families were minimal. In more technologically developed nonliterate societies, where these differences became more prominent, a mixed pattern sometimes existed. In Samoa, for example, commoners were permitted premarital sexual freedom but princesses were carefully guarded and were expected to be virgins until they were married.[24]

Illegitimacy was not a problem in the nonliterate societies that permitted premarital sexual liaisons since marriage occurred shortly after puberty—and sometimes before. Not only did young people reach puberty at a later age than in industrial societies, but protection was also provided by the biological fact that young girls are relatively infertile for a period of one to three years after the onset of menstruation.

In agricultural societies, premarital sex is generally prohibited by the culture and reinforced by religious sanctions. Discrepancies in wealth between various segments of the society become much more pronounced since improved technology permits the accumulation of a greater economic surplus. Political and religious elites, often with interchangeable personnel in the early stages of agricultural development, extract a disproportionate amount of this surplus in exchange for protective and spiritual services.

Theologies that explain the unknown and promise retribution for sufferings and wrongs encountered in this world become codified and are promulgated by a hierarchy of specialized religious officials. The traditional organized religions of East and West have not only legitimated the unequal distribution of material and psychic goods in stratified societies in the past, they have also favored sexual abstinence as an ideal.

Sexual gratification is a pleasure that all mankind can experience, and forgo, regardless of station in life. This is a possible reason for the position of the traditional organized religions on human sexuality. Faith is stronger when based on self-abnegation. The requirement of sexual abstinence or sexual gratification only for the purpose of procreation reached all members of society, rich and poor alike, at least formally.

The evidence seems to indicate, however, that in practice enforcement of restrictive premarital sexual norms was less than perfect, particularly within the lower levels of preindustrial societies. Unfortunately, since only the elite were literate, and they wrote mostly about themselves or each other, the historical record of the sexual practices of the masses is not very adequate. Love and feelings of intense physical attraction and emotional attachment have occurred in all societies, but societies have varied not only in the extent to which they have permitted sexual gratification for young unmarried members, but also in their definitions of the appropriateness of love as a basis for marriage.

In American society, today, individuals who marry without a feeling of love feel deprived or guilty. In traditional societies, particularly in the East, love was often regarded as a "laughable or tragic aberration" by the extended family.[25] In societies where the family unit rather than the individual is paramount in importance, a love relationship between husband and wife is discouraged since it detracts from family loyalty and may be disruptive of authority and deference patterns in the extended family. Love is also discouraged as a basis for marriage because of the possibility that it might cross class or caste lines.

In traditional India love was culturally prescribed as appropriate to the husband-wife relationship, but only after betrothal or marriage. In traditional China and Japan, respect rather than love was the culturally prescribed value governing husband and wife relationships. The significant emotional tie was between parent and child. Families in traditional societies used a variety of devices such as child betrothal and marriage, sexual segregation, and the isolation and chaperonage of women to prevent love and premarital sexual liaisons from occurring.

Romantic love as a positively sanctioned and culturally prescribed norm regulating the relationship between men and women arose in the West among the feudal aristocracy during the age of chivalry, in the twelfth century. But the pattern, initially, was consistent with Christian attitudes toward sex in that norms of courtly love applied outside of the marital relationship and were grounded on the principle of chastity. The lady and her knightly love, who was not her husband, did not consummate their relationship. They suffered and fetishized instead. The European nobility of the seventeenth and eighteenth centuries finally joined sex and love—but still outside of the marital relationship.[26]

As societies industrialized in the West, the middle classes rose to prominence and it is they who joined love, sex, and marriage. But premarital sexual abstinence remained the norm. The language of love became part of the courtship procedure, but only after betrothal —which was still arranged by the family with an eye to the economic status of the prospective bride or groom. Chaperoning was used to prevent premarital sexual consummation of the relationship.

In highly industrialized societies, the norm of premarital chastity persists, although it is honored less and less and becomes more difficult to enforce. The family is less able to control the economic and marital future of its offspring. Nepotism is displaced increasingly by merit, skill, and drive as a basis for recruitment of workers and elites. Family farms and businesses are replaced by impersonal corporations that recruit personnel on the basis of rational rather than traditionalistic standards such as ancestry, noblesse oblige, or paternalism. Social status becomes less a matter of birthright and more a matter of achievement.

The decline in the restriction of the mating and premarital sexual behavior of the young in contemporary industrial societies is a logical concomitant of the decreased significance of the extended family as an economic and social unit: individuals are freer from family control to work out their own destinies in all spheres of life. Mate choice has less implication for the fate of the entire family and, for the individual, the personal qualities of a potential marital partner become more significant than ancestry and inherited social status.

The much talked about sexual revolution, in which there was a relatively sudden and widespread increase in the frequency of premarital and extramarital intercourse in this country, occurred, actually, in the 1920s. A parallel phenomenon, but on a less widespread scale, took place at the same time in European countries such as France and England.[27] The studies by Alfred Kinsey and his associates, and a small number of more limited and less publicized studies that had been conducted in this country since the 1920s, exposed the fact that premarital sexual intercourse was far more prevalent in America that the official norms would indicate. The most startling finding of the Kinsey studies was that approximately 90 percent of the married males and 50 percent of the married females interviewed had experienced intercourse before marriage. Kinsey and his co-workers also found, incidentally, that about one-half of the married men and one-fourth of the married women respondents had engaged in extramarital affairs by the time they reached the age of forty.

The gap between sexual values and actual behavior in the United States that was revealed by these studies precipitated a reaction of agitated indignation and attack by representatives of the traditional morality in the United States, who feared a band wagon effect. It is probably for this reason that the Kinsey studies have not been repeated, although the data by now are quite old. Funds have not been forthcoming as yet from foundations or the government for a new nationwide study of contemporary sexual practices and attitudes in the United States.

What precipitated the sexual revolution in the 1920s? A large number of factors, acting in combination, played a role. Science and technology provided safer, more convenient birth control devices and some control over venereal disease. Increased industrialization, spurred by World War I, uprooted people, encouraged the movement from country to city, and thereby weakened family and community controls. The shorter work week provided more leisure time for sexual activities. The automobile, hotels, the spread of commercial, nonfamilial forms of recreation and the concomitant invention of dating diminished the effectiveness of family chaperoning.

The growing equality of women in education and employment, which was also accelerated by World War I, was another important factor. Educated and economically independent women are less likely to accept the double standard, which grants sexual freedom to males but not to females. Women who are least educated and most dependent economically on their husbands are most apt to express tolerance of their husbands' infidelity on the grounds that they are "good providers." [28]

Increasing secularism and knowledge about the facts of human sexuality also played an important role. The late nineteenth-century work of Richard von Krafft-Ebbing and Havelock Ellis and the publications of Sigmund Freud, at the turn of the century, became enormously popular among intellectuals in the United States and, in watered-down versions, affected the attitudes of the educated middle classes.[29]

Since the 1920s, in America, the pattern of sexual freedom has spread gradually, continuously, and in an evolutionary, not revolutionary, way. Individuals who are most liberal in their sexual practices are those whose ties to traditional organized religion and to the conventional morality are weakest: the highly educated, men in general, blacks, political radicals, and nonchurchgoers.[30] This is true of all age groups, including adolescents.

Young, unmarried people in our society today abide by one of four different sets of norms governing sexual behavior: 1) abstinence for both sexes—which is declining and is relatively rare now; 2) the double standard—which is also declining, particularly in the middle class; 3) gratification, but only on the basis of love or the expectation of future marriage—which is increasing most rapidly; and 4) promiscuity, or unqualified gratification, regardless of the object—which is uncommon, and is growing, but not significantly, at the present time.

The fact of recent continued increases in premarital sexual intercourse in our society is indicated by constantly rising rates of illegitimacy and of pregnancy at the time of marriage, in spite of advances in birth control technology. Another bit of evidence is the decline in organized prostitution which is, in part due to economic affluence (more women have other alternatives), in part, due to the rising status of women but also, in part, due to the fact that legitimate sources of sexual gratification are more readily available to males.

What has changed, actually, in recent years is not so much sexual behavior but attitudes toward sex: the two are coming closer together.

Those who are involved in nonmarital sexual liaisons are less furtive and feel less guilt about their behavior than in the past. Despite the changes that have been occurring, however, the majority of adolescents still experience sexual frustration in varying degrees and for a more prolonged period of time than in nonindustrial societies.

In coping with the biologically based changes of adolescence and the needs and energies that become more pronounced at this time, the family in industrial societies has lost its previous effectiveness. It can no longer provide satisfactory outlets in productive work and early marriage for its young. Here again the problem can be formulated as a cultural lag in which other agencies—the government, in particular, but also the church—the economy, education, and recreational institutions have failed to recognize and channel the adolescent's drives and energies adequately. And this failure is costly in terms of human life. Accidents by auto, drowning, falls, and firearms are the major cause of death in the age group fifteen to nineteen years in the United States. Suicide rates are also high. Fortunately, the adolescent's reflexes are fast; if not for this fact, deaths by accidents would be even more frequent.

CONFLICTS WITH PARENTS. The great majority of adolescents do not rock either the societal or the familial boat despite contrary images in the mass media. At the extremes, however, the sexual maturity of offspring can have profoundly disrupting effects on family functioning.[31] This, too, will vary according to class. Among the poor, for example, father-daughter incest is not infrequent. In the middle class, particularly the upper middle class, parents may seek extramarital sexual gratification, often for the first time in the marriage. The heightened sexuality of the adolescent can be contagious; Lolita fantasies are not uncommon in middle-aged men with adolescent daughters. An attractive nubile daughter may be a serious threat to an impaired husband-wife relationship.

Parent-child rivalry and envy also become intensified at this time: the adolescent is at the height of his powers; the middle-aged parent is experiencing unequivocal signs of physical decline. The menopausal mother is confronted with a daughter whose reproductive capacities are budding; the father may no longer be able to defeat his son in tests of athletic prowess.

Depression is a common response to loss, and guilt is a frequent component of depression. The adolescent may experience depression in response to the loss of his parents as primary love objects in his life and guilt in response to unconscious erotic feelings toward the parent of the opposite sex that become reactivated during adolescence. He will experience heightened envy and hostility toward the parent of the same sex and will often defend against erotic feelings toward the parent of the opposite sex with aggressive and hostile behavior.

Parents may feel guilt about their envious feelings and may respond with depression to the anticipated loss of their maturing child. These feelings are intensified in competitive, mobile industrialized societies. Depression over the potential loss of a child is not unrealistic, particularly in the middle class, since the child is increasingly unlikely to settle next door or in the family compound when he grows up.

I want to emphasize at this point that negative feelings between parents and their children are a matter of degree, as is mental illness for that matter. Parent-child conflicts occur in most extreme form in families where overt and obvious mental illness is present, but the difference is relative rather than absolute. Another point to remember is that these feelings coexist with positive feelings, which are usually stronger. Ambivalence is man's unique fate, in familial as well as in other social relationships.

Feelings of envy and aggressive and hostile impulses are not likely to be captured in survey research questionnaires, however. Deeper, less acceptable, feelings between parents and their children tend to be repressed, particularly in authoritarian homes, where the conventional morality is strongly supported and where hostility and aggression on the part of children is not readily tolerated. For this reason, survey research studies that attempt to measure the existence of a generation gap, or conflict between the generations, usually obtain negative results.[32] What these studies uncover is a basic agreement in attitudes, values, and role conceptions between most parents and their adolescent children. In study after study, a clear majority of students have reported good communication and understanding and a close relationship with their parents. Even in the realm of sexual behavior, young people often feel their standards are not so different from their parents.[33] Parents become more conservative about sex with age, but their children apparently recognize the disparity between what parents say and what they do or have done. The present adolescent generation is more open about their sexual behavior and more apt to set up premarital housekeeping arrangements, but otherwise their behavior is not so different from their parents.

At a psychological level, however, conflict between the generations is not likely to be tapped by attitude questionnaires. One way to gauge the actual prevalence of conflict at deeper, less consciously accessible and less readily admissable levels would be to use projective tests of the Rorschach and Thematic Apperception variety on a widespread scale. At the moment, these tests are too costly and time-consuming to administer to large, statistically representative samples of the population. As research techniques continue to be refined and improved, however, survey instruments that tap deeper feeling levels and penetrate psychological defenses may yet be devised. Only then will it be possible to answer accurately the question of the extent of intergenerational conflict in contemporary societies.

Sociologists can, however, point to cultural and social structural conditions that reduce or exacerbate feelings of psychological conflict between the generations and, particularly, between parents and their adolescent children. As I mentioned earlier, the fact of nuclear family structure removes potential mediators and buffers such as grandparents and aunts and uncles from the daily interacting family unit, thus probably intensifying both negative and positive feelings. Rapid social change and ambiguous, contradictory, or changing role definitions disrupt family functioning and intensify psychological sources of conflict particularly in the area of authority patterns within the family.

The increasingly protracted economic dependence of adolescents on their parents also promotes conflict and mutual resentment, particularly in a society that values independence and self-reliance. While many adolescents have the opportunity to change the economic circumstances of their lives in modern societies, in the process they become impaled on a series of contradictory cultural values and experience severe role conflict. In the middle class—particularly in America—creativity, independence, work, and achievement are highly valued and are incorporated into the role prescriptions for adolescents of both sexes, increasingly. Adolescents are exposed to these values and, at the same time, to the imperatives of conformity in bureaucratic settings, protracted dependency in an economy that cannot use them, and the fun morality of a wealthy society. They have been taught that all men are equal, but they must compete to show their superiority. They must compete and at the same time love their fellow human beings. And they are more apt to take the latter admonition seriously than their disenchanted elders.

Males have a particular problem in that the culture defines aggressiveness as masculine. Very intense relationships with the mother in the middle-class nuclear family may encourage passivity, however, particularly where the mother is college educated, ambivalent about her homemaking role, and turns mothering into a career. Studies on the phenomenon of momism and maternal overprotection in middle-class America have been accumulating since the 1940s, reflecting the existence and the seriousness of this problem, particularly in the upper middle class.

Male adolescents probably suffer more severely from the economic dependence of adolescence since the culture prescribes greater independence to the male than to the female. On the other hand, males generally are less sexually repressed than females and are less apt to experience conflict with the requirements of impulse gratification in an era of greater sexual freedom. Females are freer in their sexual behavior than previously but they are still less apt than males to experience orgasm.

Female adolescents have their own unique culturally based conflicts that become more pronounced during adolescence. They are taught to be aggressive and competitive with males in school and later on jobs —although not at the highest levels of either. At the same time, however, feminine role prescriptions require that they be dependent, nurturing, and receptive in their relationships with other human beings, and particularly with males. The requirements of passivity, dependence, empathy, and conformity, furthermore, ill-prepare females for the resourcefulness, impersonality, and self-direction that are often required in rapidly changing, bureaucratic, and anomic American society.

These sources of conflict stem from role prescriptions and are additional to or may reinforce psychological conflict. The nature and intensity of role conflict varies, however, by class. In competing for marital partners and occupational statuses adolescents who are rich are more protected by family power and privilege from the worst ravages of competition and insecurity. Adolescents who are poor are often not even in the economic race and marriage is frequently the result of a drifting together and a fatalistic acceptance of the inevitable, particularly if the girl becomes pregnant.

Adolescents have reacted to their unique stresses and frustrations by withdrawing, by fighting, or by persevering and enduring—which is the most common adaptive response. Each path has its own particular subcultural trappings and peer group supports. Time, if not the major social institutions in industrialized societies, is on the adolescent's side, fortunately. Biologically, at least, adulthood is inevitable, for those who survive.

MIDDLE AGE AND OLD AGE

BIOLOGICAL CHANGES. During childhood and adolescence, biological changes in human beings are pronounced and easily observable. During the years of young adulthood, physical change is slower: youth tends to ebb unremarked and almost unnoticed.

In middle age, beginning somewhere around forty-five, and varying with social circumstance as well as genetic predisposition, physical changes once more become marked. Family roles in highly industrialized societies, however, are affected more by social definitions and expectations than by the actual biological changes that occur as family members age, as we will see.

Aging individuals experience cumulative, irreversible, and progressive losses of energy and muscular strength, a decline in sex hormone production, a slowing in speed and reaction time, impairment of the functioning of the five senses—vision, hearing, taste, smell and touch—and some changes in intellectual functioning.[34] The question of just how much, if any, intellectual deterioration occurs in healthy older people is a matter of controversy. Measurement devices are imperfect and psychological factors, such as motivation and drive and the level of initial intellectual endowment, affect the fate of the intellectual faculties of particular individuals differently in old age. Investigators tend to favor and report studies that support their own beliefs and attitudes about the topic. Detachment about the aged is difficult to achieve, particularly in a society such as ours, which places such a high value on youth.

Intelligence is a complex attribute. Some of the components in problem-solving ability may decline with age, while others increase, and still others remain unchanged. Generally, individuals over seventy, who are healthy, tend to perform better than young adults on tests of vocabulary, verbal comprehension, and simple arithmetic. They perform less well on tests involving speed in decoding information.

Much of the evidence that has been cited to show a decline in overall intelligence with age reflects, rather, the decline in reaction time, which affects I.Q. scores negatively. The basic ability to learn new material, furthermore, does not seem to decrease with age. The ability to perform finely coordinated voluntary movements is impaired but is counterbalanced by the longer experience (where this is not made obsolete by technological development) and better work habits of older individuals. For this reason, studies of worker performance in industry show little change in productivity up to age sixty or sixty-five. Older workers are removed from the economy less for reasons of biological decline than for reasons of pressure from below—to make room for younger people who need employment and who are less expensive to employ since they start at lower salaries.

AGING AND FAMILY LIFE. The effect of biological aging on family functioning varies according to the stage of technological development in different societies and largely according to class within a particular society.

In nonliterate societies, very few individuals and only those with exceptional health, strength, and luck were able to survive to old age.[35] Physical strength and quick reflexes were highly prized attributes in these societies. Older people, who could no longer perform tasks that required speed or strength, such as hunting, were given less physically demanding work. They dressed the kill, processed hides, repaired equipment, or helped with young children. The aged often worked until their death. Labor intensive economies, which have few sources of energy available other than manpower, utilize the old in less physically taxing but socially necessary tasks.

The burden of caring for the aged who were incapacitated was distributed among the many members of the extended family. Euthanasia was sometimes practiced in societies where life conditions were extremely harsh and brutal. The majority of nonliterate societies, however, did not detach, disengage, or disaffiliate their aged members from the world of the living and the productive.

Since the aged were so extraordinary in having survived in these societies, their survival was frequently attributed to the benevolence of supernatural forces. Gentle treatment by younger family members was often sanctioned by the fear of ghostly revenge. The aged were also a socially valuable repository of oral tradition, knowledge, magic, and skills in societies that had no written language. This was another factor that enhanced their prestige and encouraged good treatment by the younger generation.

As societies have developed technologically and become more stratified economically, the treatment of the aged has been less benevolent and has varied largely according to their power and economic status. A close reading of the historical records of the ancient Hebrews, Greeks, and Romans, and of medieval Europe and colonial America, reveals that the ideals of respect, deference, and kindness toward the aged were little more than the official rhetoric of these societies. In fact, only a few old people and largely those who were within the upper strata, were able to command good treatment. The majority suffered neglect at best, and cruelty at times. The wife shared the fate of her husband, and lost her privileged status, if she had it, upon his death.

In highly industrialized societies, physical strength and speed become less socially necessary attributes in the population, but social conditions—increased population and the possibility of operating the economy with far fewer people, for example—disqualify the more numerous aged from economically productive work. They lose status dramatically upon compulsory retirement, and those who suffer most are those who have been most highly achievement-oriented during their work years.[36]

It is an irony of modern times that men and women who have been most successfully socialized into the traditional masculine and feminine sex roles during earlier stages of their life cycle experience the greatest stress in old age. Very dependent, nurturing women are less able to redirect their energies into nonfamily activities when their children leave or if their husbands die; [37] very aggressive and highly achievement oriented men have more difficulty shifting to the affiliative and expressive role that is appropriate to the status of retirement.

Definitions of the obligation toward the aged of the family and the state in modern Western societies have varied largely in relation to the course and nature of technological development, the degree of urbanization, and the value placed on economic productivity and success in the society.

As the mobile, nuclear family becomes the typical form in modern societies, and as the aged are increasingly removed from the work situation in economies that cannot or will not use them, the burden of support of the aged becomes increasingly difficult for the family. Three-generation households in which the aged live with their grown children are not desired by a majority of old people or by their middle-aged children. In America, the pattern exists more frequently in the working class, which has less choice in this respect. A widowed mother may live with her grown daughter. Even here, however, it is an atypical arrangement and is becoming less frequent. The middle class is more apt to provide cash income supplements for their needy aged parents.

The role of the state in sharing the responsibility for the aged with the family varies in Western industrialized societies. The United States, in this respect, compares unfavorably with other Western democracies. In England, for example, government-subsidized home service is provided for those who cannot perform domestic tasks or who need temporary nursing care. In America, the incapacitated old person must move in with an adult offspring or be disengaged from the household and the community and placed in an institution. A society that values youth and success to the extent that America does is not tolerant of those who are left behind. Breaking ties is less painful than daily confrontation with human frailty and vulnerability. Nevertheless, in both societies, only a small percent of the aged live in institutions. A little more than half of the old people in America, further-more, live near at least one grown son or daughter whom they visit regularly.

In Sweden public housing for the aged is extensive and Old Age pensions are tied to the cost of living and provide completely for the material needs of old people. These pensions are granted to all, re-gardless of private means or the amount of previous tax contributions.

England and Sweden industrialized earlier than the United States and are still, at present, more highly urbanized. This explains part of the difference in government policies, but ideological factors have also been operative. The American belief in rugged individualism and in-dividual responsibility for one's fate, and the concomitant dislike of paternalistic government, also account for some of the relative delay in increased government assumption of the responsibilities toward the aged that the small nuclear family cannot adequately fulfill, in America—or anywhere else, for that matter.

BIOLOGICAL SEX DIFFERENCES

Differences in hair color are not regarded as having a necessary rela-tionship to behavior and are not accorded great significance in human societies. Differences in skin color, however, are a very important basis for evaluation and behavioral expectations. Biological sex differ-ences have also been a major source of cultural definitions of expected behavior, particularly within family groups. The biological fact of maleness or femaleness has been elaborated into conceptions of mas-culinity and femininity that have varied greatly in different societies. Almost any personality trait or human activity, even the care of young children (which was assigned to secondary husbands in polyan-drous Marquesan society) has, at one time or another, been defined as either masculine or feminine or both in various societies.

HORMONAL DIFFERENCES

In nonhumans, the relationship between the sex hormones and behav-ior is clear and direct. Injection of female sex hormones intensifies nurturing behavior; injection of male sex hormones increases aggressive behavior. Nonhuman females do not have territorial defense patterns, nor do they usually engage in competitive and dominating behavior, typically.

The relationship between the sex hormones and human behavior, however, is much more difficult to establish. Culture intervenes, and biological factors are not easily isolated. The cortex, which is most highly developed in human beings and is the seat of memory and learning, can override hormonally based predispositions.

Studies of newborn infants, who have experienced minimal cultural influences, have not demonstrated consistent, reliable, or extreme sex differences in such areas as emotional response or sensitivity to various stimuli. Adult males do have a somewhat higher metabolic rate on the average than females, but again, numerous studies that have been conducted have not found typical and consistent differences in the activity patterns of female and male infants. These studies have limited value in relating behavior to sex hormones, however, because differences in male and female sex hormone production do not become pronounced until puberty. By this time, typical differences in the socialization experiences that males and females undergo from the moment of birth obscure the role of the hormones in determining sex role behavior.

While there is evidence that high levels of the female sex hormone estrogen are associated with positive mood states and low levels with negative emotions in many women, this does not have crucial implications for sex role prescriptions. The fact that a large number of women seem to be somewhat more irritable, depressed, and anxious just before menstruating, after delivering a child, and during menopause does not mean that women should be excluded from certain statuses. Occupants of all statuses are irritable, depressed, and anxious, at times, whatever the state of their hormone levels, and men also experience mood swings that correspond to changes in their hormone levels, although they are less apt to express vulnerable moods because of male sex role prescriptions which stress fortitude and stoicism.

The topic of the relationship between sex hormones and the emotions in men and women needs much more study. Many of the investigations on women that have been conducted up to now have failed to distinguish between the effect of changes in hormone levels and preexisting personality traits of the women who have been studied. They have also failed to allow for the power of suggestion since the subjects of these studies have been aware of the investigators' interest in their menstrual cycles.

The most obvious biological differences between males and females, in physical size and strength and in reproductive functions, have been most clearly tied to sex role definitions, particularly in the past. Hunting, for example, required not only great physical strength but greater mobility and freedom to roam, often great distances, and for weeks and sometimes months at a time. Women, who gestate and nurse the young, have been less available for these activities. On the other hand, in many societies women have been assigned more physically arduous tasks than men.

With technological development, the tie between biological sex characteristics and behavior becomes more tenuous and the possibility of modifying sex role norms in more radical ways arises. Push-button technologies and weaponry in highly industrialized societies do not require physical strength. Women are less apt to nurse their young, and biological scientists may yet devise a substitute for the womb to gestate the young. The dead hands of culture and biological and economic necessity weigh less heavily in modern societies, and individual choice and inclination have freer play.

In the past, the differences between males and females in reproductive roles have had highly significant implications for the restriction of the sexual behavior of the female, particularly in economically stratified societies. The reasons are obvious: paternity cannot be established if the sexual outlets of the female are unlimited, and it is the female who is directly burdened with an illegitimate child. Advances in the technology of birth control in industrialized societies have been a very important facilitating factor in the decline of the double standard.

The recent explosion of a number of myths regarding female sexuality will change sexual practices and attitudes and values even more once they become widely publicized.[38] It has been established, for example, that the clitoris and the lower third of the vagina are the primary erotic zones in female orgasmic response. The female-superior coital position has, however, been unpopular in this country and has been defined as unfeminine. When it becomes more widely known that this position allows for more direct clitoral stimulation and is thus more likely to be gratifying to the female, notions of the relationship between masculinity and who is on top are likely to be discarded.

In the sexual folklore of the West and the East, the size of the penis has long been equated with masculinity and the capacity to gratify women. Recent empirical investigations have revealed, however, that there is little anatomical difference in this respect between males, when the penis is erect. The publication of this kind of information and the knowledge that female sexual response derives largely from external stimulation and does not depend on the depth of penetration is likely to promote more rational sexual techniques, devoid of anxious and irrelevant male concerns about their comparative anatomical adequacy.

CHROMOSOMAL DIFFERENCES

Other biological differences between males and females have had less obvious effects on sex role definitions and are significant, largely, as they affect the sex ratio. The human female has an XX chromosomal makeup; the male has XY chromosomes. Genes of the X chromosome have been found to provide greater protection against a variety of infectious and noninfectious diseases.[39]

The greater vulnerability of males to disease results in a higher percentage of male prenatal deaths, higher male infant mortality rates, and a shorter average life span. The sex ratio, however, does not become greatly imbalanced for biological reasons since more males than females are conceived and born.

The longer life-span of women, a trait that characterizes the female of the species throughout the animal kingdom, has been enhanced in recent decades by the increased control over deaths during childbirth. The earlier occurrence of puberty in females has enabled them to marry earlier and to marry older males. Combined with their greater resistence to disease and their longer life-span, these biological facts have led to a surplus of approximately five million women in the United States—particularly in the older age categories. The surplus has implications for female behavior insofar as it encourages competition for males, with emphasis on seductive behavior and beauty aids as secondary consequences.

The surplus of females will probably not get out of hand, however, because scientific medical advances, particularly in the control of the major noninfectious diseases to which males have been more susceptible (heart disease and some forms of cancer, for example) will diminish the consequences of women's biological advantage in this respect at earlier stages of the life cycle. The upper limits of life expectancy for either sex will not change much, but men as well as women will be more likely to reach these limits.

If it becomes possible to predetermine the sex of offspring, and this seems quite likely, the sex ratio may be adversely affected, however. A surplus of males will probably no longer be produced to compensate for their lower survival rates. Most American parents prefer one male and one female child, at least. If the present decline in the birthrate and in the desired number of children continues, two rather than three children will probably become the national ideal. The sex ratio at birth will then be equal, but survival rates will continue to be unequal unless the infant mortality rate is zero.

At present, the preference in most American families is to have a male child first. If this can be realized, incidentally, it will reinforce and promote certain definitions of appropriate male behavior in our society. First-born children are more apt to be self-reliant, independent, and achievement-oriented. They also, on the other hand, have a higher incidence of neurosis and suicide.

OTHER DIFFERENCES

Males also differ from females in that they do not experience a sudden and dramatic decline in their capacity to reproduce: they do not go through menopause. The desire to father a child can be gratified up to age eighty for some males. This can be disruptive of the monogamous system of marriage, particularly in societies such as ours where the values of loyalty and duty toward marital partners are declining in favor of standards of personal happiness and self-fulfillment. The pattern in which an older male divorces his wife of many years, marries a much younger woman, and starts a new family is becoming more frequent.

Intellectual functioning has also varied typically between males and females, but no demonstrable biological basis for these differences has been established. The female brain weighs less on the average, but brain size has not been found to be related to intellectual capacity. The effects of typical differences in life experiences and different cultural expectations of male and female intellectual qualities and strengths can, on the other hand, account for most, if not all, of the observed variations. Girls, for example, exceed boys in verbal performance: they speak sooner, articulate more clearly, use longer sentences, read sooner, need less remedial help, and excel in grammar, spelling, and vocabulary throughout the school years.[40]

A factor which strongly affects verbal fluency and intellectual functioning generally is the amount of contact with parents, particularly with the mother. First-born children, only children, and children of small families tend to score higher on I.Q. tests, on an average. Twins, who must share contact with parents from birth, and who tend to communicate with each other rather than with adults, score lower, on the average. Girls are given less freedom than boys, are kept closer to their mothers, and have more contact with adults. Their earlier development of certain intellectual skills is very likely related to this fact. Their greater tendency to conform and to be less active and aggressive is more consistent with student role requirements in the school situation. They therefore earn better grades than boys, even in subjects such as the natural sciences, where boys score higher on standardized achievement tests.

In adulthood, no typical male-female differences show up on various tests of intelligence. On more specialized tests, differences that appear are clearly culture-bound. Women, for example, tend to have a better memory for names. This is a reflection of their stronger interest in people and interpersonal relations, which, in turn, stems from cultural role expectations.

THE GENETIC BASIS OF AGGRESSION

Aggression is a trait that has been culturally defined as masculine and desirable for males in almost all societies, the differences in these definitions having varied in degree rather than kind. Throughout human history men have usually been required to suppress emotions related to love to a greater extent than women and have been allowed greater freedom to express emotions related to hate.

The question is then, and this is a very important question, bearing on the fate of human societies and the inevitability of war: To what extent is male aggression genetically determined? The relationship between male sex hormones and aggressive behavior in nonhumans has been clearly demonstrated, as I have already pointed out. Females are more apt to engage in nurturing, withdrawing and pacifying, and grooming behavior than males. When male sex hormones are injected into pregnant monkeys, the female offspring are more active and aggressive than the female young in control groups. Injection of male hormones upsets the dominance order in adult animal groups.

The fact of hormonally-based aggressive behavior stemming from the sex drive is of a different order of significance, however, than the recent claims that have been made for an independent, spontaneous, genetically based aggressive or "killer" instinct in men. The work of Konrad Lorenz and Robert Ardrey, positing the existence of an indigenous, nonreactive urge to kill in human beings, which they believe is phylogenetically programed, has convinced many who seek explanations, and perhaps absolvement, for the persistence of war.[41]

These authors and their compatriots in the currently fashionable pursuit of futility and despair ignore the evidence of zoology, anthropology, psychology, and physiology in their arguments.[42] Animals kill for survival—to satisfy hunger needs; they do not kill for the sake of jealousy, rivalry, or pleasure. Man elaborates the notion of killing for survival, often irrationally, but this is not proof of genetic predisposition.

Territorial defense patterns in nonhumans, which are a means for establishing differential food and sexual privileges in animal groups, involve threatening display rather than killing. Furthermore, man's closest relatives, the primates, do not have the pattern of territoriality and are not usually belligerent except when provoked. Even prehistoric man, according to the anthropological evidence, did not hunt to satisfy a "predatory instinct" but to satisfy his hunger needs and those of his dependents.

Physiologists have not been able to demonstrate the existence of chemical and physical changes in humans and other animals, comparable to the drop in blood sugar levels as hunger builds up, that indicates a continuous internal accumulation of aggressive energy without reference to an external stimulus.

From the field of psychology we have a vast body of data demonstrating that much of the aggression manifested by human beings is a reactive response to frustration—the blocking of needs or goal-directed behavior.[43] If aggression is universal in human societies, it is because frustration is universal. Social conditions affect the amount of frustration in the population and the culture encourages or inhibits the expression of aggression. It also identifies the objects of aggression: strangers, minority groups, noncomformists and, currently, adolescents. The list of individuals and groups who have served as objects of displaced aggression in human history is long.

War, if it is inevitable, is programed not in the genes but in frustration-inducing social conditions, abetted by cultural values that make extreme distinctions in definitions of feminity and masculinity, equating masculinity with killing and stoicism and repudiating love-related sentiments as effeminate. Societies pay a price not only for their requirement of extreme aggressive behavior in the male, but also when they ascribe extreme passivity to the female. They lose the potential contributions to the culture of many of their citizens, who are encouraged to contribute to the growth of population rather than culture. We now need knowledge, ideas, and direction far more than we need people. Masochism, the correlate of passivity in the human female, can also have tragic effects on the family. It promotes resentment and subtle retaliation of those who suffer and encourages the aggression of those who benefit.

Long-haired youths in contemporary societies exalt love and repudiate killing in their slogan 'Make love, not war." They also deemphasize differences in male-female sex role definitions. The sex act is not only a nondestructive alternative to militarism, it also contains an element of aggression and allows for a partial release of these impulses. To make love and not war is grounded in profound psychological truth.

Nonliterate societies that have made little distinction between the ideal personalities of males and females have emphasized physical and love-related pleasures such as eating, drinking, and sex. This type of society, however, has been very rare and survived, when it did survive, because it was isolated from other societies.

If we are to redefine the cultural ideal of masculine aggressiveness it will have to be a worldwide phenomenon. The balance of love will have to replace the balance of terror; otherwise the pioneers in this undertaking will perish. Economic abundance has encouraged impulse gratification, freer emotional expression, and a greater honesty and sense of responsibility in at least some of our young citizens. I think we can anticipate continued changes in this direction. But the have-not nations will have to be carried along in the sweep of future auto-mated splendors; otherwise, the envy and frustration of the other four-fifths of the world will undo us.

It should now be clear that the basic biological needs and traits of human beings throughout the life cycle establish certain broad limits to the content of family roles, but it should also be clear that role conceptions and definitions can vary greatly within these limits as so-cieties industrialize. If biology is destiny, it becomes much less so in modern times, with the aid of science and technology.

Biological maturity and all that this implies, including the intensi-fication of the sex drive, coincides less with provisions for sexual grati-fication and marriage in modern societies. Biological changes during other phases of the life cycle also tend to be less relevant to cultural dictate as retirement, for example, becomes compulsory, largely for technological and economic rather than biological reasons.

Sex role typing declines, in certain respects, as basic differences be-tween males and females in size and strength, particularly, become less significant for economic functioning. Differences in reproductive functions continue to define parental roles, but less so than in the past, and limited ultimately by the basic biologically grounded emo-tional needs of the human young—needs which underlie and strongly effects physical and intellectual development and growth. The content of the role of mother or father changes as societies de-velop technologically, but the status of parent is unlikely to be elimi-nated because of these basic biological needs.

A look into the past with an eye to changing social conditions, par-ticularly advances in science and technology, will further illuminate this point. We will also see, then, how certain values—particularly the values of individualism, secularism, equalitarianism, rationalism, and achievement motivation—arise, become widespread, and are incorporated into family roles as societies move toward increasing control over their material environments. Our heritage is an ever-expanding possibility for deliberate and rational change in family life and in social life, given the values that guide us. Scientific knowledge accumulates, however it is used, misused, or ignored by those whom it would benefit.

3

TYPES OF HUMAN
SOCIETIES

Human societies, and the major institutions within them—the family, religion, government, economy, education, and recreation—can be seen to have varied in rather typical ways, when these societies are classified on the basis of the level of technological development and the state of scientific knowledge that has characterized and distinguished them.

In science, typologies are constructed for the purpose of classifying observed facts according to some explanatory or interpretive principle. Scientific typologies, ideally, meet the standards of all inclusiveness and mutual exclusiveness: all relevant facts can be classified, and the location of any particular fact or item, once the classifying principle is established, is logical and irrefutable.

THE PROBLEM OF TYPOLOGIES

When human beings, their activities, or their societies are being classified these standards are difficult to meet. Individual variability and cultural complexity may defeat the most enthusiastic typologists in the social sciences. It is currently voguish to attack typologies as sterile or oversimplified. This is a symptom of the anti-intellectualism that has always characterized American society and that has been enhanced recently by severe political and economic strains and a growing ethic of despair. Scientific typologies have, in fact, played an important role in the history of science and in the progressive accumulation of information and understanding about human beings and their material and nonmaterial worlds.

When viewing human societies as falling into several major categories on the basis of the level of scientific information available to them and the primary means by which resources are produced and energy is obtained, it is important to bear in mind that the model and the concepts are abstractions. Reality is almost infinitely complex: societies usually present a mixed picture and boundaries are often blurred and hard to establish.

Many societies, furthermore, have not changed in a pattern of step-by-step progression and advance in the ability to harness energy, manipulate the environment rationally, and accumulate verifiable knowledge about the world. Some societies have regressed, usually after a defeat in war—Western Europe and the Mediterranean nations after the fall of Rome are examples. Other societies have stood relatively still—hunting and gathering societies that have survived into the present, for example. And still other societies have skipped stages, sometimes quite dramatically—the industrializing societies of sub-Sahara Africa, for example.

Social conditions and social trends that have been associated with gradual technological development in the West, such as increased urbanization, rationalism, secularism, bureaucracy, and mass literacy have occurred and proceeded at varying rates in the newly developing nations of the Third World. The very rapid introduction of advanced industrial techniques and scientific methods for controlling disease and curbing death has produced transitional conditions, such as the population explosion, that have little precedent in Western history. These nations may or may not emulate the West in the economic, ideological, political, or familial patterns that will ultimately characterize them. They are living, natural experiments that may provide additional answers to the question of the relationship between ideology, technology, and institutional forms. They are ongoing, readily observable case studies in rapid social change and are a unique challenge to practitioners of the sciences of man.

Whatever the problems of typologizing—of definition, placement, and judgment—if the thousands of separate and discrete societies that exist and have existed, from small bands or tribal enclaves of 50 to 200 souls to behemoths of almost 8 million toilers and dreamers, are classified on the basis of tools and weaponry, the state of scientific knowledge, the amount and kind of property and economic surplus, and the nature and degree of mobility within and between their borders (and all of these are interrelated), we find certain associated patterns and regularities in family life.

A TYPOLOGY OF SOCIETIES

The major types of societies that have existed can be classified, in broad perspective, as nonliterate hunting and gathering and horticultural societies, agricultural societies, and urban, industrial societies. It is possible, also, to construct a highly generalized portrait of family life as it has varied within these major types of settings, focusing on courtship and love, and husband and wife and parent and child relationships. This particular task I will leave for the following chapter, after I have traced the major changes in values that have accompanied technological evolution.

PRELIMINARY CONSIDERATIONS

Two major technological innovations that have occurred in human history have had such enormous consequences for social life that they can be called revolutions.[1] The two revolutions are the Agricultural Revolution and the Industrial Revolution. The concept of revolution, in this case, refers to degree rather than speed of change. The changes associated with the Agricultural Revolution—the increase in the size and permanence of settlements and in the amount of occupational specialization of labor, the increase in trade and commerce, the differential accumulation of wealth, the development of class structures, and the elaboration of political and religious forms into more formal structures—took thousands of years to unfold. The effects of the second major technological revolution have been progressively speedier, largely because cultural borrowing and diffusion occur more quickly as mobility and communication increase and isolation and provincialism decline. By and large, and sooner or later, however, more efficient techniques for adapting to the environment have tended to replace less efficient techniques, although values have played an enormously inhibiting or facilitating role in this process.

The Agricultural Revolution, in which the technique of cultivating plants was discovered, is believed to have first occurred in the Middle East about ten thousand years ago. Horticulture, the first stage in this revolution, involved the knowledge and use of the hoe and digging stick (but not the plow) in plant cultivation. Animals were domesticated in horticultural societies and used as a source of additional food production, but the use of animal power to replace manpower (the harnessing of oxen to the plow, for example) was not known.

Archeologists do not agree about whether the techniques of horticulture developed independently in the New World or whether they diffused throughout the world from their origin in the Middle East —to Britain in the West and to Asia in the East, and then across the Bering Straits to the New World. Whatever the path and the vicissitudes of this particular technological innovation, however, the consequences for the quality of human life and for human values were tremendous.

With the advent of the Industrial Revolution in England in the eighteenth century, machine power gradually replaced manpower and standardized goods came to be produced by standardized machines using interchangeable parts. Mass production and mass consumption are a paramount consequence of this additional source of power. Industrialized technology enhances the material comfort of all segments of the society—albeit disproportionately—in a way that the Agricultural Revolution did not. Inhabitants of modern urban slums wear fashionable factory-made clothing that is often in sharp contrast to the shabbiness of their shacks and tenements.

In my description of nonliterate and agricultural societies, I shall rely mainly on studies and observations of isolated surviving agricultural and nonliterate communities made before these communities began to change dramatically through contact with industrialized so-

cieties. Since the rate of social change in these isolated societies has
been very slow, it is likely that family life and social life has not varied greatly through the ages.

NONLITERATE HUNTING AND
GATHERING SOCIETIES

Man as a distinct animal species has inhabited the earth for at least
two million years and possibly even longer. Modern man (Homo sa-
piens) appeared sometime between 70,000 and 35,000 years ago. Until
the discovery of horticulture, man survived as a hunter and gatherer,
moving constantly (sometimes every week) as local food supplies were
exhausted, living in small, isolated, homogeneous bands, with little or
no specialization of occupations other than on the basis of age and sex
and no surplus food. Life was short, but not necessarily brutish and
nasty. While there was no leisure class and all who were physically
able participated in the quest for food, the average work week (three
or four days) has yet to be attained by a majority of humans in modern societies.

The realm of the sacred, that part of the world that is set aside,
treated with reverence and awe, and regarded as unmanipulable and
uncontrollable, was all-powerful. Animism, the endowment of the
physical environment with supernatural properties and forces, was
common. Man in nonliterate societies often did not distinguish between himself and the material environment with respect to such
qualities as life, motivation, and power.

Superstition, chance (including games of chance rather than games
of skill and strategy), and fatalism were rife; knowledge of rational
techniques for adapting to the environment was very limited.

The rate of social change was so slow as to be almost impercepti-
ble. The number of elements of technology and knowledge in the culture that could be combined or recombined into new forms was small,
and the rate of invention neglible. The number of people comprising
the intellectual and motivational pool from which could arise innovation and new solutions to the problems of existence was limited. Contact with other societies and the possibility of borrowing more efficient or effective techniques was sporadic or nonexistent.

Most hunting and gathering societies had leaders who emerged temporarily at times of decision-making to mediate discussions of when and where to migrate or how to plan food-foraging expeditions. These individuals were usually not full-time leaders, however. No permanent, widely recognized status of leader existed, typically, to which was attached automatic rights of deference and authority regardless of the personal qualities of the occupant. Leaders returned to the mundane survival activities of daily life when their stewardship talents were no longer required. And this was true often of the only other specialized occupation in these societies—the shaman or medicine man, specialist in magical salvation or destruction.

Magic occupied the life space that organized religion and science occupy in more technologically developed societies. The shaman coerced the spirits and demons into intervening in the concerns of his clients, bringing them health, long life, love, or the defeat of enemies. The shaman was self-employed; he was not a functionary in a permanent religious organization. Priests have represented a moral community; shamans worked alone and without the backing of a systematic, all-embracing theology.[2] They neither competed with or supported family values, beliefs, or behavior.

While monotheistic religions existed in a small number of nonliterate societies, rarely was there a conception of an omniscient, omnipresent supreme being who was actively concerned with sanctioning and implementing a system of ethics.[3] This development is associated with more complex technology, more populous and more heterogeneous societies, and the decline in the effectiveness of the family and the community in exercising social control.[4]

Private property as we conceive of it was unknown in hunting and gathering societies: the ownership of land that was soon to be abandoned was pointless and the accumulation of liquid capital, or its equivalent in shells or other media of exchange, was impossible in the absence of an economic surplus and trade. The notion of personal property, however, did exist and was vested in such items as ritual rights (to songs, dances, and names and the small amount of portable items (tools, weapons, or clothes) that individuals were able to transport on their backs. It was easy to discard and duplicate new equipment that was simply and quickly constructed out of materials that were readily available at the new site. The impetus for both possession and accumulation was lacking in hunting and gathering societies.

Men hunted and fashioned spears, axes, and bows and arrows out of wood, stone, and bone. Women collected edible vegetation, bore and nursed children (often throughout the entire span of their short lives), and succored the ill, the wounded, and the dying. Communal sharing of the kill was common. Luck and chance were powerful forces; families and individuals could ill afford the independence that stems from economic security. They might be next in the capricious battle with the forces of accident and destiny.

Villages rarely contained more than fifty people and were often even smaller. Sometimes villages sharing a common culture and language were united into a tribal structure, but these were usually not under the effective rule of a centralized authority. It was difficult for one family to accumulate the equipment and the power to subdue the rest.

Population remained fairly constant, automatically regulated by balanced and very high birth and death rates. Where this balance was upset, infanticide was often practiced. Inefficiency was the rule in reproduction and in survival—in all areas of life, in fact, except art, music, and religious ritual, where the standard of efficiency did not apply.

Except where protected by natural, geographic barriers, most hunting and gathering societies that did not discover the use of metals in fashioning tools and weapons and the technique of deliberately cultivating plants were doomed to extinction by the expansion of societies that did make these self-preserving discoveries.

NONLITERATE HORTICULTURAL SOCIETIES

With the introduction of horticultural technology in human societies, the press of the search for food lightened. Population increased, since population in nonindustrialized societies tends to expand in proportion to the available food supply. Settlements become more permanent; the exhaustion of the land took longer to accomplish than the exhaustion of the local supply of wild animals and vegetation by hunting and gathering societies.

Tribal federations became more unified and effective political units, under the control of families that had forged ahead in power and wealth. The families who achieved this initial advantage probably did so because they happened to have produced more sons, and sons who were more aggressive than their compatriots. Expelled misfits of extended families or survivors of decimated, weaker families sought the protection and swelled the ranks of the more powerful families, bringing still more manpower and fighting power to these families.

More efficient food-procuring techniques made an economic surplus possible and a new source of distinction between families and individuals appeared. Humans evaluate people, places, and things. They arrange objects in their environment in a hierarchical order and judge them as more or less good, or more or less desirable, according to their values.

In hunting and gathering societies, prestige was differently allocated to members of the society on the basis of age, sex, and personal qualities such as physical strength, bravery, or enterprise. With the development of an economic surplus, the differential possession of the land and its fruits became an additional criterion for evaluating families and individuals.

Religious ideologies provided the motivation for families to produce more than they could consume and the justification for turning over this surplus to the priests and to the heads of more powerful families, who traded protection for tribute. Hereditary, family-based advantage in property, power, and prestige became established and class structures came into existence.

More efficient techniques for supplying food released some members for full-time specialized occupations in the arts and crafts, religion, and politics. Pottery and weaving appeared and the use of metals (other than iron) was discovered. Specialized occupations meant the production of more goods of a particular type than the individual, his family, or the village could use. These new and often luxurious products were either transferred to the elite or were traded by barter. Trade and commerce encouraged cultural diffusion and mobility; the rate of social change increased somewhat.

Women usually did the work of planting and harvesting in horticultural societies. Men often did the heavier work of clearing fields. They continued to hunt to supplement the subsistence needs of the society, their contribution in this respect varying from society to society. In societies where hunting continued to be more important than plant cultivation in providing for subsistence needs, the status of males relative to females was usually higher.

Cannibalism, headhunting, human sacrifice, and the taking of slaves are practices associated with horticultural technology and the accumulation of an economic surplus. In the absence of written records, scalp collecting became popular in many societies—a prototypical form of conspicuous consumption in which the number of accumulated scalps served to validate the status of the brave and the strong.

Not all societies developed a more advanced technology—some for reasons of geographic isolation or climatic idiosyncracy, others for lack of an ideology that encouraged accumulation, aggression, and innovation. On the ruins of the less isolated of these societies arose the great agricultural societies of historic times.

AGRICULTURAL SOCIETIES

Agricultural societies appeared in Egypt and Mesopotamia approximately five thousand years ago. These societies not only had the plow, they harnessed oxen to the plow, thus taking a giant step in the direction of conserving human energy and supplementing the sources of power available to the sociey. With rare exceptions, these societies were distinguished from hunting and gathering and horticultural societies by three features: the development of a written language (limited to the elite), the existence of urban centers, and the yen and capacity for empire-building.[5]

Horticultural societies such as the Maya of Yucatan, who possessed an ideographic system of writing, a calendar and a numeral system that included the concept of zero, the Incas of Peru, who were empire builders, and the Chinese during the Shang and Chou dynasties, who had a written language, urban centers and a feudalistic system of government, were unique exceptions.

Other differences, that distinguished horticultural from hunting and gathering societies became even more pronounced in agricultural societies: the size and permanence of settlements, the variety of occupational specialization, the extent of trade, the degree of social inequality, the level of productivity, the size of the economic surplus, and the size of the non-economically productive class all increased.

Warfare in horticultural societies was usually sporadic—limited to raiding, plundering, the capturing of slaves, or the driving off of interlopers. In agricultural societies, wars of conquest and occupation became the preferred form. Conquest and subjugation were faster and more efficient ways to increase wealth than patiently to await the rewards of continuing technological development. Technological innovation in agricultural societies, furthermore, was discouraged by the fact that the fruits of new discoveries were likely to be preempted, promptly and mercilessly, by the religious and political elites.

Occupation, governing, and tax collecting from huge, heterogeneous territories require organization and personnel. Agricultural societies developed vast political and military bureaucracies to handle these tasks as well as religious bureaucracies to cope with the problem of social control.

Bureaucracies develop when it is necessary to coordinate the activities of large numbers of people in the carrying out of large-scale tasks. If one man is collecting taxes from ten people, he can keep track of who is paid up and who isn't. If a thousand collectors are collecting taxes from a million people, somebody back at the home office has to keep records, coordinate functions, and provide supplies to avoid waste, loss, duplication, and chaos. And so the administrator is born.

As the tasks of protecting, controlling, building, and expropriating economic resources grew in scope in agricultural societies, bureaucracy proliferated in the political and religious spheres. No single extended royal family could provide the talent or numbers to coordinate the activities of governing and worshiping. And so they recruited administrators, tax collectors, and professional armies from other elite but less powerful families.

Literacy is also a usual precondition for governing large territories (and, incidentally, a precondition of bureaucracy). Records must be kept of tribute exacted and rewards dispensed to loyal functionaries. Since the written language was very complex in less technologically developed agricultural societies, a specialized occupational group of scribes came into existence. Here, again, recruitment was largely from the wealthy and powerful families, since only they could afford to release their sons from productive work and could pay the costs of long years of education.

Formal legal systems developed in response to the need to control large populations with local and varying cultures and conceptions of justice. Codified law represents an attempt to substitute impersonal, universalistic principles for the blood revenge tactics of family-dispensed justice. Where formal law and agencies of law enforcement are lacking or ineffective, injured parties and their families usually engage in the spiraling and interminable cycle of retributive acts characteristic of blood revenge. This can be disruptive of the civic order and predictability required for the effective operation of centralized governments.

Technological development proceeded unevenly and slowly in agricultural societies, but most of them eventually learned how to harness wind and water power and developed increasingly more efficient tools and weapons, particularly with the discovery of iron.

Centralized governments were usually monarchical and autocratic. Oligarchic republican forms of government appeared in maritime societies, where land was less significant as a source of wealth. The degree of centralized control by a king or emperor was related to the size of the territories governed, the existence of natural barriers, and the consequent ease of transportation and communication within the society. Feudalism, a system in which power is dispersed among lesser elite families within a loose federation headed by a king or emperor, existed where highly centralized control was difficult to maintain.

Conflict was a constant feature of agricultural societies, stemming from economic, religious, and ethnic differences in interests and values and from the barely endurable life conditions of the peasants. Spontaneous peasant revolts, particularly in more advanced agricultural societies, were standard occurrences.

While the royal family and the governing class together comprised probably less than 2 percent of the population in these societies, they owned from one-half to two-thirds of the national wealth.[6] Religious faith and political coercion (where faith was inadequate) kept the supply of tribute, rents, and taxes flowing from the masses to the elite. Privilege was divinely sanctioned; excellence, for those who were chosen, was measured by success in extracting the surplus to the fullest extent possible. Good works served God, not man. The haves and the have-nots worshiped, usually, with equal conviction. The privileged were as convinced of their right to wordly goods as the masses were resigned to their suffering.

Land was the most important source of wealth in agricultural societies, and wealth and power truly walked hand in hand. Political power was viewed not as a public trust, even ideally, but as a proprietary right to be exploited to the fullest for family and personal gain.

Urban settlements developed as seats of government and religion and as centers of industry and trade. In the towns and cities, peasants could exchange what little was left of their surplus for tools, spices, and other products they could not produce. It was in the urban centers that the middle class became prominent, consisting of merchants, self-employed artisans, and minor clergy and officials who served the governing classes. The emergence of a middle class had great significance eventually for the redistribution of power and for changes in family life. The urban middle classes have been the innovators and the leaders not only in political and religious revolutions but in many of the significant changes in values that have characterized family roles and functioning in modern times.

Despite the fame of urban centers in agricultural societies, they contained only a small proportion (5 to 10 percent) of the population. The masses continued to exist close to the land, illiterate and short-lived, subject to unremitting hardship and the unrelenting coercion of economic necessity and authoritarian political power.

Magic, superstition, and fatalism were preeminent features of peasant society as they had been in less technologically developed, nonliterate societies. For the masses, knowledge of rational techniques for coping with the environment had increased somewhat, but control over one's fate and the availability of recourse and options had changed very little from prehistoric times.

INDUSTRIAL SOCIETIES

With the Industrial Revolution, man took a mammoth stride in the direction of increasing control over his environment and edged that much closer to destroying it. Probably the most important precipitating factor was the invention of the steam engine. The shift to manufacturing as an important source of national wealth, and the establishment of the factory system, transformed Western economies and societies and led eventually to the dominance of the West in world politics, prerogatives, and privileges.[7]

The effects of the Industrial Revolution have reverberated throughout the world over a period of almost two hundred years as man has shifted his energies increasingly from extracting activities (farming, mining, lumbering, and fishing) to manufacturing, from stoking and operating machines to watching and adjusting machines, from flying shuttles and spinning jennys to automated plants and computerized services, from producing to selling and distributing, and from accepting and obeying to innovating and experimenting in all spheres of life. Creative energies have been released that lay dormant for thousands of years in agricultural societies, curbed by repressive economic conditions, fatalistic ideologies, and highly effective social controls.

To explain a complex social phenomenon such as the Industrial Revolution, it is necessary to select from a multitude of historical events, those that seem most relevant. History is objective fact; interpretations of history vary with time, place, and the world views, predispositions, biases, and interests of societies and their citizen-writers of history.[8] Causal explanations in science, furthermore, are subject to the process of infinite regress.

Where should one begin?

Contemporary Western historians and social scientists usually trace the sequence of events that culminated in the Industrial Revolution to the voyages of exploration and discovery that began in the fifteenth century in Europe. Natural science, mostly concerned at that time with understanding and explaining the mysteries of the solar system, was given a tremendous boost by the knowledge that became available about the shape of the earth. Physicists, academists, and biologists were also stimulated to seek a more empirical, experimental basis for their propositions and predictions, to venerate past authority less, and to trust in observation more. Technology, the practical application of scientific knowledge, benefited accordingly.

Myths about the material universe and, much later, the social order began to be struck down, gradually but inexorably. Rationalism came to be valued; its fruits apparent in profit and power and, less immediately and less obviously (even now), in benefit to human life.

The age of exploration and the colonization of the New World resulted in a flood of previously scarce metals into the mother countries and a great acceleration in world trade and commerce. One important consequence of the influx of gold and silver into European countries was the spread of the money economy and the decline of the barter system.

In the less technologically developed agricultural societies of antiquity, grain served as a medium of exchange where simple barter was inadequate. Since grain is cumbersome and perishable, scarce metals of various kinds came into use as substitutes for payment in kind or in grain. At first the size and weight of metals used in commerce were standardized for local areas. Then, as empires were consolidated by ruling families, centralized governments assumed the responsibility for minting standardized metal currencies.

The spread of the money economy in the fifteenth and sixteenth centuries had tremendous implications for social life. It facilitated trade: with a less cumbersome medium of exchange, it was easier to calculate profit and loss rationally, to invest and reinvest in business ventures, and to accumulate the kind of wealth that could later be easily diverted into industrial enterprises. Liquid capital gradually replaced land as the major source of the wealth of nations, families, and individuals.

As trade and commerce increased, merchants and artisans multiplied. Merchants stimulated new needs and acquisitive impulses among the populace. Their mobility in agricultural societies provided an important channel for cultural contact and diffusion. Their pursuit of gain and their calculation of profit in monetary terms were prototypical manifestations of the values of individualism, rationalism, competitiveness, and active mastery over the environment which are basic to achievement and innovation-oriented industrializing and industrialized societies. These new values eventually undermined the cooperative, conservative, fatalistic, nonventuresome, and nonrisk-taking values of the landlocked peasant in traditional societies of the West and had enormous implications for family life.

In addition to the material benefits that derived from the era of exploration and colonization, the Protestant Reformation, in the sphere of ideology, is also credited by some scholars with having had a major facilitating effect, if not an independent causal effect, on the social trends that eventually resulted in the Industrial Revolution in the West.[9] No comparable innovation in religious beliefs and values occurred in the East; Eastern religions continued to value other-worldly spiritual goals and future-worldly rewards. For life on earth their advocacy of patience and resignation remained unchanged.

The Protestant Reformation was itself a response to social conditions that had been changing at least since the time of the crusades. The Crusades opened up new culture contacts and new trade routes, stimulated new material wants, and enhanced the importance of urban centers. The doctrines of Protestantism, as enunciated by Martin Luther and John Calvin in the Sixteenth century, provided a set of values and beliefs that eventually filled the spiritual needs of urban merchants and craftsmen, supporting and reinforcing their interests and endeavors.

Luther exalted honest work in one's calling as a way of serving God, thus removing the association of work with punishment and sin, which was the view of the medieval Catholic Church. The Church had frowned upon accumulation beyond that which was necessary for existence, and had stigmatized the merchant and the moneylender as thieves and parasites.

Calvin regarded profit-making as a respectable source of income, as respectable as wages and rents. His doctrine of predestination, which held that individuals were destined at birth for salvation or damnation and could do nothing to change their fate, had the unintended consequence of promoting rationalism in business life. This-worldly success came to be interpreted as a sign that the individual was favored by God in the lottery of fate and was, therefore, among those who were destined to dwell in His house forever. Continuous work, thrift, self-discipline, and self-denial brought not only worldly success, but relief from the constant anxiety that Protestants felt (difficult for secularized modern man to imagine) about whether or not they were in fact among the chosen.

The Puritan sects, prominent in England, Scotland, Holland, and New England declared that man was alone before God. His closest friends might be among the damned. He must seek success at the expense of his competitors and must rely ultimately only on himself. Individualism was given powerful ideological legitimation, and loneliness, the corollary of individualism, eventually became the existential condition of the most independent, the most self-directing, and the most steadfast of the practitioners of the success ethic.

Certainly the founders of Protestantism had no idea of the far-reaching consequences of their movement, particularly in promoting, at least indirectly, profit-making enterprise and industrialization. That there was this association initially is indicated by the fact that the first nations to become highly industrialized were Protestant. But the wealth shipped in by the colonies to many of these nations was an antecedent, if not sufficient, factor. In the East, the most highly industrialized nation, Japan, experienced no great change in the religious sphere prior to industrialization; it was, however, a colonizing power.

MODERN SOCIAL TRENDS

The social conditions accelerated or sent into motion by the Industrial Revolution and the values that became widespread have profoundly changed the quality of life in contemporary industrial societies. Briefly, I want to sketch some of these changes, focusing on those that seem most clearly associated with recent trends in family life.

In highly industrialized societies, developments in medical science and public health diminish the death rate and lengthen life—almost doubling the average life span in the past one hundred years. Reproduction becomes more efficient (fewer babies die) and birth rates decline. Even with the decline in birth rates, however, world population has increased nearly sixfold in the two hundred years since the Industrial Revolution.

The high level of technological development makes for an increasing emphasis on mental skills and selling and distributing in the economic sphere. The middle class eventually becomes the numerical majority; the class pyramid moves toward a diamond shape, with the rich at the apex and the poor at the bottom and most people located in the middle. Movement up the class structure becomes common;

movement down becomes feared. In traditional societies, movement either way was rare and irrelevant to the dreams and hopes of the majority of the populace.

Psychological mobility, the subjective counterpart in expectation, identification, and aspiration of actual, objective change in group membership, also becomes common. The mass media, to which all gradually become exposed, encourage this process by serving as sources of information about life styles, would views, roles, etiquette, speech, dress, consumer goods, distant places, and distant people. Models proliferate, as do socializing agents. Superficial differences, urban-rural, regional and, to a lesser extent, class differences are increasingly leveled by the standardized images promulgated in the mass media. The leveling process is underwritten by the efficiencies of mass production and the reality of mass consumption.

Geographic mobility is also common: mobility in search of jobs, education, better housing, greater political freedom or social acceptance, new experience, adventure, or escape from family and community controls. The more highly industrialized the country is, the higher the mobility rates. The United States has the most mobile population in the entire world.

Factories and offices require concentrated populations; urban centers contain a majority of the population in industrialized societies. In the United States, over 70 percent of the population lives on 1 percent of the land; 6 percent of the work force can produce enough food on the farms to feed more than thirty times their number.

The degree of urbanization in a society is not determined by the growth of cities but by the proportion of the total population that lives in cities. In India, cities are growing, but the high birth rates in rural areas maintain the urban-rural population ratio at a fairly constant level. The movement from farm to city is a finite process; eventually, the United States will be a nation of cities. Farms will be factories to which workers will travel from their urban homes to perform their daily shift of work.

Technological development proceeds at such a rapid rate in industrialized societies that economic growth can increase national wealth faster than wars of conquest. Invention and creativity underlie this technological development; governments with an eye on the future become highly involved and concerned about the quality of education and the level of achievement motivation of their citizens.

The specialization of occupations increases constantly: the *Dictionary of Occupational Titles in the United States,* published by the Department of Labor, lists over 20,000 separate and distinct kinds of jobs in this country. Ever-narrower specialization in training and knowledge becomes the only way to keep the pace of technological change and the accumulation of information from becoming an intolerable strain on human intelligence.

The clock and the traffic light replace sunrise and sunset as regulators of human activity. Time becomes an obsession, particularly for those who have much to accomplish. Human contacts become increasingly segmented, impersonal, superficial, ephemeral, utilitarian and, ostensibly, rational.[10] The cash nexus replaces emotion and sentiment as the foundation and lubricant of social relationships. Loyalties to place and group decline; sophistication—flexibility and a capacity to adapt to constantly changing social situations—becomes a useful quality of character and often an absolute imperative.

Democracy—nominal, formal, fictional or actual—becomes the preferred governmental form and the wistfully desired organizational principle in other spheres of life. Educated, skilled, better fed, and more economically secure people are not submissive or compliant; they want a greater role in determining their fate, whether they are workers, women, ethnic and religious minorities, or young people.

Democracy and bureaucracy become the competing and antithetical ways of organizing authority and decision-making; they are antithetical because authority in bureaucracies flows from the top down. In democracies the process is reversed, ideally. The preservation of individualism, where this is valued, becomes a new challenge: not only do political coercion and authoritarianism suppress inventiveness and creativity but so does bureaucracy. It is an organizational form that is intrinsically inimical to unpredictability and change and, therefore, to initiative and to the restless, achieving spirit, although authority in bureaucracies, based as it is on skill and training, is usually not as arbitrarily oppressive as traditional forms of authority.

Intellectuals in highly industrialized societies, whatever the form of government (as long as it allows intellectuals to express themselves) decry the increase in anomie and alienation, the fragmentation of identity, and the endless quest for meaning and purpose. They deplore the breakdown of community and extended family and the decline in solidarity and belongingness. They point to the destructive possibilities of runaway rates of unbalanced and uncontrolled social change. They bemoan the apotheosis of technology, bureaucracy, the functionary, and the expert. They fear the concentration of power and the availability of vastly more efficient and effective means for obtaining and maintaining power. And they mourn the loss of innocence, the decline of utopia, and the disappearance of chiliastic visions.

As societies have changed from traditional (nonliterate and agricultural) to modern (urban, industrial) the family has also changed, particularly with respect to the values that become incorporated into family roles. The proliferation of urban values in industrialized societies—values such as individualism, equalitarianism, secularism and rationalism, tolerance and cosmopolitanism, and active mastery and achievement—is increasingly reflected in all aspects of family life—in courtship patterns, in marital interaction, and in parent-child relationships.

We now have a basis for understanding why these values arise as societies develop technologically. Let us go back, then, and trace in greater detail typical variations in family role conceptions and performance in nonliterate, agricultural, and industrialized societies so that we can better understand survivals and trends in contemporary family life—in America, particularly, and elsewhere.

4

VARIETIES OF FAMILY
LIFE

How has technological evolution affected the family? How has the family changed from the time when human societies consisted of bands of roving hunters and gatherers, to the time when land became an anchor and a source of wealth, to the time when mobility is once again an everyday condition of human existence and wealth is far more abundant, somewhat less equally distributed, and more movable and liquid in form. How have the values that I have called urban values affected family roles and relationships and family problems and conflicts?

The trail is not easy to follow: the historical record favors the literate and the privileged and those who achieved greatness or eternal notoriety. The prehistorical record, as reconstructed by archeological studies of weapons, tools, and art forms, says little about family roles, childrearing practices, or intergenerational relations in nonliterate societies that are extinct. Again we must depend on data from isolated surviving traditional societies that have been studied in modern times. We assume, as I mentioned earlier, that family roles and values in these societies are not so different from those of their extinct predecessors, at least in major respects, given the very slow rate of social change in these societies.

THE FAMILY IN PREHISTORY AND HISTORY

Prehistory and history are time perspectives. Prehistory refers to the era in human societies before the invention of writing and written records. Culture and subculture are associated with place—with territory and society—and with groups.

A single culture may be viewed historically, through time. Since rates of social change vary, the two perspectives do not always coincide when we compare societies, using the level of technological development as a basis for classification. In the very long run, however, and I am thinking now in terms of thousands of years, certain typical trends in family life have emerged that are associated with major breakthroughs in technology. I am refering specifically to the Agricultural and the Industrial revolutions.

In the late nineteenth and early twentieth centuries, scholars of the Social Darwinist persuasion attempted to reconstruct step-by-step stages in family structure and functioning that they believed were associated with each step-by-step unilineal advance in technological development. Underlying these exercises was the assumption of progress toward human perfection and the assumption of a progressive intellectual superiority in the population base that supported technological development and a moral superiority in the family forms associated with different levels of technological development.

Usually the family was depicted by Social Darwinists as having advanced from a state of primitive sexual promiscuity, to group marriage, to matriarchy, to patriarchy and, finally, to the most perfect union—Victorian monogamy. Among the more famous scholars who applied this model to family life were Herbert Spencer in his *Synthetic Philosophy* (1860), Johann Jacob Bachofen in *Das Mutterrecht* (1861), Lewis Morgan in *Ancient Society* (1877), and Edward Westermarck in *The History of Human Marriage* (1891).

Frederick Engels in *The Origin of the Family, Private Property and the State* (1902) also rested his analysis on technological development and assumed unilineal and universal stages in family structure and functioning. His analysis, however, focused on technological development as it affects the accumulation and distribution of economic resources in human societies and was devoid of assumptions of historical progress in family life. Engels, in fact, felt that family life had deteriorated morally from a presumed original state of equality between man and woman in societies where property was communal.

We now know as a result of accumulated anthropological researches and more complete and accurate historical information that there has been no universal, step-by-step, inexorable pattern of family development and change in human history. Matrilineal societies, for example, have been common in Asia, Africa, Oceania, and aboriginal America. These societies, in which descent is traced through the female line and where newlyweds usually reside with the wife's relatives, have typically preceeded patrilineal forms, because horticulture usually precedes agriculture and matrilineal family organization tends to occur where women make primary contributions to subsistence needs by doing the cultivating in the society. But this is not an inevitable consequence in horticultural societies; in fact, a majority of these societies are patrilineal.

The economic role of women in a particular society may be a necessary but it is certainly not a sufficient determinant of patterns of calculating descent in that society. Given similar technological conditions, the discovery of horticulture, for example, preexisting traditions, values, and myths, the origins of which are forever lost to the scholarly and the curious, have played an obviously important role in affecting the direction of change in family roles in particular societies.

We cannot argue, on the other hand, that family values and ideologies have been an "independent" force in social change as one sociologist has claimed. William Goode has pointed to the communal experiments in China, Russia, and Israel, and the retreat to more traditional forms in the latter two countries, as evidence of the "independent" effect of family patterns on technology and economy.[1] The decision to institute communes in China, Russia, and Israel was made by political leaders, not by families; preexisting family values have promoted the commune movement in China and undermined its success in Russia and Israel. The family, however, did not initiate the communal experiments in these countries.

Basic human needs and basic human emotions are universal; similar material conditions are associated with similar institutional characteristics. While there is no necessary and inevitable connection between the two, in particular societies we have ample evidence of certain major directions of change in family roles and values as societies have developed technologically and as they have achieved greater scientific knowledge about the world and its inhabitants.

To present an overview of family life throughout human history is an enormously complex task. We can simplify this task somewhat if we select out certain major aspects such as family structure and functions, courtship and love, marital interaction, and parent-child relationships and describe typical variations that have appeared in nonliterate, agricultural, and industrial societies, particularly as these variations reflect major changes in values.

FAMILY STRUCTURE

The concept of structure refers to a number of units—molecules, individuals, social classes, for example—that are related to each other in certain interdependent and recurring ways within some sort of bounded whole: a cell, a family, or a society. In the family, structure refers to the totality of socially recognized statuses or positions occupied by individuals who are engaged in regular, recurring, and socially sanctioned interactions and relationships. With death, divorce, separation, marriage, and childbirth, family structure changes: statuses are lost or added; roles are redefined or redistributed.

Family structure, historically, has been either nuclear or extended. Anthropologists have preferred the designations "conjugal" or "consanguine." The conjugal or nuclear family structure is one in which the marital tie is paramount. In extended or consanguinal family structures, biological descent is the primary fact of family life and the marital tie is deemphasized.

The pattern that predominates in a particular society will depend in large measure on the mobility of its members as they pursue economic goals—both movable game and the vicissitudes of the job market are associated with nuclear family structure.[2] The extended family is a cumbersome unit, ill-suited to situations where individual members or nuclear families are frequently on the move.

The type of food supply, the size of the economic surplus, the kind and amount of property and wealth and whether it is family owned or individually obtained, are related factors. All in turn are tied to the level of technological development. Because of the importance of the mobility factor, the nuclear family, relatively independent from the larger familial unit with respect to authority and economic functioning, predominates in hunting and gathering societies and in urban, industrial societies.[3] In horticultural and agricultural societies, the family is less mobile or is immobile, is bound to the land as a major source of sustenance, and strives to maintain the extended structure as the cultural ideal.

Ideals and reality, however, have rarely coincided for the masses of human beings. While the extended family has been the cultural ideal in a majority of societies, it is very likely that the common man has lived, throughout history, predominantly in modified extended units. Certainly this has been true in the West. The rich and the powerful in stratified societies, whether horticultural, agricultural, or industrial, could afford to maintain the extended form better than their poorer contemporaries. Harsh living conditions, inadequate food supplies, and little empirical knowledge about the control of disease and the environment subverted this type of family structure. Death frequently removed key figures in the three generational unit.

Polygyny (the taking of multiple wives) has also been a cultural ideal in a majority of human societies, but here too, from all evidence, monogamy has been the actual condition of the majority of men and women. It was mainly the upper strata who could support a polygynous family structure and then largely in societies where women performed important subsistence economic activities.[4]

Monogamy becomes the ideal as well as the actuality in agricultural societies. While a higher level of technological development permits a more efficient utilization of manpower in these societies, the wife's direct contribution to subsistence (the extraction of raw materials) declines and polygyny becomes more difficult to support.

Among areas of the world where polygyny has survived in agricultural societies are the Arab countries. Women in Arab societies have performed the lion's share of subsistence activities. Men sowed and helped harvest, but women were largely responsible for the daily activities that kept families alive. Work was defined as demeaning, and more suitable for the female sex. Cultural definitions of masculinity emphasized bravery, sexual virility, and idleness. Males valued talk and gossip (with other males) and adornment. They marketed because marketing was not defined as a chore, as it is in Western societies, but as an occasion for social interaction and pleasurable talk.[5]

The practice of polygyny, incidentally, promoted and reinforced social inequality in economically stratified societies. Strong, wealthy extended family groups were in a position to obtain more wives who, in turn, produced more sons, thus adding to the family pool of warriors and enhancing its claims to protective prowess and its right to rule over weaker families.

In highly industrialized societies, extended family patterns are most pronounced among the very rich and the very poor. Wealth is the source of the authority of the matriarch or patriarch among the rich —wealth and concomitant power and social contacts that facilitate careers and guarantee security to younger generations of the family. Among the poor, necessity and custom bind the extended family together. The maternal grandmother in the black slums cares for the illegitimate grandchildren while the mother works. The aunts, uncles, cousins, comadres, and compadres provide food and other essential goods and services within segments of our society characterized by extremes of insecurity, illness, deprivation, and distrust and suspicion of government and nonindigenous professionals.

The extended family structure is more functional in traditional societies where land is the basis for subsistence and wealth. The family provides services that cannot be obtained elsewhere. It works as a productive economic unit, pooling and sharing economic resources. Children are essential to economic survival and well-being. A widow with a large number of children is a desirable mate because she brings needed field hands and household helpers into the new marriage.

In highly industrialized societies, children do not earn their keep and are not necessarily a source of support in old age. Family members are employed on an individual basis. The head of the family does not control the employment of his wife and children. Recruitment into jobs is based, at least ideally, on talent and skill rather than on membership in a particular family group. Economic resources are in the form of money paid to individual members of the family.

In early stages of industrialization, however, the traditional patterns survive to the extent that families tend to work in the same factory under the supervision of the male head of the household.[6] Wages, particularly those earned by children, are turned over to him. Women can rarely sustain themselves on their earnings in a labor intensive economy. The income that married women earn is used to provide essentials for the family that the labor of husband and children are unable to provide.[7] Only in highly industrialized societies do some married women work for psychological reasons and only in this kind of society can a large number of women earn enough by their own labors to sustain themselves (but not their children) adequately.

Family businesses, headed usually by the oldest living member of the family, also promote the continuation of extended family patterns in early stages of industrialization. With increasing industrialization, family firms are bought up and absorbed by nationwide corporations. The son and heir becomes a bureaucrat or an employee in the national office rather than the one-man boss of the local textile mill, glass factory, or shoe factory in Middletown, Yankee City, or Springdale, U.S.A.

Nepotism still persists, however: in working-class districts of London, fathers "speak up" for jobs for their sons when the latter finish school.[8] Unions in the United States show preference to sons of members. The children of movie stars have an edge over equally talented children of nontheatrical family origins. But even the former cannot succeed without some talent, at least, as fate and family origin become somewhat less intertwined in modern societies.

The extended family fights a losing battle with the necessities of geographic mobility and the attractions of social and psychological mobility in industrialized societies. The young leave the old behind, on the farms and in the older areas of the city, as they seek better jobs, better living conditions, and new experiences. The relocation of factories and offices out of the city, urban renewal, public housing projects, and planned New Towns (for the middle classes) provide additional impetus for the separation of extended family members.

Social mobility usually leads to geographic mobility. Extended family ties are further weakened by differences in interests, values, and life styles that characterize members who achieve a higher status or descend to a lower social status than their families of origin. Where geographic mobility is forced, as in urban renewal areas, the severing of extended family ties can be a major reason for severe conflict with public agencies who enforce this mobility. This is particularly true of certain ethnic groups such as Italian-Americans, who have very strong extended family bonds. The second and third generation tend to stay together in older, urban, working-class neighborhoods where the immigrant grandparents originally settled, even though the younger generations, at least, have the choice of moving to middle-class neighborhoods.[9]

Extended family contacts survive in urban industrial society but in much-modified and attenuated forms.[10] The completely isolated nuclear family with no relatives within easy visiting distance is relatively rare. It is most likely to be found where there has been extreme intergenerational mobility—where a daughter or a son has risen from the working class into the upper middle or the upper class, for example, or where children have married across racial or religious barriers. Most extended families maintain contact by visiting, letter, and telephone; help is exchanged in the form of gifts, loans, baby sitting services, and advice, particularly during emergencies, even in the middle class, where extended family ties are weakest.

These patterns are qualitatively different, however, from the daily contact and interdependence based on economic necessity that characterized extended families in traditional societies. At least some of the stresses that families experience in modern societies can be attributed to a lack of adequate substitutes for the services that the extended family performed in the past: care and support for the aged and incapacitated, daily child-care and housekeeping help, and a built-in supply of wider social contacts, confidants, and companions in recreational activities.

Loneliness was rare where the extended family provided a network of stable social relationships. Working-class wives in contemporary industrialized societies who have moved away from their mothers and sisters are the loneliest of women, particularly if they do not work.[11] They are not as apt as their middle-class counterparts to be involved in church, club, volunteer community activities, or friendship relationships.

The decline of the extended family and familistic values and the concurrent rise of individualism in modern times is reflected in language. Many traditional societies contained no word meaning "self" or "individual." These concepts did not reflect a meaningful or significant aspect of social and psychological reality. The question: "Who are you?" was answered in terms of familial rather than occupational status: "I am Jacob, son of Isaac and grandson of Abraham." The question in modern societies is not "Who are you?" but "What do you do?" or, in its less direct form, in the United States where status distinctions are more subtle, "Where do you work?"

The type of family structure that is associated with industrialization can and does appear in agricultural societies. In the United States, for example, the nuclear family, sometimes enlarged by unmarried individuals who were forced to attach themselves to a family unit in order to survive, was typical even before industrialization, which occurred largely after 1850.[12] Preexisting conditions promoted the nuclear family structure and the values associated with this type of family, values such as personal autonomy, achievement, and equalitarianism. Probably the most important of these unique conditions was the shortage of women (which promoted equalitarianism within the family), the existence of a frontier (which provided escape from community controls and encouraged independence and individualism), the absence of a medieval past (with its cultural rigidities and authoritarian values), and the selective, continuous, voluntary settlement of this country by restless, independent people who were escaping economic and political oppression.

While the trend in family structure has been in the direction of the nuclear form, as societies have industrialized and as people have become more mobile, technological development is neither a necessary or a sufficient cause of this development. In present-day mainland China, for example, Maoist ideology, which extols collectivism and impugns individualism, has resulted in a continued de-emphasis of the nuclear family unit, even as the country has industrialized. This is true on the provincial communes which are industrializing as a result of deliberate government planning. It is also true in urban areas, however, where the aged, if they are not incapacitated, are encouraged to move in with an adult offspring.

In mainland China, the preexisting pattern of familism, with its emphasis on the needs of the family rather than the individual, has been utilized in the fulfillment of planned social goals. The individual continues to be submerged within the larger unit: extended family, commune, and state. In Japan, the stem type of extended family structure, consisting of three generations—grandparents, parents, and grandchildren—is still the typical pattern,[13] despite the fact that Japan is now among the top three countries of the world in level of technological development. While preexisting values in Japan, particularly a very strong tradition of familism, have preserved the extended family, at least with respect to residence patterns, the other aspects of extended family life, however, are declining: three generational hierarchical authority, the de-emphasis on the marital tie relative to the parent-child tie, and the economic dependence of the younger adult generation on the elders. This is true certainly in urban areas.

It is possible that the isolated nuclear family is a type of family structure that will never exist in certain countries. It is also possible to predict that traditional values in these countries have had only a temporary delaying effect on what will ultimately be the worldwide pattern. And, finally, it is possible to argue that the isolated nuclear family in countries like the United States is a transitional form that will never become typical.

The New Towns and urban collectives that are springing up in the United States may be a harbinger of social arrangements that will become established in this country and throughout the world, either by government fiat or by spontaneous popular choice. Communes (where property is commonly owned) and cooperatives (where private property exists but where certain goods and services are shared and exchanged cooperatively and without monetary compensation) can be viewed as functional equivalents, in some respects, of the traditional extended family. The commune or the cooperative provides collective security for nonproductive members, shares homemaking and child-rearing functions, and helps overcome the problem of loneliness.

These forms differ from the traditional extended family in that membership in the group is nonconsanguineal, is based on mutual interest and voluntary choice (in non-Communist countries), and authority is not rigidly hierarchical, arbitrary, and unquestioned. In the spontaneous give and take of the collectives that are currently springing up in this country, authority tends to settle on those who have needed skills and who are older and more experienced.[14]

One other type of family structure, which is neither nuclear or extended, becomes significant in highly industrialized societies—the female-headed family.[15] This type of family structure, which arises as a result of illegitimacy, death, divorce, or desertion is not nuclear, since an essential aspect of the nuclear family is the marital tie. It is not necessarily absorbed into the extended family either, however, as it is in traditional societies.

Higher income levels are associated with lower divorce rates and lower illegitimacy rates. For this reason and because of the anticipated decline in the incidence of widowhood during earlier stages of the life cycle as a result of continued advances in the control of diseases to which males are more susceptible than females, an overall decline in the proportion of female-headed families in automated societies would seem to be a reasonable prediction.

Divorce rates may continue to rise, however, for reasons that I will take up later. And the future of illegitimacy rates cannot be predicted simply on the basis of anticipated rises in the overall standard of living in automated societies. Right now, for example, in slum areas in New York, legalized abortion is not having the immediate predicted effect on illegitimacy rates among Puerto Ricans. Machismo, the standard of masculinity in which manhood is defined in terms of virility (demonstrated by fertility), is still strong in these areas and impedes family planning efforts, at least temporarily.

In black areas, other subcultural supports exist in the ready availability of the maternal grandmother to care for illegitimate children. On the other hand, sociological surveys have indicated that illegitimacy is disapproved among the poor and that girls who bear illegitimate children experience lowered self-esteem. Will the pattern of illegitimacy continue to persist, even if preventive measures such as birth control counseling and alternative measures such as legalized abortion become readily available to all?

The ultimate answer lies probably in the realm of psychology—in deep-seated, unconscious needs. This level of motivation will not be easily recognized and unearthed by behavioral scientists using paper and pencil surveys. Nor will it be easily dealt with if the goal is to eliminate illegitimacy entirely. Technological development and the rising economic status and psychological independence of women may result in a spreading pattern of voluntary illegitimacy. Even now, unmarried women of high status, even though only a handful, are opting for mother-child families as a matter of conscious and deliberate choice. The reasons for this choice have little to do with economic deprivation or subcultural role definition, however, at least at present. These are idiosyncratic actions rooted in the unique psychological life histories of the women involved.

The breaking down of rigid, traditional male-female role prescriptions is an enabling factor. The notion that marriage and the marital tie are essential to parenthood is on the decline, as indicated by the fact that adoption agencies are now granting babies to single adults.

The feminine equivalent of "bachelor" is "spinster"—a word with negative associations. We can anticipate the addition to the English language, eventually, of a more neutral label to describe this status, a label that will reflect its voluntary nature for an increasing number of women. Spinsterhood implies a lack of choice and settling for less.

As voluntary single status for women becomes less stigmatized than it has been in the past, a growing number of women are likely to opt for motherhood without the responsibilities of marriage. This pattern, however, is far from becoming a matter of subcultural preference for women of high or of low status. The two-parent family and child relationship is still the prototypical human relationship, whatever its variations. Unless that is eliminated, we can predict that the heterosexual pairing relationship, whatever its problems, will survive and endure for most adults who have a choice, in all societies.

FAMILY FUNCTIONS

Societies have a need to survive. So do individuals in family groups. The two levels of need not only may not coincide, they may be in direct opposition to each other. The need to protect the total society by means of war results in the death of individual family members. Tax policies, and the allocation of societal resources for defense or for the benefit of one particular segment of a total society, may deprive certain other families in the society of the possibility of providing for adequate physical care, intellectual growth, and emotional security of its members.

It is for this reason that I have explained the universality of the family in terms of its role in fulfilling human rather than societal needs. People do not ordinarily live their lives to fulfill abstract societal goals. If families do fulfill these goals, they do so coincidentally and incidentally. The process of fulfilling the needs of family members, in fact, can be potentially destructive to the total society. The need to procreate may endanger the survival of the society by overpopulation and related problems of famine and contamination, for example.

Functionalists have defined several major social tasks, called "functional prerequisites," that must be fulfilled if human societies are to survive.[16] The major institutional areas in modern societies—the family, government, religion, education, and the economy—are organized around the carrying out of these tasks.

The maintenance of society requires some sort of institutionalized (widely accepted and deeply internalized) patterns for regulating sex, reproduction, and the care and socialization of the young. This is the province mainly of the family and the educational system.

Every society must also have a system for producing and distributing essential goods and services to its members. This is the area where technological and economic institutions operate, and also, government, insofar as it is involved in taxation and redistribution of the national wealth through public services.

The total society and individuals within it must have protection against human destructiveness. This includes protection against the destructive behavior of others and self-destructive behavior. The government performs this function also.

Another function, the fulfillment of which is considered by some to be necessary for survival, is the presence in societies of a shared system of beliefs that gives meaning and purpose to life and furnishes motivation for its continued existence. In traditional societies this is the monopoly of religion. In industrializing societies, various secular equivalents of religion appear in the form of social movements. Unlike religion in traditional societies, the goals of these secular movements are this-worldly and the means are empirical. The supernatural is regarded as irrelevant to the daily affairs of men.

The controversy over this functional prerequisite centers on whether the motivation for group or individual survival can or must be derived from group goals and ideologies. In highly industrialized societies, where individualism is a dominant value, who is to impose shared beliefs and on what basis shall most, many, or some people accept these beliefs?

It may be that in highly complex, heterogeneous, rapidly changing societies, individuals increasingly must work out their own unique life plans on the basis of personality, opportunity, and constantly shifting social conditions. Certainly the direction of the most recent social movements in highly individualistic America is away from systematic ideologies, long-range goals, and widely agreed upon means.[17] Families, in their socializing efforts, are also much less certain about what is, what must be, and what will be.

In nonliterate societies, particularly of the hunting and gathering variety, all functions that sustain the society are fulfilled by the family as an automatic consequence of its daily operations. The distinction and possible discrepancy between societal needs and individual and familial needs are minimal in societies not economically stratified. In these societies, the family regulates sexual behavior, reproduces, socializes, protects, works, distributes available resources, and performs religious rituals—largely without the aid of experts, specialists, and outsiders. The head of the household is soldier, preacher, worker, and teacher.

As societies develop technologically and become more differentiated, the family also becomes more specialized in its functions. Its province in the protective, economic, religious, educational, and recreational spheres is contracted and its functions delegated, in part, to outsiders. The economic functioning of the family becomes curtailed as other agencies take over the production of items formerly manufactured in the home: prepared foods, clothing, soap, candles, and numerous other items.

Married women, unless they work outside of the home, perform services that have not been entirely farmed out to factories, bakeries, launderies, and other agencies. The economic value of their services, while considerable, is not readily measurable and evaluated. An important determinant of self-esteem in a business civilization (how much one is worth economically) becomes a problem for women. Employed wives tend to have higher self-esteem than nonworking wives.[18]

Men, because of more efficient technologies and higher levels of wealth, are often able to earn enough to purchase the goods and services no longer produced or provided in the home. If they cannot, the wife may work also. In the 1900s, in America, the typical woman employee was unmarried and in her twenties; in the 1970s, the typical woman worker is married and in her forties. Economic motivations apparently are more important than psychological reasons (a strong need for achievement and recognition, boredom, loneliness, or isolation, for example) in determining the decision to work. Most working wives claim they would not continue to work if their husbands earned what they would consider an adequate salary or wage.

The trend in highly industrialized societies is away from the evaluation of children as economic producers, as a source of security in old age, or as proof of sexual virility. While the birth rate declines, children continue to be desired but increasingly for psychological rather than economic reasons; they are a source of love and companionship, at least ideally, and they can provide meaning and purpose to life.

Protective functions are also shared with specialized agents and agencies—police, lawyers, judges, and all others involved in law enforcement and defense. The courts and law-enforcement agencies are used, in fact, by one family member against another where family authority is disputed or where definitions of family obligation or tolerable behavior are not shared. Parents have usually invoked the law against children; aged parents have sued for nonsupport, for example.

It is a sign of the times that laws making this type of legal action possible have been repealed in the United States recently. On the other hand, there have been several instances where children have brought suit against parents on the grounds that failure to conform to family norms is insufficient reason for withdrawal of economic support. This type of suit would have been unimaginable in colonial America. Several colonies had laws that specified the death penalty for sons over sixteen years of age who repeatedly disobeyed their parents.[19] The decline in patriarchal authority is probably the single most dramatic change that has occurred in family life in the transition from agricultural to industrial societies.

Families no longer provide all possible role models that the child may want to emulate, nor do they have the necessary skills and knowledge to train their children to fulfill adult roles available in the society. Schools constantly expand their jurisdiction, claiming expertise to legitimate their authority when there is conflict with parents over the content, goals, and techniques of teaching.

Passive recreation, commercialized and provided by skilled professionals, replaces the taffy pull, the barn raising, folk dancing, and other activities which usually involved the family as a unit in traditional societies. Active participant recreation—golf, tennis, and swimming, for example—is now more often an individual than a family project.

For a while, during the 1950s, it looked as though television would bring the family together again, in the recreational sphere, in front of the television set in the living room. Two-, three- and four-television set families have dispelled these earlier visions of a recreational renaissance within the family.

Families tend less and less to pray together. The family altar is gone in industrialized societies. The saying of grace at mealtime is disappearing. The discrepancy between religious ethics and daily conduct grows wider. Rationalism tends to drive out dogma, where the two are in conflict. The use of contraception, for example, other than the rhythm method, becomes widespread among Catholics, despite the official position of the Church on birth control.

One function of the family—the provision of emotional support and gratification—becomes more, rather than less, important in modern societies. The expectation of happiness as a by-product of family interaction was absent or minimalized in traditional societies. Happiness is a concept that is closely linked to to the value of individualism. The remorseless struggle for life in preindustrial societies did not foster sentiment, kindness, and the luxury of concern about self-esteem, self-fulfillment, and personal growth in family relationships.

LOVE AND COURTSHIP

LOVE DEFINED

Love, a most elusive concept, has been perceived differently in human societies with respect to its relevance to courtship and to marriage. In all societies, since human beings possess the same basic needs and proclivities whatever the cultural and material context, the emotion of love in the man-woman relationship has consisted of two distinguishable, but not always separable, aspects.

What we call romantic love is a feeling of intense physical attraction and a desire for sexual contact with a person of the opposite sex. The personal qualities of the loved one are usually idealized. These feelings are often most intense at the beginning of a relationship and they remain very intense if sexual consummation of the relationship is frustrated.

Sigmund Freud attributed the depth of feelings of love to the strength of sexual impulses (first experienced in relation to parents) which are frustrated or, in his words, "inhibited in their aim." [20] He regarded romantic love as a neurotic compulsion which derives its compulsive nature from the fact of frustration.

Historically, in the West, romantic love as a subcultural prescription regulating the man-woman relationship first appeared during the Age of Chivalry in twelfth-century France. The intense pinings and yearnings of noble ladies and their knights was a direct consequence of the fact that these relationships usually occurred outside of marriage and were not consummated—usually.

An analogous situation in modern societies is found in the infatuations that adolescents are prone to develop toward unavailable individuals who are often authority figures or who represent the adolescent's ego ideals. The intensity of longing and desire is in direct proportion to the unattainability of the loved one.

Romantic love is narcissistic; the individual is preoccupied with his or her needs and frustrations. In its pure form, it is distinguished from mature love, which has an additional aspect—mutual identification and concern with the needs of the person who is loved.

LOVE AS A BASIS FOR MARRIAGE

Whether or not romantic love has been prescribed as appropriate to courtship and mate choice in various societies has depended, in large measure, on their level of technological development and, within each society, on the social status of marriageable men and women. Arranged marriages have been prevalent where there has been extreme inequalities in wealth between families, and where the choice of a mate had great significance for prestige, power, and wealth and the inheritance of these attributes by linear descendents of the extended family.

Romantic love as a basis for marriage, on the other hand, implies free choice and a disregard of family needs and wishes in the making of this choice. Expedient criteria—money, power, actual or anticipated social status—are unimportant or irrelevant. This pattern is prevalent in the simplest and in the most complex societies because the fate of the family is less affected by the marital choice of offspring in these kinds of societies. All are poor in hunting and gathering societies and, ideally, all have the possibility of social mobility in highly industrialized societies.

If parents are not apt to live with their daughters- and sons-in-law, and are not likely to depend on their children for economic aid or support, and if education, skill, and talent become more important than inherited social status in determining economic fates, parents will be less concerned (but not unconcerned) about the social origins and personal qualities of their children's marital choices.

The fact that families often arranged marriages in stratified traditional societies, because to do so was vitally important to their fate, explains the motivation of parents. But what of the young people who complied with the family's matchmaking decisions? Why was it so easy for families to prevent and control disapproved erotic attachments between the young in traditional societies?

The obvious explanation is that the complete economic dependence of the young, reinforced by rigid cultural definitions and highly effective social controls, repressed spontaneous or negatively sanctioned love impulses. It has also been argued that widespread premarital sexual freedom in nonliterate societies reduced the intensity of an emotion that thrives on frustration. Another possible explanation that is often given is that love relationships in traditional societies were less intense and thus easier to control because the prototypical parent-child relationship was less intense in societies where the extended family existed.

Intensity of feeling is extremely difficult to assess, particularly when the individuals involved are long dead. Despite the presence of other relatives to help with child rearing, mother-child relationships appear to have been quite strong in many traditional societies. Certainly this was true in polygynous societies. In matrilineal societies, fathers, who had little authority over their children, seem to have had very warm, affectionate relationships with their offspring. And the mythology, folklore, art, and written products of many traditional societies attest to the presence of individual cases of romantic love regardless of cultural dictates and social pressures.

Whatever the answer to this historical puzzle, the situation changes dramatically in modern societies. In automating societies, as the standard of living rises for all classes, and as the discrepancy in income between classes narrows (however slowly), love as a basis for marriage is more apt to operate not only ideally but actually. The greater economic independence of women in modern societies also fosters this trend. In the past in the United States, surveys of reasons for marital choices have indicated that women have been strongly influenced by such factors as the intelligence, education, earning potential, and ambition of their prospective mates. This is changing and should continue to change in the direction of freer, less opportunistic mating.

Nevertheless, and however prevalent and effective the ideal of romantic love, marital choices in modern societies are usually restricted to individuals who are of similar class, race, religion, ethnic origin, and educational level. Sociologically, like marries like with respect to location on various prestige and privilege hierarchies. This has been conceptualized by sociologists as the principle of homogamy in marital choice. It also applies, incidentally, to the age, intelligence, physical appearance, physical attractiveness, and the previous marital status of individuals who decide to marry. People tend to sort themselves out spontaneously on the basis of similar interests and life experiences, and in a way that usually does not offend family standards.

Where like does not marry like, males have usually married down, trading superior social status for the personal attractiveness of lower status women and, incidentally, reinforcing cultural values of male authority and female deference. In interracial marriages, in the past in the United States, the tendency has been for an economically successful minority group male to marry a woman of the dominant race but of a lower class. This too is changing. More recently, interracial marriages have been taking place between status equals, presumably on the basis of love since expedient considerations are not obviously present.[21]

Until recently, area of residence has also been a very important factor in determining marital choices. Most marriages have taken place between people who live in the same neighborhood or community —"the girl next door" phenomenon, which sociologists have conceptualized as the principle of propinquity, or nearness, in determining marital choices.

Both standards, homogamy and propinquity, decline in highly mobile societies for obvious reasons. Geographic mobility and greater exposure to individuals of different social origins diminished ethnocentrism (the fear, dislike, or intolerance of strange people and strange ways) and territorially based group ties and group loyalties.

College campuses in the United States, particularly the fastest-growing residential public colleges and universities, are giant mixing bowls that recruit from an increasingly wide spectrum of the population. Almost half of our high-school graduates now attend college and we are heading in the direction of universal higher education. It is in these enclaves that the sorting and the seeking of the mating process is most free of traditional trappings and family intervention.

THE PSYCHOLOGICAL FACTOR

In analyzing the basis of attraction between potential marital partners, the adage "opposites attract" is part of the folklore of American society. How is this reconciled with the tendency for like to marry like, for which we also have an adage: "birds of a feather flock together"?

Here, the answer lies in the distinction between sociological and psychological factors in determining marital choices. Sociological factors (locating characteristics such as class, race, and religion) affect conscious, deliberate choices—those based on obvious similarities in interests, values, and beliefs. Psychological factors, deeper and often unconscious needs and motivations, may not be congruent with the more obvious bases for mutual attraction. It is at this level, largely, that the principle that "opposites attract" operates.

In the sociological literature, much confusion has resulted from a failure to appreciate the distinction between conscious and unconscious motivations in the trial and error explorations of the mating game. Psychological needs are often repressed by human beings, particularly those needs that do not conform to culturally prescribed role definitions. These motives will not show up on survey questionnaires because they are not recognized, or if recognized, they may not be admitted. Very few men are apt to state that they sought out an aggressive and dominant woman because of strong dependency needs, even if they are aware of this fact.

The evidence that on a psychological level opposites attract is not, therefore, overwhelming. Sigmund Freud formulated an early version of the notion that individuals with complementary needs and personality traits tend to seek each other out in love relationships. He distinguished between narcissistic love, which he attributed to males, and anaclitic love, which he attributed to females. The former is characterized by a strong need to be admired and revered; the latter by a strong need to be dependent, deferent, and vicarious in the realm of achievement.[22]

In the field of sociology, Robert F. Winch and his associates have elaborated on the notion of complementarity of needs in marital choices.[23] The theory of complementarity suggests that individuals are attracted to each other at the level of psychological need to the extent that they have opposite needs, or different levels of intensity of the same need. The theory has been tested with respect to such traits as dominance-submissiveness, nurturance-receptiveness, achievement-vicariousness, and hostility-abasement.

The evidence for complementarity in personality traits of marital partners is impressive but not yet conclusive. Projective tests and depth interviews are most apt to get at this kind and level of information but, as I indicated earlier, these techniques are costly and time-consuming to administer. For this reason, they cannot be used on large, statistically representative populations. Qualitative data, furthermore, are even more subject to investigator bias in interpretation than are survey data which, while superficial, are at least more concrete and less subject to misinterpretation.

Irrefutable support for the theory will have to await further refinements and sophistication in social science methods. The use of projective rather than direct questions on survey questionnaires is one such refinement. Rather than ask directly: "Would you like to have an extramarital affair?" most experienced investigators would now ask instead: "Do you feel that most married men (women) would like to have an extramarital affair?" With the second type of question, the respondent can project impulses that he cannot or will not admit, and the social scientist may come closer to the truth.

It is important to obtain more evidence on the theory of complementarity of needs in marital choices because free choice on the basis of romantic love is becoming institutionalized for all classes in industrialized societies. Psychological needs may override the homogamous principle and homogamy is associated with marital stability. We can have a better basis for understanding the persistence or failure of marriages if we understand what affects choices at the psychological as well as the sociological level and how the balance in psychological needs may be disturbed if husbands and wives develop differently during the various stages of the life cycle.

Romantic love as a principle of mate selection may not turn out to be as irrational as is often claimed since a balance in the satisfaction of unconscious psychological needs is also important for the stability of marriages. As religious, familial, community, and legal sanctions lose their traditional effectiveness in stabilizing marriages, and as the marital tie becomes paramount in family relationships, the principle of mutual gratification of needs at the deepest psychological levels becomes, in fact, the essence of marital stability.

MARITAL INTERACTION

One major aspect of husband and wife roles that has varied considerably in human societies has been the amount of sharing or segregation of activities and obligations that has been allowed or pre-scribed by the culture, and this in turn has tended to vary with the strength of the values of patriarchalism and authoritarianism in var-ious societies.

MARITAL ROLE SEGREGATION

Generally, as with types of family structure, the least technologi-cally developed societies and the most technologically developed so-cieties have had similar patterns: marital sex role definitions have been less rigid and exclusive in hunting and gathering and in highly industrialized societies. In agricultural societies, the differentiation of marital roles according to sex tends to be most pronounced.[24] The husband's responsibilities and the wife's responsibilities are sharply distinguished and the crossing of sex lines results in conflict and ten-sion.

By and large, and in many societies, wives and mothers have per-formed what has been called expressive functions: they have been more involved in reducing conflict and in providing comfort and emotional support to family members. Husbands and fathers have usually performed instrumental tasks, requiring leadership, authority, and disciplinary powers.[25]

In highly industrialized societies the expressive-instrumental divi-sion of labor blurs; in fact, the nuclear family becomes largely an ex-pressive unit, with authority shared, deemphasized, and more negotia-ble in terms of who has it and when and how it is used. In a reversal of the traditional pattern, in which mother and child were often in-formally allied against the patriarchal father, the child may even ap-peal to the father to intervene in decisions made by the mother.

The amount of sharing or segregation of homemaking or child-care activities in highly industrialized societies varies according to class and according to the stage in the family life cycle. The urban upper middle class is least traditional in this respect, the lower middle class is intermediate, and the working class, which is closer to its rural ori-gins, is most traditional.

The honeymoon stage of the family life cycle (the early years of marriage before the arrival of children) and the retirement stage are characterized by the greatest amount of joint husband-and-wife activ-ity, within and outside the home, for all classes. In the retirement stage there may even be a role reversal if the wife is younger, is employed, and continues to work. The retired husband usually becomes more expressive. His relationships with grandchildren, for example, in which he is not typically an authority figure in modern societies, are often characterized by more warmth, indulgence, and spontaneity than he was able to express toward his own children during their childhood. Older wives, on the other hand, tend to become more openly aggressive and less self-sacrificing, probably a response to the greater independence and freedom they experience when the children are grown.

The childrearing stage of the family life cycle is characterized by the greatest amount of role segregation: the wife is least apt to work and is usually deeply involved in child care; the husband is invested in his work, the amount and degree of his commitment depending on the prestige of his job, his opportunities for advancement, and the extent to which he can utilize his ability, judgment, and initiative on the job. Time permitting, in all stages of the family life cycle, where the husband does participate in activities that have been traditionally defined as feminine, he will feel less tension and less shame if he is middle class than if he is working class.[26]

The wife's dependence on the husband is highest during the childrearing stage, particularly if she does not work. Previously negotiated, and possibly modified authority relations and household activity patterns tend to shift back toward the traditional forms during this stage of marriage. And it is this period that is characterized by the greatest amount of marital role conflict for the middle-class highly educated woman who has been encouraged to be independent and self-reliant in other areas of life.

Marital satisfaction, incidentally, at least as reported by wives, tends to parallel the pattern of joint or segregated activities throughout the family life cycle. It is highest when joint activities are high: during the honeymoon stage and, in the middle class, during the "empty nest" stage, after the children have left. The childrearing years diminish joint activities and responsibilities in the husband-wife relationship and, given the modern values of sharing and reciprocity in marriage, marital satisfaction declines.[27]

The sexual satisfaction of married women is also related to the degree of equality, interchangeability, and flexibility in marital roles. The sexual adjustment of women, far more than that of men, is situational: it reflects the amount of mutuality in other spheres of marital life and it fluctuates according to changing marital circumstances. In the working class, where marital roles are most segregated, wives are least responsive sexually.[28] And changing circumstances (unemployment, for example) diminishes the wife's sexual responsiveness more than it does the husband's potency, although both are affected by this crucial change in the husband's status.

Husbands tend to evaluate their marriages in terms of the sexual relationship. Wives, who are more bound to the traditional morality, are less apt to value sex for sex' sake. In the United States at present, women in all classes, except the most economically deprived, place companionship above economic support, sexual gratification, or the possibility of having children, as the prime value in marriage. College students who are about to be married usually emphasize this aspect and, also, communication. They hope to be able to express feelings, negative or positive, openly, directly, and for the purpose of enhancing the honesty and the intimacy of the relationship. This is a modern orientation.

COMMUNICATION

Communication becomes an important value in modern marriages because the effectiveness of talking things out is more recognized and accepted than it is in traditional societies. Freudian psychology, the talking cure, has left its mark on the cultural heritage—in America particularly. The Freudian formula for diminishing conflict is to promote awareness of unacceptable, unconscious impulses. This diminishes guilt and the anxiety which is often a defense against destructive impulses. Diminished anxiety facilitates communication.

The Freudian emphasis on insight and communication has filtered outward and downward from the urban, professional upper middle class, via the mass media, in disguised but recognizable ways. One has only to look at the man-woman relationship as depicted in the movies of the 1930s in this country to appreciate the changes that have occurred in human relationships in the past forty-odd years. The modern viewer, particularly those who are under thirty, reacts with impatience, if not irritation, to the coyness and to the comedy or tragedy of errors that is based on the inability of the hero and the heroine to be direct and honest with each other—to tell it like it is, in today's language.

This century has been called the century of psychological man. The psychologically sophisticated husband and wife are more aware and more accepting of destructive impulses, are better able to discuss and control these impulses, and are less likely to suffer the agonies and the anxieties of blindly defending against them. These patterns are most prevalent within the urban, professional upper middle class, but they represent a trend that is slowly spreading up and down the class structure.

Communication between husband and wife also improves in modern societies because communication is freest between status equals. One doesn't joke with an authoritarian parent, teacher, or employer. The modern family, increasingly equalitarian, is more spontaneous, less repressed, and less inhibited in its parent-child, husband-wife relationships. Members are freer to communicate love, hate, dreams, fears, fantasies, and realities.

DEFERENCE PATTERNS

Deference rituals such as bowing, kneeling, and the use of titles and polite forms of address symbolize differences in prestige and authority in human relationships. These patterns tend to disappear in modern societies as the absolute authority of monarchs, popes, employers, and patriarchs declines and the prestige of citizens, workers, parishioners, women, and children rises.

In all societies, the norms of togetherness in eating, sleeping, working, and playing and the extent of sharing of material and psychic goods have reflected status differentials within the family.

In traditional societies, particularly those in which the status of women was low and the marital tie deemphasized, husbands and wives were often separated: they slept separately, ate separately, walked separately, and sat separately at public functions. Sex taboos —menstrual or post-partum, the latter sometimes lasting two or more years (since this was a major technique of birth control)— reinforced the norm of separateness.

Public display of affection—by look, gesture, speech, or touch —was taboo. Wife-to-husband deference was expressed by a meek demeanor, soft and restrained speech, downcast eyes, speaking only when spoken to, sitting on lower, less comfortable chairs or at the foot rather than the head of the table, and eating the leftover and less choice portions of food.

The patterns of chivalry that developed in the West—the opening of doors, or relinquishing of seats for females, for example—are not deference patterns in this sense. They signify female fragility. As biological sex differences become less important in determining sex roles in machine economies, chivalric patterns disappear.

Where relationships are formal and rooted in authority rather than love, inhibited communication is typical. The exchange of confidences and what sociologists call self-disclosure is a parent-child phenomenon in traditional societies; in modern societies, it is a husband-wife imperative.

DIVORCE

Divorce is another phenomenon that has reflected male-female status differentials and economic roles in various societies. In a majority of societies women have had less freedom than men to initiate divorce. Patrilineal societies have had low divorce rates; matrilineal societies have had higher divorce rates. Whether or not societies have permitted divorce, socially sanctioned alternatives or additional liaisons (with concubines, mistresses, and prostitutes) have usually been available to men. Polygyny was common in nonliterate societies; polyandry was rare.

Customs such as the payment of a bride-price to the bride's family or the rendering of service by the groom to her family for varying lengths of time, served two functions: they compensated the bride's family for the loss of a productive worker, particularly in horticultural societies, and they encouraged the stability of marriages, since the time spent in service was lost and the bride price not returnable in the event of divorce. The custom of providing a dowry to the groom or the groom's family arose among the upper strata in traditional societies where the bride did not perform essential economic functions. In modern societies, these practices tend to disappear. The status of both marital partners becomes more equal and economic factors, as I've said before, decline in importance where the extended family is not the economic productive unit.

Divorce rates also tend to rise. This fact is usually cited to argue that the family in modern societies is breaking down. The United States, which has by far the highest divorce rates in the world and where the divorce rate has increased at least tenfold within the past hundred years, is regarded by many analysts as a bellwether in the trend toward the disappearance of the family as a social form in urban, computerized societies.

A calm and unbiased look into world history and cross-cultural variations in divorce customs does not support the fears (or, perhaps, the wishes) of the prophets of doom. In many nonliterate societies there have been higher divorce rates than in the contemporary United States.[29] If we take into account all causes of nuclear family breakdown—death as well as desertion and divorce—we find, furthermore, that more families are remaining intact for longer periods of time than ever before.[30]

In certain agricultural societies such as Japan, Egypt, and Algeria in the late nineteenth century, there have been higher divorce rates than in today's United States.[31] And finally, there is no necessary and inevitable connection between level of industrialization and divorce rates—Japan, for example, has low divorce rates, at least at the present time.

The tendency, however, is for divorce rates to rise with the level of technological development. The reasons are obvious: the rising status of women and the possibility of obtaining self-supporting employment other than in domestic service; the possibility that men have to purchase necessary goods and services—clean laundry, cooked food, clothing and shelter—from commercial establishments; increased urbanization and geographic mobility which diminish the effectiveness of family, community, and religious social controls and sanctions; and finally, the modern psychological orientations and expectations in marriage—for love, happiness, and mutual fulfillment—which are more difficult to achieve than the traditional goals of economic cooperation and physical survival.

Divorced individuals in modern societies are not absorbed into extended family structures. They experience varying degrees of loneliness, anomie, confusion, and depression.[32] The culture contains few clear-cut norms defining the role of the divorced man or woman. Alcoholism and suicide rates rise. Old friends are lost, since the eligibility of the newly divorced person, particularly the woman, is a threat to intact marriages.

And yet the majority of those who are divorced remarry. Despite the steady rise of divorce rates in the United States, the institution of marriage is far from being on the decline. Higher percentages of people are getting married than ever before.

Humans cannot survive without love and love (and hate) is virtually a family monopoly. Friends are shed more readily than family as individuals move up and down the class structure; in crises and emergencies, the nuclear family, if it has a choice, turns to the extended family first; and adolescents, according to the evidence of many surveys, are more influenced by family than by friends in the most important decisions of their lives—in the educational and occupational spheres, particularly.

Divorce laws in this country lag behind the changing expectations and conditions of modern marriages. The concept of guilt of one partner—for cruelty, adultery, desertion, or nonsupport—underlies most present divorce laws. The notion that mutual incompatibility or irreconcilable differences are more realistic reasons for divorce is yet to be widely recognized and accepted by lawmakers. The new divorce laws in California, in which the guilt of one partner is neither assumed or required for divorce, represent an attempt to close the perennial gap between law and reality in rapidly changing societies.

THE PARENT-CHILD RELATIONSHIP

Childrearing practices vary on a continuum from permissive to authoritarian. The essence of the permissive parent-child relationship is not overindulgence and overprotection. This has been a popular vulgarization and distortion of the concept and practice of permissive childrearing, particularly in the upper middle class in America, until recently.

The permissive parent-child relationship is one in which the child's needs and wishes are taken into account in the process of socialization. Parents do not set arbitrary feeding schedules for the newborn infant; the child's weight and hunger needs are taken into account. Decisions and demands made upon the child are flexible rather than absolute and the parent's comfort and convenience is not the foremost consideration in disciplining the child. Children are seen, heard and, frequently, listened to.

Authoritarian parents demand absolute obedience and submission. Power is used openly and physical punishment rather than explanation or reasoning is used to obtain unconditional conformity. The spontaneous display of affection as well as aggression within the family is curbed. The hostility that the child cannot express at home may be displaced onto subordinates, strangers, and out-groups in later life. The bully and the sadist are products of authoritarian upbringing.

Prejudice, where it is not a subcultural norm, is often a psychological result of authoritarian childrearing practices.[33] Prejudice tends to decline in highly industrialized societies because permissive childrearing practices become more widespread. The need to project and displace repressed hostilities is diminished if the child can express aggression more freely within the home.

The early excesses of runaway permissiveness in childrearing in this country have been curbed in recent times by common sense, supported by the findings of social science. These findings filter down, sooner or later, to the middle classes, and even beyond. It is pretty well established now that children identify with parents more strongly and are most apt to internalize parental values when parents temper their affection with reasonable and nonarbitrary controls.[34] Neither extremely permissive nor extremely authoritarian parents do as well in this respect. The new and current childrearing formula in America, and the trend in all classes, is firmness, combined with affection and respect for the child's needs.[35] (Compare the first and the latest editions of Dr. Benjamin Spock's *Baby and Child Care*.)

Permissive childrearing practices are most common in noneconomi-

cally stratified traditional societies and in highly industrialized societies, particularly in the middle class. Agricultural societies, with their
rigidly hierarchical authority structures, are characterized by authoritarian father-child relationships. Conflict is a typical by-product of differences in authority. Where these differences are extreme, conflict
will often be extreme, even if it is suppressed. For this reason, mother-child relationships in the course of human history, have usually
been more warm, affectionate, and relaxed than father-child relationships.

As I pointed out earlier, in matrilineal societies, where the mother's
male relatives had more authority over a child than the father, fa-
ther-son relationships were usually warm and unrestrained. Affection
rather than fear characterized these relationships. A modern parallel
is found in kibbutz communities. Parents have little authority over
their children and are not responsible for their discipline and custodial care. Most sources report that the emotional tie between parent
and child in these communities is relatively unambivalent and uncon-
flicted.

In newly industrializing societies, the father becomes more permissive, particularly in his relationships with his sons, as he loses the
economic basis of his absolute authority.[36] In highly industrialized societies, personality traits such as intelligence, energy, needs and drives,
and other resources such as time, education, skills, and interests become at least as important as cultural norms in family decision-making and authority relationships, especially in the middle classes.

In very rapidly changing societies, parents are more influenced by
their children and may even follow their childrens' lead in certain
areas of life. Margaret Mead's thesis in *Culture and Commitment* is
that children in rapidly changing societies are more adaptable than
parents.[37] The young are more in touch with what is new and
changing—by inclination and by circumstance. By identifying with
their young, parents can better understand and perhaps better cope
with the present and the future.

The mass media reflect this latest trend in parent-child relationships. In television advertising the young mother, with an air of impatience, introduces her not-quite-with-it mother to the latest product
advances in disposable diapers, or household conveniences, for exam-

ple. In one currently popular commercial, a young unmarried daughter has a heart-to-heart talk with her mother. She makes known to her mother, in whispered and confidential tone, that the best way to promote feminine hygiene is with the use of a vaginal deodorant spray. The mother is impressed and convinced. This vignette reflects far more serious occurrences in contemporary America as many young people, particularly in the upper middle class, have managed to persuade their parents to accept such innovations as the living together pattern, communal living, and the hang-loose ethic of impulse gratification.

The urgent necessity for economic cooperation from all members of the family declines in industrialized societies, and fathers become less authoritarian. What other factors promote permissive parent-child relationships in modern societies?

Parents project their world views and their life circumstances into their relationships with their children. If life is brutal, if parents are rigidly controlled by powerful authorities, if strict obedience and conformity to social demands is their lot, and if there is little hope or expectation of changing circumstances for their children, parents will bring up their children to obey strict rules and regulations.

If authority is more diffuse, if cultural norms are vague, contradictory, constantly changing or even absent, if opportunities and choices exist in the social environment, particularly in the occupational shere, if the future is unpredictable, if self-control, independence, and flexibility are more adaptable than mechanical conformity to unchanging, situational norms, parents will be more permissive. Children in modern societies make many decisions and choices on their own; uncertainty, unpredictability, and constant change are the essence of their taken-for-granted world.

The availability of opportunities affects values even in nonindustrialized societies. It is for this reason that many values in family life that are regarded as modern were prevalent in America before industrialization. America was a relatively open society from the beginning: the frontier with its vast quantities of land and other natural resources provided unparalleled possibilities for mobility and achievement.

Foreign travelers to this country, from colonial times to the present, have commented on the lack of discipline and parental restraint in parent-child relationships in America.[38] The spoiling and overindulgence of American children, their rudeness and their refusal to be properly respectful and obedient to elders, are recurrent themes in travelers' accounts of American family life.

Permissiveness and its corollaries in personality traits—individualism, particularly—facilitated industrialization and the accumulation of scientific knowledge in this country. Since the end of World War II, America has produced a far higher number of patented inventions than any other country in the world. While it is true that the technological base is more complex in the United States and more elements are available for combination or recombination into new forms, the desire and ability to innovate, to go against the prevailing wisdom and norms, to seek new knowledge—in short, to create—is a tendency that has been promoted in this country by less-repressive parent-child relationships.

The values that have been labeled middle-class American values, achievement motivation, for example, are values that are associated with the availability of opportunities, whether these opportunities precede or follow industrialization. They are urban values. It is no accident that the Protestant Reformation, which emphasized the values of individualism and achievement, took hold among the urban middle classes before the Industrial Revolution. The old European adage "City air is free air" referred to the autonomy and opportunities that existed in urban environments. The relationship between the availability of opportunity and family values and roles will become more apparent as we look into present-day subcultural variations in family life in America. We will see, then, how the values that have become increasingly paramount in human relationships, historically, as societies have industrialized are more or less prominent in American family relationships, depending on ethnic origin and class.

5

AMERICAN VARIATIONS:
ETHNIC CONTRASTS

In modern America, family roles and family relationships vary typically according to class, ethnic (national) origin, and urban-rural residence. These locating factors are the major sources of subcultural differences in role conceptions and expectations. Race and religion are also sources of difference but these characteristics tend to correspond to ethnic origin and are increasingly included under this heading by social scientists and social reformers.

Compound nationality labels—Afro American, Mexican American, or Indian American—are replacing "color" racial labels (black, brown, red) in an era of cultural pluralism. The concept of ethnic origin is less ambiguous and less loaded than the concept of race. In modern times, the constant movement of populations, and the inevitable miscegenation that sooner or later occurs when diverse populations are in contact, blur racial categories and distinctions. It is often more realistic and more meaningful to classify a particular family as Puerto Rican, for example, than to attempt to categorize the family racially. Distinctive family patterns, furthermore, are more readily explained and understood as a survival of unique historical experience or of cultural traditions of the country of origin (or tribal origins in the case of the American Indian) than as a result of genetic, racial heritage.

With the exception of American blacks, whose African heritage was largely destroyed upon their arrival in this country, ethnic cultural traditions of the country of origin have been the most important source of variation in family life in this country in the past, certainly in the first generation after immigration, and often beyond.

As societies become highly industrialized, however, class tends to replace ethnic origin and urban-rural residence as the most significant source of variation in family values, behavior, and role conceptions. The process of acculturation is actually the process whereby families and individuals take on the dominant values and norms of urban, industrial societies. These values—rationalism (pragmatism, efficiency), equalitarianism, secularism, individualism, and achievement —have usually been called middle-class American values or dominant American values.[1] Actually, they are also urban values. They become more pronounced in highly industrialized societies, and they become incorporated into the roles of husband, wife, parent, and child in modern societies, at least in the West.

The expanding middle classes in these societies are urban and national in identification and are more oriented toward modern values than they are to the traditional values and identities of local community or country of origin. Middle-class, urban American Indians, for example, are the leaders of the current pan-Indian movement in this country—a movement which is attempting to supplant local, tribal identities and values with a more generalized urban value system and ethnic identity for American Indians.

The modern values reflect high levels of technological and scientific development and the opportunity structures and ideologies that have been associated with these developments, in the West. These values are most strongly emphasized among the upper strata but they are the direction of change for all classes. The distinctive family roles and values of rural families and diverse ethnic groups tend to disappear slowly as families and individuals rise in the class structure.

A similar tendency exists with respect to the relative significance of class and religion for family and individual values. The greater authoritarianism and lower levels of achievement motivation that have been attributed to Catholicism [2] are less a matter of religious belief and church affiliation than of class membership and related factors such as level of education and type of occupation in the contemporary United States.[3] Whatever the presumed disadvantage of the emphasis of the Catholic religion on spiritual and other-worldly goals historically, Catholics in America have been more socially mobile (from the working class into the middle class) than have Protestants in recent years.

Catholic immigrants settled in large numbers in northern metropolitan areas. The second generation has had educational opportunities and nonmanual jobs more readily available than Protestants who have been concentrated in rural areas and in the South. Whatever the effects of the Protestant ethic on achievement motivation and social mobility in the past, large numbers of Protestants in this country have been downwardly mobile in recent years as they have left their farms and taken manual jobs in urban areas. At the present time, nationally, Catholics have higher median levels of income and education than do Protestants.[4] This fact is somewhat misleading, however, since blacks who are and have remained disproportionately poor are also Protestant.

Race is also increasingly supplanted by class as a determinant of family values in modern times. American middle-class black families, for example, are more "middle class' than their white counterparts: they have fewer children, are more equalitarian, are more achievement oriented, and place more emphasis on respectability, status validation, and participation in community activities, both religious and secular.[5]

We see, then, that the process of acculturation is actually one of adoption of urban, industrial values. These values are found in all classes; the upper strata are more likely to act them out, by virtue of objective circumstances centering on the greater availability of opportunity.

The survival of traditional values such as fatalism, religiosity, ethnocentrism, authoritarianism and familism will be stronger within some ethnic groups than others. The rate and extent of acculturation of newly arrived immigrants or migrants from rural areas in a particular society varies, depending on a number of circumstances. The most important of these circumstances are the availability of educational and occupational opportunities in the new environment; the isolation or exposure of the new groups to urban values; the strength and compatibility of preexisting values with the new values; and the receptivity of the dominant group to the newly arrived groups, a condition that is closely tied to racial differences.

These factors promote or discourage social mobility, and social mobility tends to homogenize ethnic and rural-urban differences in family role conceptions. This process is underwritten by the efficiencies of automated technologies, which diminish gross material differences in living standards. At the same time, other factors such as higher general levels of education, widespread exposure to the mass media, and increased opportunities in growing economies, subvert traditional values.

Class as well as ethnic differences in life conditions and life styles decline in modern times, more slowly in some societies than in others, more noticeably between the middle and upper class than between middle class and the poor. But the trend is clear. However, while poverty becomes less extensive in highly industrialized societies, inequality, which is relative, will always be with us.[6]

The final stage in the process of acculturation is assimilation, or the fusing of group identities into a single national identity.[7] This is the melting pot ideal of old, discredited now, but not yet dead. Assimilation, so defined, has not occurred in America except for north European Protestant immigrants to this country. We have no concept of English Americans.

Nevertheless, and despite the current trend away from the goal of assimilation and toward increasing pride and emphasis on ethnic differences and cultural pluralism in America, the process of assimilation is very likely inexorable. Social mobility, aided by the exigencies of urban, industrial economies, and ideologies, is the great leveler here.

Racial differences and barriers slow the process for some groups more than for others, as do religious differences. This will become clear as we discuss ethnic variations in family life in this country along a three-generational time perspective. But whatever the starting point, wherever culturally and physically dissimilar groups have been in contact for any length of time, an interchange of values, behavior patterns, and genetic traits has almost always been an inevitable consequence, regardless of the inhibiting or delaying effect of ethnocentric ideologies, cultural prohibitions, and powerful negative sanctions.

Despite the leveling tendencies of mass production, mass consumption, mass education, and mass recreation in modern societies, and in the United States, particularly, family roles continue to vary typically on a scale from the traditional and rural to the modern and urban. Since, with time and acculturation, ethnic variations in family life tend to merge into class variations, an analysis of typical family role conceptions and performance within various ethnic groups is a logical preliminary to a discussion of class differences in American family life. For this reason, also, I will spend much less time on ethnic than on class variations.

ETHNIC VARIATIONS

The recent emphasis on cultural pluralism and ethnic heritage in America seems to contradict my contention that ethnic groups tend to shed their distinctive family patterns as they become socially mobile. The movement toward the celebration of national origins, however, does not represent an attempt to reconstruct the traditional family values that more or less characterized almost all of these groups. Nor does it represent an attempt to reinstate or perpetuate the historic economic misery of these groups—a misery of which movement leaders may have little memory or knowledge. The new pan-nationalism in America represents, rather, an extolling of distinctive ethnic art, language, dress, and food patterns for the purpose of promoting a positive identity and ancestral pride in those who have had little of either.

If we examine the contemporary family roles of various ethnic groups in this country, we can see illustrated the process of acculturation, as this has been accelerated or delayed by the availability of opportunity in the new environment, by the extent of discrimination, and by the degree of cultural and physical similarity or difference of the acculturating group from the dominant society—the last two factors tending to vary together. I have chosen to describe just a few of the incredible number of ethnic minorities that comprise American society, but these few groups will illustrate the wide range in variation of the acculturation process as affected by enabling or hindering ideological and material factors.

BLACK FAMILIES

More has been written about the American black family in recent years than about any other ethnic group. Because of limited space and a desire not to repeat what is generally known, my focus here is primarily on the traditional-modern value dichotomies and how black families vary along this particular dimension and is meant to supplement more familiar and more comprehensive approaches to understanding black family life.

Probably the most significant factors affecting the family roles of American Negroes are the lack of a strong patriarchal tradition and the concentration of a majority of black families at income levels that are grossly inadequate, particularly if we apply the Department of Labor's standard of a modest income for a family of four in making this judgment. That this is largely a result of racial discrimination, which is more severe for American blacks than for other less identifiable groups, is indicated by a recent Census Bureau survey, in which it was found that American Negroes have a significantly lower median income than families of Spanish-speaking ancestry, even through the latter have a lower median level of education.[8]

The new opportunities that have opened up for the black community in recent years, furthermore, have benefited mainly upper working-class and middle-class black families. The poorest strata have not gained proportionately, as indicated by the fact that illegitimacy rates, the percentage of female-headed households, and the percentage of blacks on welfare has risen gradually in the two decades from 1950 to 1970.[9]

Lower working-class black families are traditional in many respects—familism (along the female line, particularly), superstition, religion, and fatalism are strong. The lack of a powerful patriarchal tradition, on the other hand, stems historically from the slaveholder's definition of the adult black male role as that of breeder rather than of economic provider for mate and children, and this role conception is reinforced currently by the greater difficulty that black males experience in fulfilling their economic obligations.

The fact of an absence of a strong patriarchal tradition can be viewed as having potential positive implications, however, at least for the future of the black family. While at the moment black males have less authority in the home than any other ethnic group in this country, regardless of class,[10] black husbands and fathers are also, at the same time, more expressive in their marital and parental roles and are more helpful and willing to share in childrearing and home-making chores.[11]

These distinctive variations in the husband and father role are in the direction of modern patterns in family life, patterns such as the sharing of obligations in the home, companionship, and psychological support. And these preexisting norms facilitate the adoption of urban values, given enabling economic opportunities for the black male. Whites, in fact, are moving in the direction of age-old black family patterns with respect to masculine expressiveness, mutual sexual grati-fication, and declining role segregation in the marital relationship.

The relative absence of patriarchalism, furthermore, bodes well for the realization of two other modern, urban values—rationalism and achievement orientation. Black women are far more apt to take advantage of family planning programs and legalized abortion for ex-ample, than are Puerto Rican women, whose traditional husbands continue to define virility in terms of fertility. Black women are, gen-erally and from long experience, more pragmatic, more resourceful, and more flexible than women who have been protected within the patriarchal structure for centuries.

Black children, since they do not typically have authoritarian fa-thers, do not experience one of the psychological sources of low achievement motivation. Increased economic opportunity enabling black fathers to become instrumental role models for their sons, com-bined with an early emphasis on independence which is typical among black families, and the confident setting of high standards on the part of black mothers, should conceivably result in higher levels of achievement motivation in black children than in children of fam-ilies where the father plays a more authoritarian role. And, in fact, there is some evidence indicating that middle-class black children have more intense achievement needs and higher levels of aspiration than their white counterparts.[12]

Black wives and mothers who are poor want strong, supportive husbands as much as wives and mothers in any other segment of our society.[13] Black husbands and fathers, in all classes, share these values, and where economic and educational opportunities permit, they live by them.

The possibility of achieving the psychological rewards that become a paramount value in nuclear family relationships in highly industrialized societies is closely tied to the economic resources available to the family, particularly at the extremes. Since American black families at comparable levels of education receive less income than whites, the higher divorce rates of black families at all social class levels are at least partially understandable.[14]

In many respects, however, black families become very much like white families in form and function as each succeeding urban generation continues to acculturate to modern values, a process that is hindered much less by preexisting cultural values among American blacks than by racial discrimination and inadequate objective opportunity, despite the heavy concentration of migrant blacks and their descendents in the industrial Northeast.

THE MEXICAN AMERICAN FAMILY

Mexican Americans have been the forgotten minority in the United States, possibly because the American Southwest has been a region that has been relatively neglected by both academicians and writers, with the notable exception of the late John Steinbeck. Even Steinbeck, however, returning to the Southwest in the early 1960s, romantically bemoaned the loss of the traditional values among urbanized Mexican Americans, values that he and others, from the vantage point of a different kind of misery, have fancifully equated with happiness and the good life.[15]

The more than five million Mexican Americans, mostly second generation offspring of peasant immigrants from Mexico and concentrated in the border states of Texas, Arizona, New Mexico, and California, are the second largest minority group in the United States, far outnumbering the million and one-half Puerto Ricans whose plight and problems are more familiar to the American public, at least in the Northeast.

Since World War II, particularly, the isolation of Mexican Americans has been declining, initially, as many Mexicans went off to war, and since then as the border states have become increasingly urbanized. Gradually, also, the American population of Mexican origin has shifted from Texas to California and from farm to city. With this mobility has come new opportunity, new perspectives, and changes in family roles that reflect the increasing adoption of modern values.

Because this particular segment of the population lives in a variety of geographical settings, it provides an excellent illustration of the differential process of acculturation of the same ethnic group as this has varied according to available opportunity.[16] The effects of length of residence in this country and social class on acculturation have varied dramatically according to the degree of acceptance Mexican Americans have experienced in their host environments. In San Antonio, for example, as compared to Los Angeles where there has been less discrimination and more objective opportunity, Mexican Americans who have been in this country for similar lengths of time, have significantly lower median incomes, lower median levels of education, are more apt to reside in segregated barrios even if middle class, and have appreciably lower rates of intermarriage with Anglos. The contrast in these respects with Los Angeles, which is at the extreme end of the rural-urban continuum, are even greater in the smaller cities and towns of Texas.[17]

Physical difference from the Anglo population continues to be a significant factor in acculturation in less cosmopolitan areas, where distinctions are still made, both within and outside of Mexican American communities, with respect to degree of Indian and Spanish ancestry. But in Los Angeles, the association between skin color, income, and segregation almost disappears, and the trend toward assimilation is more pronounced.

Familism is the strongest surviving traditional value within the older Mexican American community, along with patriarchalism and machismo—the cultural ideal of masculinity which equates maleness with sexual prowess. Some social scientists have attributed the economic adversities of Mexican Americans to the machismo ideal, arguing that this standard channels male energies into expressive and affiliative rather than achievement goals. I will return to this question shortly.

With respect to familism and its persistence among Mexican Americans, the most recent evidence on Mexican American families in large cities indicates that extended family households are rare, that family visiting is declining in younger generations, even among the poor, that the mutual obligations of godparents and parents (who act as comadres and compadres) are not taken seriously by younger people, and that younger marital partners are more apt to turn to each other than to the extended family for advice, support, and psychological gratification.

Patriarchalism, ideally a situation where the husband makes all decisions unilaterally and is obeyed unquestionably by wife and children, has always been a cultural ideal that has been ameliorated in practice by informal manipulation and negotiation. Among younger, higher status Mexican Americans, however, particularly those who live outside of the barrios, even the verbalization of this cultural ideal declines, and the male role is redefined in the direction of less dominance and less rigid segregation of functions and obligations within the home. The female role, however, continues to be more traditional and confined to domestic activities. Most Mexican Americans still consider it shameful and a threat to masculine pride to have an employed wife, although this is changing within the third generation in more cosmopolitan areas. The traditional definition of the female role is less apt to be modified than the definition of the male role, since it is closer to the still dominant ideal of femininity within the wider society.

The standard of machismo requires validation of masculinity through sexual conquest. Machismo is inextricably intertwined with patriarchalism, since it rests on masculine privilege and narcissistic ego need. Here, again, the pattern declines quite dramatically among the young in urban areas, particularly outside of the barrio, where it receives little support. With the decline of machismo, attitudes toward birth control become more positive, but in this case, the cultural heritage is a powerful inhibiting factor, particularly among poor and more recent immigrants from Mexico. As an inhibitor of hard work and competitive achievement, however, the persistence of the value of

machismo, as well as other tendencies to maximize immediate pleasure, is more likely a consequence and a compensation for deprivation
rather than a cause of achievement failures. This has been quite
clearly demonstrated in more recent community studies of other impoverished groups in American society.

Since the traditional values decline in direct relation to the availability of education and occupational opportunities, especially in more
accepting and less isolated urban environments, we can anticipate
that as father and son relationships become less authoritarian, and as
fathers become more supportive of individualistic, educational goals,
high levels of achievement motivation will become characteristic of
the Mexican American population also, particularly in the third generation in more cosmopolitan and less ethnocentric urban areas.

THE JAPANESE AMERICAN FAMILY

The modernization of the Japanese family in America has proceeded
more slowly in some respects than in Japan because the isolation of
the Japanese American from the effects of technological development
and rapid social change has been more pronounced here.[18] Nevertheless, in California, which has the largest concentration of individuals
of Japanese ancestry, this segment of the population has the highest
median levels of income and education of any minority group, with
the possible exception of the Jews. Japanese Americans also have very
low rates of crime and delinquency, indicating at the same time, the
greater persistence of the traditional values of obedience and conformity to parental values and norms. The generational pattern of increasing acculturation is very clearly illustrated in the contemporary Japanese American community since other factors—urban-rural
residence, for example—do not vary significantly.

A majority of the Issei generation, first-generation immigrants who
were born in Japan, arrived here some time between the end of the
nineteenth century and up to 1924, when immigration from the Orient and Eastern Europe was sharply restricted by the Johnson Act.
While the Issei came largely from rural agricultural areas and occupations, they were unusual in that they were relatively literate, compared with peasant immigrants from Europe, and they valued education even before their arrival in this country.

Second-generation Japanese Americans, the Nisei, born largely before 1940, experienced an unusual push into modernity not only by their parents' preexisting emphasis on education, but by the West Coast evacuations of Japanese Americans during World War II. Familistic values were weakened by the loss of confiscated family homes and businesses, which removed an important source of Issei control over their second-generation offspring. After the war the Nisei, who were forced to seek out independent, nonfamily occupational opportunities, were thereby more speedily acculturated into the modern values of individualism and equalitarianism in family relationships, although a cultural lag in this respect is still quite pronounced among Japanese Americans.

The third generation, the Sansei, born largely since World War II and now in high school or college or in the adult occupational world, are the most totally acculturated of all. And yet certain subcultural differences remain in family role conceptions, even within the third generation, that are traceable to the survival of traditional ethnic values in marital roles and in childrearing practices.

In the Orient, the patriarchal tradition was more intensely crystalized than in the West. The deference and obedience of wife and children toward husband and father, and of younger generations towards elders, while mitigated in practice, was more intense and more formalized in ritual, ceremony, religion, and law in the Orient than in Western society.

The extended family form, the ancestral clan or house as the basic family unit, was far more salient in the Orient as reality and as cultural ideal, for all social strata. Arranged marriages and emphasis on lineage, important indicators of the value of familism, were common even among the poor in Japan, particularly after the Meiji Restoration in 1868.[19] The values of obedience, deference, duty, and responsibility were constantly reinforced by pervasive mechanisms of control that elicited shame and guilt for the slightest deviation from established convention.[20]

Survivals in contemporary Japanese American family life, and a frequent source of role conflict in the Sansei generation especially, are found in the greater prevalence of strict disciplinary measures in childrearing, the greater emphasis on conformity and unconditional obedience, on humility and emotional reserve (particularly the supression of anger), the continued extensive use of shame and guilt as mechanisms of control, the greater submissiveness of women, even within the higher strata, and the greater strength of extended family pride and intergenerational emotional dependence.[21]

The pattern of male dominance is stronger in Oriental American homes, at all class levels, than in any other ethnic group in this country.[22] While the emphasis within Japanese American homes on achievement and competiveness has promoted educational and occupational success, the continuing stress on familism and authoritarian values has retarded the flexibility, the independence, and the self-reliance that are important attributes of individualistic achievement in highly industrialized society.

While recent studies of the Sansei generation have indicated a shift toward greater independence in this generation, both males and females remain, typically, less assertive, more deferent and conforming, and more emotionally reserved than Caucasian Americans of the same age.[23] The rigid conformity, status distinctions, and authority relations of traditional Japan that continue to affect family roles of Japanese Americans in this country, are likely to disappear with time, but more quickly in the occupational world than in the world of the family, where they are less immediately dysfunctional.

THE JEWISH AMERICAN FAMILY

A majority of American Jewish families trace their ancestry and surviving ethnic values to the small town or village shtetl communities of Eastern Europe.[24] Since Jews from the European Pale of Settlement (where they were confined by law) were not permitted to own land, they were a commercial people, for whom at least a limited social mobility was possible. Certain of the urban values, particularly a rational active mastery approach to their environment and high levels of achievement motivation, were a significant feature of their cultural heritage prior to immigrating to America. Their very rapid social mobility, relative to peasant immigrants to this country, is usually traced to these preexisting values and skills which are similar to other immigrant groups (the Levantine Greeks, for example) with a commercial heritage, who have also experienced rapid occupational mobility in the United States.

The traditional Jewish religion fostered a devotion to sacred learning, searching analysis and critical questioning. A life devoted to learning brought the highest status in the shtetl community, overriding even lowly economic occupation as a source of prestige. Wealth brought with it the divine commandment to bestow charity on the less fortunate.

Familism was strong but individual achievement was highly valued, fostered by mothers who strongly encouraged and rewarded competitive achievement in their children at a very early age. Excelling the fate of the father and the mother was a source of pride rather than envy to the parental generation and great sacrifice toward this goal was not unusual. This was unlike the pattern in other traditional families in Europe, where a son's achievement might be viewed as a threat to the strongly patriarchal father.[25] As another indication of the strength of familistic values, powerful sanctions were also used to regulate marriages, which were arranged for all except the poor. The patriarchal tradition in shtetl society was present but was mitigated by the economic role of women in family commercial enterprise, the husband often abdicating his instrumental role, in part, to pursue the goal of learning.

Arriving in America, largely during the period of mass immigration that ended in 1924, most Jews settled in the great metropolitan centers, at first in the East and gradually in the Midwest and West. Encountering occupational discrimination, they tended to concentrate in self-employed occupations and in the newer light industries.

From the first to the third generations, the acculturation patterns of American Jews, overwhelmingly urban and encountering a moderate and varying degree of discrimination, illustrates the close fit between certain of their preexisting values and the opportunities that were available in America, but it also reveals the persistence of certain ethnic values in family roles.[26]

Preexisting achievement, educational, and philanthropic values were transferred from the sacred to the secular by Jewish immigrants and their descendents through an emphasis on the learned and helping professions as occupational goals and an interest in reform politics. Studies of occupational differences of Jewish and Italian groups in this country have revealed distinct variations in parental role expectations within the two groups that can be traced to their differing European cultural heritages and life circumstances.[27]

Education was neither valued or necessary in southern Italian peasant society where agricultural occupations did not require literacy and where even limited social mobility was rare. Fatalism (*que sera sera*) rather than an active mastery approach to the world was more appropriate to life circumstances that were grimly impoverished and not likely to change. These traditional values and the conception of the child as an economic asset lingered longer among Italians in America, who were less willing to sacrifice for the educational goals of their children and who were more apt to encourage early employment and economic contributions from their children than to support individualistic long-term training and achievement goals.

Equalitarianism, particularly as enacted in parental roles, has been strong in Jewish homes, as indicated by the greater tendency within this group to be permissive in childrearing. The value of equalitarianism is also indicated by the apparent greater prevalence of the partner marital role within this ethnic group, which probably reflects, in part, the traditionally more active economic role of Jewish women in the European shtetl.

Familism and ethnocentrism, on the other hand, have been more persistent among Jews than among other immigrants. The intermarriage rate is lower than among Catholics and Protestants, although this rate is increasing, especially among highly educated, more mobile, and more secularized professionals.[28] When compared with other ethnic groups of the same social class, the Jewish divorce rate is lower; extended family ties, as measured by frequency of visiting and exchange of services among relatives, are higher; [29] and permissive childrearing is more prevalent.

The concept of the Jewish mother is currently popular in literary and academic circles. What does this concept mean and to whom does it apply? The Jewish mother is the traditional mother who looks to her children rather than her husband for psychological gratification and empathy. The stereotype of the Jewish mother has been applied to Jewish women particularly possibly because the syndrome is more characteristic of women in a subculture emphasizing strong achievement motivation and intense involvement and identification with children.

Second generation American Jewish men and women have been

strongly represented in the communication and entertainment industries. They have depicted their manipulating, guilt-inducing mothers in novels, plays, movies, and in the academic literature. But they are not unique in their relationships with their mothers. Traditional women, who do not have gratifying relationships with their husbands, tend to invest in their children instead. And they expect a payoff, in psychic and material rewards, which in fact, and until recently, they very often received.

In part, familism has been more persistent among Jews of all classes in succeeding generations in this country, because of the concentration of first- and second-generation Jewish immigrants in self-employed, commercial, and professional occupations which tied them to local communities. Geographic immobility reinforced the traditional religious, familistic, and philanthropic values. Subsequent generations, preponderantly in the middle class, are more apt to be salaried employees in large organizations and thus more mobile and more subject to the secularizing and individualistic trends of the wider society.

Despite continued differences in family roles, complete acculturation of American Jews to the modern, urban values is very likely inevitable in the long run, barring a severe economic and political crisis in which the Jews might once again become the target of displaced hostility by the frustrated and the desperate. Eventually, and ironically, the Jews will probably fulfill the vision of the nineteenth-century German Jewish immigrants to this country. Social class will completely override ethnic tradition and the Jews will retain their separate identity, if at all, as simply another religious denomination in the American firmament.

The key to family change in modern times should be clear by now: acculturation to urban values depends ultimately on the cultural baggage and, even more importantly, on the existence of real and effective economic and educational opportunity. Social mobility is the prize and class location is the major and prevailing factor in the persistence of traditional values or the adoption of modern values in contemporary American family life.

6

AMERICAN VARIATIONS: CLASS DIFFERENCES

Man is an evaluating animal and in all societies human beings have evaluated and ranked each other on a scale from superior to inferior. In most societies, furthermore, there is pretty general agreement about where people belong in this hierarchy. According to the prevailing values of a society, people with similar amounts of prestige will be placed in layers or strata above or below each other on a rank order from high to low.

Historically, the ranked categories, layers, or strata that have differentiated people in terms of prestige have been called castes (if position was hereditary, unchangeable, and sanctioned by religion), estates (if position was sanctioned by law and extremely difficult to change), and classes (if position is theoretically open and achieved by individual talent and effort).

In hunting and gathering societies, age and sex were the major bases for categorizing individuals and for assigning overall prestige in the society. Age and sex were also the major determinants of the roles people played. Within the broad categories of male or female, and young or old, individuals differed in esteem, which derived from personal qualities such as strength, bravery, resourcefulness, and temperament. Families, however, were not differentiated with respect to relative prestige and all families played out their roles in very similar ways.

In horticultural and in agricultural societies, the bases for evaluating and ranking human beings expand to include wealth, power, and ancestry. The family becomes the social unit that is ranked and family roles vary in certain typical ways according to the position or status of the family in the overall society. Individuals are ranked according to family membership and this rank does not change, typically, from birth to death.

In urban, industrialized societies, ancestry declines in importance, although it by no means becomes insignificant, and achievements and personal qualities become increasingly significant in establishing the overall prestige that human beings enjoy. Individuals are born with the social status attributed to their families, but the possibility of changing this status, and the material and psychic disabilities or rewards that go with it, are much greater.

In modern societies also the differential effects of social status on family roles declines somewhat as cultural and subcultural prescriptions become less imperious. Individual differences in resources such as intelligence, skill, time, and energy become more significant in defining the scripts that family members enact in particular family settings, as I mentioned earlier.

Class permeates and colors all life experiences. It affects, if it does not largely determine, not only the quality of life but the duration of life, on the average. Location in the social structure obviously determines the material resources that are available to families and individuals, but much more than that is attributable to membership in a particular class. Class position is associated with typical attitudes, values, and behavior, with self-confidence and self-esteem, with alienation and prejudice, with type and extent of mental illness and degree of sex role conflict—with patterns of thought, generally, as well as with patterns of speech, dress, and recreation. Ultimately, many of these are psychological attributes but their extent and frequency is affected by social location in the society.

In the contemporary United States the upper strata travel more, read more, have more education, vote more, have more friends and entertain them more, receive more mail, and join more organizations. They are less apt to divorce, separate, or desert each other. They raise their children differently. They are less apt to commit crimes of violence and they will be punished differently if they do.

One of the most important things sociologists can know about families or individuals is their location in the class structure. This is widely recognized, as indicated by the fact that journalists in this country often use the phrase "sociological" as a synonym for class in describing class-based attributes or attitudes of particular groups or populations.

Empirical, social scientific studies of the class structure in America largely date from the early years of the depression, another time of heightened class awareness. Many of the pioneering studies treated the family only incidentally in their attempted profiles of class-bound worlds, however.

More recently, a great deal of knowledge has been accumulating on class differences in family roles, in family values, family functioning, family problems, and family destinies. In the 1970s, in America, the family as well as the economy is viewed as an institution in crisis. Both are very topical areas of concern in the mass media and in scholarly research and publications.

A summary of all of the data that we have on class and family life is beyond the limits of a short, general essay on the past, present, and future of the family. What is possible, however, is to utilize once again the model of technological and scientific development and the transition from traditional rural to modern urban values that tends to occur with these developments, as a basis for selecting, organizing, and interpreting some of the information that has been collected on class differences in contemporary family life in America.[1]

THE AMERICAN CLASS
STRUCTURE

Except at the extremes of poverty and wealth, the American class structure is characterized by a vagueness and blurring of boundaries. The value of equalitarianism, and the realities of mass production and mass consumption, obscure the existence of class in America, as objective fact and as subjective state of consciousness.

This has not been true of other economically stratified societies. In medieval Europe, for example, estates were rigidly demarcated and were symbolized, among other things, by dress. The type of dress worn by members of the various estates was often sanctioned by law —peasants were not permitted to wear silk. This greater rigidity in class patterns persists. European workers are more likely than their American counterparts to wear their workers' caps and clothes to work. American workers do not usually wear identifying caps and, in any case, keep their work clothes in lockers. On the street they are often not readily distinguishable as working class, in either dress or demeanor. Their speech, less articulate and "grammatical," may identify them as working class to those who listen, but it is not as distinguishing a mark as the cockney speech of working-class Londoners.

The value of equalitarianism and the relatively high standard of living in America has dulled the consciousness of class, but it has not eliminated the fact of class: the existence of objective, observable, and measurable differences in prestige, power, and privilege in our society that separate people from each other—intellectually, emotionally, and physically. Position in the class structure is still a crucial factor in determining valued friends and eligible marital partners.[2]

Americans have tended to deny the validity of class because class consciousness is not as strongly developed in this country as it is in others. The very term "class" is painful to many ears in America. In American sociology, concepts such as socioeconomic status, interest groups, democratic pluralism, and national elite have been more acceptable (and respectable) than concepts such as class, class conflict, and ruling class.

Why has the level of class consciousness been low in this country? Feelings of class solidarity and the extent of identification with others in similar class positions will not be strong in societies characterized by the existence of a strong set of common values that deemphasize conflicting interests of different classes—national integrating ideologies such as facism or socialism, for example. This is not applicable to the United States, despite the existence of a democratic ideology which is accepted, ideally, by many Americans.

Awareness of class will also be less extreme where the possibility of moving out of one's class is accepted, desired, and believed in, a condition that certainly has characterized the United States in the past.

Individuals who identify with members of a higher class and who believe in the possibility of rising in the class structure will feel little class solidarity.

On the other hand, blocked social mobility (that is recognized) and a higher general level of education in a society enhance feelings of class identity and the understanding of class interests and how these are or are not being promoted in a society. For these reasons, awareness of class and class solidarity have increased recently in the United States, at least for the lower strata. The upper class has always had this kind of consciousness and understanding.

In describing the class structure of the United States, or in plotting out this structure in towns, villages, and small and middle-sized cities, sociologists, particularly if they have limited funds, determine the occupational distribution of the populations they are studying. Occupation is the single most valid indicator of social class, social class referring to the entire complex of attitudes, values, and ways of life that tend to coincide with occupation. This concept is broader and more inclusive than the concept of economic class, which is based on income but which may blur the kinds of distinctions in the sphere of values and role conceptions that interests us here.

Sociologists often subdivide the three broad classes in America— upper, middle, and working class—into upper and lower levels: the upper and lower upper class, the upper and lower middle class, and the upper and lower working class. Despite the trend toward the adoption of common urban values in all classes, material life conditions, world outlooks, family roles, and life experiences generally continue to vary in rather typical ways within the six major strata.

The typical differences between skilled blue-collar workers— carpenters, electricians, plumbers, mechanics—and lower level white-collar workers—civil servants, salesmen, secretaries, clerks —illustrate this point. What do these large categories of people have in common and how do they differ, typically, in the way they live out their lives? Recently, both have been combined in the designation "middle American" because they have shared a common political orientation toward the civil rights movement. There are real differences that separate these two segments of our society, however.

While the skilled worker's occupation is manual, his income is

often higher than middle-class middle Americans. Construction workers often earn more than secretaries and school teachers. But their
consumption habits are different. The skilled worker, futhermore, has
experienced a typically different kind and quality of socialization in
his home, his neighborhood, at school, and at work.

He is more apt to identify with semi-skilled workers than with the
lower levels of the middle class. His family relationships, sexual ba-
havior, reading habits, organizational memberships, attitudes toward
foreign affairs, and consumption patterns reflect this fact. The skilled
worker is less apt than a white-collar parent to value higher education for his children as an absolute good, for example. He is less likely
to encourage his daughters, equally with his sons, to seek higher education. He will be more approving of concrete vocational fields such
as teaching, accounting, or engineering than he will of the humanities and social sciences, where preparation for specific occupational
roles is less obvious. If his child drops out of college, he will consider
the time spent in college wasted. The middle-class parent is more apt
to view whatever time spent in college as a valuable growth experience and a status symbol.

World outlooks as well as what has come to be called "the quality
of life" differ in typical ways within these two large segments of
American society regardless of common features (the increasing adoption of urban values) and individual exceptions. To ignore these typicalities and differences defeats understanding of the social reality in
America even as it reinforces the cherished American values of individualism and equalitarianism.

While there is considerable disagreement about where to establish
class boundaries, the percentage of upper-class individuals in contemporary American society is probably no more than 2 percent (including the newly rich) and is relatively stable. The upper middle class
consists of about 10 percent of the population and is a segment of our
society that is growing rapidly. The increasing affluence that accompanies higher levels of technological development and the growing
need for expert management of organizations and expert professional
services for people creates additional jobs at this level, given an expanding and rationally planned economy. About 40 percent of the
American population is lower middle class. This segment of our so-

ciety is growing most rapidly as industries engaged in distributing, selling, educating, and communicating continue to proliferate. The balance of American society is working class, including the 20 to 30 percent who are lower working class, or poor. The working class is contracting, slowly, as unskilled, semi-skilled and skilled manual occupations are automated out of existence.

In my sketch of family life in the various classes in the United States, I will focus on typical or statistically most frequent patterns. It is important to remember, however, that in a changing and mobile society there are many exceptions and there is much overlapping within the various strata in the behavior and values that I will be describing.

THE UPPER WORKING-CLASS FAMILY

Working-class occupations in America are those in which individuals work with things, primarily—tools, equipment, machines— rather than with knowledge and communication skills.[3] Secretaries work with machines, but symbols and ideas are essential to their work since they must know spelling, grammar, and the elements of style. Sales people use persuasive ideas and a knowledge of their product in the performance of their jobs. Physicians use equipment of all kinds, but their work is grounded on a large body of theory and knowledge about the human body and the human psyche.

The upper and lower working classes are distinguished among other things by the circumstances of their employment—by type of job, the level of skill and knowledge required, the pay, and the steadiness and security of employment. The lower working class, usually referred to as the poor, is unskilled, unemployed, underemployed, or irregularly employed. The upper working class, also known as the stable working class, is steadily employed in semi-skilled jobs, requiring a few days on-the-job training, or in skilled jobs requiring vocational training, lengthy apprenticeships, or fairly extensive on-the-job-training.

Semi-skilled and skilled workers are likely to be unionized. They have higher and steadier incomes than their unskilled counterparts, and more security and self-esteem. While survival is not as precarious as it is among the poor, the upper working class has less autonomy and less control over their lives, on and off the job, than the middle class. Their alternatives in the face of catastrophe—unemployment, severe illness, or dislocation by urban renewal, for example—are fewer and less adequate than in the middle class. Their limited education, lack of savings, and their traditional values often hinder rational accommodation to the blows, uncertainties, and rapid changes of modern life.

The percentage of high-school dropouts is high among skilled and semi-skilled workers but not as high as it is in the lower working class. Wives often have more education than their husbands, since females are less likely than males to drop out of high school. For this reason, if they work, they may have more prestigious white-collar jobs. The husband usually earns more, however, and authority patterns within the home, superficially at least, seem to follow the traditional patriarchal pattern.

The blue-collar worker puts forth the image of toughness, courage, unsentimentality, and command, and his wife supports his self-proclaimed status as boss and ultimate authority in the household. Both husband and wife verbalize the traditional values and sex role definitions and they believe that what they verbalize is what actually exists.

But ideal and reality, often disparate, here too do not coincide. The working-class wife, in fact, usually has more unilateral authority than the middle-class wife in managing the budget, the home, the children, and relationships with the extended family and her husband. Effective authority within the family reflects the community status of the husband and his personal resources, as well as subcultural definitions and expectations. This is evident in the working class, as elsewhere, despite the stronger hold of the traditional values in this class.

In the working class, the husband abdicates in many areas of decision making that involve the home and the children. When on sporadic occasions, he does assert his will, more often he does so in a coercive and unilateral way. Hence, the working class wife views her husband as dominant and controlling, despite her very real authority (by default) in day-to-day activities.

The authority of the father is also less than it appears to be in relation to his children, particularly his sons. The middle-aged father, not as restrictive and repressive as his immigrant or farmer father was, complains of lack of respect, particularly from his adolescent son—of being called "beer belly," "hard hat" or "fascist pig." The modern working-class father has not demanded the arbitrary respect and obedience that his first-generation urban father demanded from him. And he cannot command this respect on the basis of superior education or economic resources.

Conflict between the generations tends to be more repressed in this stratum (and in the lower middle class), but where it is overt, it cuts deep into the basis of whatever self-esteem the father may have. The upper middle-class father who is called dishonest or a "sell-out" by his adolescent progeny suffers a different order of disesteem, one that is not confirmed, furthermore, by low social status in the world at large.[4]

Other traditional values are real as well as apparent in this segment of the working class. Familism, for example, is a meaningful aspect of daily existence and is reflected in frequent visiting and exchange of services. The extended family continues to serve interests and psychic needs to a greated extent than do experts, friends, clubs, or formal organizations.

An active mastery approach to the environment is discouraged by realistic economic and educational barriers. Individualistic achievement, furthermore, usually means estrangement from family, neighborhood, and peers. The fruits of rationalism are not readily apparent to those who have few real alternatives: luck, chance, the breaks are more persuasive explanatory principles for evaluating individual destinies, as well as life itself, particularly where the onus of individual responsibility is the only other possible explanation.

Religious beliefs are strong, particularly among wives and daughters, but churchgoing is less frequent than in the middle class. Churchgoing does not serve the purpose of status validation and it is also less frequent than in the middle class because organizational affiliation, generally, is less frequent in the upper working class. Organizational memberships are usually confined to labor unions and patriotic organizations where participation is often perfunctory and marginal.

Ethnocentrism is strong, reinforced by lower levels of education and more restricted contact with strange people and strange places.

Exposure to the mass media, particularly to television, diminishes ethnocentrism, but working-class men and women tend to limit their exposure in the mass media to entertainment and sports rather than to informational programs and articles.

Tolerance and a strong belief in equalitarianism and democracy stem ultimately from childrearing practices and parent-child relationships that emphasize these values. While the upper levels of the working class in the United States are more permissive in their relationships with their children than similarly located parents in England, Italy, Germany, Russia, and other countries that have been surveyed, the emphasis in parent-child relationships in this class is still primarily on obedience to external controls. Children who have not been able to participate much in determining their fate—at home, at school and, later, on the job—are not very apt to value self-determination, equality, and cultural pluralism as adults.

Materialism is one modern, urban value that has taken hold in this class, but the emphasis on the accumulation of material goods has a different meaning than it has in the middle class. Thorstein Veblen, an American sociologist who achieved a degree of notoriety among social scientists during the early part of the twentieth century for his satirical and often bitter analyses of American business enterprise, the American class structure, and American institutions of higher learning, coined the phrase "conspicuous consumption" to refer to expenditures in excess of what is needed for physical comfort. Veblen noted that people engage in this kind of spending because: "In order to gain and hold the esteem of men, it is not sufficient merely to possess wealth or power. The wealth or power must be put in evidence, for esteem is awarded only on evidence."[5]

The working-class family does not play this particular game. They cannot afford to and, furthermore, there is no need to. The husband's level of achievement is obvious. He is not doing the bureaucratic crawl in a large firm, nor is he taking risks, as a self-employed entrepreneur, that may lead to riches and fame.

Because most manual jobs are dull, routine, and dead end, permitting little exercise of independent judgment, resourcefulness, autonomy, or control over the work situation, the work role tends to be devalued in this class, relative to family and leisure roles. Work is a job, not a career; the paycheck is the sanction for going on. And the paycheck is used for compensatory rather than conspicuous consumption.[6]

New purchases—television sets, cars, household appliances—provide ephemeral excitement and a break in the daily routine. Purchases are made locally or in discount stores that cater largely to the working class. The working-class wife feels intimidated by middle-class stores with middle-class personnel and middle-class customers. Husband and wife buy the top of the line, on the assumption that you get what you pay for. They are unlikely to subscribe to magazines that test and give information about consumer products.

The emphasis is on the contents of the house rather than its size or location in a prestigious neighborhood. Home ownership is valued primarily because it provides escape from oppressive landlords rather than as a validation of status.

Working-class wives embrace the traditional wife and mother role more unquestioningly than middle-class wives. If they work, they do so largely for economic reasons; they are more apt than middle-class women to claim they would not work if they did not have to. Their lives, by report, are more routine than in the middle class; weekdays and weekends merge, less likely to be broken by excursions, trips, dinners out, and nonfamily visiting and entertaining.

Household work is less efficiently performed than in the middle class. Household chores usually expand to consume the time available to perform them. Employed wives, in all classes, with much less time, spend less time on the same chores. Working-class wives, furthermore, are unlikely to hire household help.

On personality tests, working-class women appear more passive, insecure, nurturing, dependent, and emotionally volatile than middle-class women. The latter have less pronounced feelings of inferiority and value personal freedom, independence, and privacy more. A higher level of education is a very important underlying reason for these basic differences as well as differences in the way female children are raised in the two classes.

The traditional values permeate all family relationships in the working class. The self-sacrificing orientation of the mother is evidenced daily and in hundreds of ways. She derives more pleasure from buying for her children than for herself. She values and stresses family solidarity and mutual responsibility above individual goals and needs, where the two are in conflict. Her world is bound, defined, and limited to family concerns and interests.

In her maternal role, she emphasizes respectability and obedience more, creativity and self-reliance less. With more children to control, she has less time to reason, spell out general principles, or to turn affection off and on as a means of exercising that control. A threat, followed up by a slap, is more effective in the short run. Since she is less ambivalently self-sacrificing, and is less questioning of traditional childrearing techniques, she feels less guilt about using physical punishment than do middle-class women.

Sex roles are also more traditionally defined and more sharply segregated in the working class. Husbands and wives share few common interests outside of the children and few common friends and recreational pursuits. Husbands are more apt to confide in male relatives, if they confide in anyone at all. Wives also confide in same-sex relatives: mothers, sisters, and daughters. Cross-sex relationships are suspect because they are viewed as inevitably sexual in motivation—a situation more pronounced in, but certainly not exclusive to, the working class.

Surviving traditional values of masculine superiority and emotional reserve restrict communication. For this reason, possible constructive solutions to marital difficulties by discussion, reasoning, compromise, or resolution are more difficult to achieve. A relationship in which one member feels fearful and inferior precludes free communication. And the tendency to turn to relatives for advice usually reinforces a fatalistic resignation: make the best of it; it is fate; God's will; woman's lot.

Given the modern values in marriage—companionship, intimacy, deep and intensive communication, and mutual emotional support—the subculturally prescribed psychological separation of husband and wife and the greater economic stresses they experience result in higher divorce rates than in the middle class. Divorces among the higher strata in our society are more publicized, but they are, in fact, less frequent.

The emphasis on traditional definitions of masculinity also restricts the possibility of mutual sexual enjoyment. Tenderness and concern for the wife's response will be rare if sexual gratification is viewed as a male prerogative. Foreplay, positional variations—any variation in technique or procedure other than the male superior, genital sex pattern—is viewed as a perversion.

The double standard, permitting sexual freedom to males but not to females, is still quite strong in the working class. Husbands, however, are less apt to engage in extramarital affairs during the later years of marriage than middle-class husbands. Here, again, the reasons probably have to do with the lesser economic resources of working-class men. With age, the money and power of higher status males can procure what youth and physical attractiveness no longer can.

The foregoing profile applies to the majority of white working-class families in this country. But change is endemic in modern society and change is a constant challenge to sociological generalization. We do not despair, however, because outdated sociology is good history and the family patterns I have just described are past history rather than present reality for a small minority of the approximately 20 million white manual workers in the United States.

Sociologists recognize this fact in their distinction between the traditional and the modern working class.[7] This distinction often parallels age and generation. The typical differences in marital, parental, and filial role definitions are usually associated with the length of urban residence of the family, beginning with the initial immigration or migration of a grandparent or parent from a rural area, outside of the United States, or within it. The generational time span for acculturation to urban values is accelerated or delayed, as I have already indicated, by such factors as the availability of educational and occupational opportunities, the degree of discrimination, and the compatibility of the cultural traditions of the area of origin with urban values.

Modern working-class families are generally younger, have a higher level of education (high-school graduation; perhaps some additional training in junior college) and have been geographically mobile (into working-class suburbs, usually). They approach the middle class with respect to a greater effective emphasis on the urban values of equalitarianism, achievement, and rationalism in family life.

With geographic mobility, the extended family is not as significant as it was in the past, and loyalties and commitments shift to the nuclear family. The separate friends and separate interests of husband and wife are shed to some extent. Friends are visited in common and instead of, or in addition to, relatives.

Sex role stereotyping within the family also declines: husbands and wives share homemaking obligations more and sons and daughters are treated more alike. Communication is freer and less strained, enhanced by the greater verbal facility that accompanies a higher level of education and by the decreased authoritarianism in the form as well as in the substance of family relationships.

The increased mutuality in the husband-wife relationship is reflected in greater sexual satisfaction and greater marital satisfaction. Sexual fulfillment for both partners is desired and accepted as the standard. Variations in sexual techniques are attempted and sexual preferences are more freely discussed and accommodated.[8]

The wife is less passive, less dependent, less fearful, and less self-sacrificing and she expects and receives more respect from husband and children. Her home territory shifts from the kitchen to the family room or the living room and, if she works, her husband is less apt to feel threatened by her employment than in traditional working-class families.

The husband is less rigid about traditional definitions of masculinity. He shows more warmth and affection to sons as well as to daughters. He helps market, clear off, wash up, and straighten out, and he may even walk the baby in the park on the weekend, if he is not moonlighting.

Modern working-class families are transitional rather than fully modern in values and behavior. As such, they experience the stresses that transition often brings, but with fewer of the safeguards and releases available to middle class families. Loneliness, isolation, and boredom are more frequent. The loss of the extended family as a daily interacting unit is less compensated by organizational memberships and extensive friendship networks. The job is a less intrinsically gratifying outlet. And more stringent economic pressures curtail commercial pleasures and diversions. Television looms large—as it does in all working-class homes—a low cost and effortless purveyor of ready-made fantasy, instant amusement, and vicarious living.

When they walk down the street in their new neighborhoods, modern working-class family members, as one researcher has pointed out, are less likely to know the faces in the crowd.[9] And the crowd has thinned out considerably in their cleaner, quieter, less violent, and somehow less exhilarating (at least to teenagers) suburban worlds.

THE LOWER WORKING-CLASS FAMILY

The traditional rural values, however modified in emphasis or overt behavior by particular ethnic groups, are strongest within the unskilled working class in this country. The poor are the most recently uprooted from agricultural environments and rural ways of life.[10]

Fatalism, superstition, ethnocentrism, authoritarianism, and familism are strong. The new urban values are visible to this segment of our population, but objective life circumstances often preclude their adoption. Achievement motivation, for example, is not a monopoly of the middle class. Young children of all classes have high aspirations. The children of the poor, however, lose these aspirations, gradually and almost inevitably, in the process of growing up in America.

If technological development brings with it real and effective (perceived and actual) educational and economic opportunity, fatalism and superstition are replaced by high levels of achievement motivation and by rationalism. Higher general levels of education, for both sexes and all ages, which are necessary to function in a complex technology, weaken the traditional values of authoritarianism and patriarchalism. The decline of simple routine jobs and the heightened interdependence of national economies promote mobility, individualism, and self-reliance on the job and elsewhere. Even the growth of bureaucracy has not led to the robot employee mentality so feared by social scientists in the past.

Modern man is far less oppressed by technology and bureaucracy than traditional man was by natural catastrophe, physical deprivation, and autocratic work situations. Much recent evidence has been accumulating indicating that employees in large bureaucracies have more autonomy than those working in small firms or organizations.[11] They are less closely supervised and can manipulate and negotiate their work conditions to a much greater extent. They certainly have more autonomy than medieval apprentice journeymen working under the watchful eye of the master, whom they often had to serve at home as well as in the shop.

Bureaucratic organizations recruit more educated workers, who have higher income, more security (workers tend to be unionized), and who do more complex work. For these reasons, upper working class and middle class men and women who work in large bureaucracies tend to be more independent, more flexible, and more open to change than employees in small organizations and firms. The bureaucratic employee who is a stickler for rules, rational or irrational, is not thereby evidencing his helplessness in a rigidly controlled situation. Often there is a choice that would better accomodate the needs of his client or customer, but he does not exercise this choice because he does not want to. Frustrated by blocked mobility and the year-to-year sameness of his job, he displaces his hostility onto the public by his insistence on form rather than function in coping with their problems.

Since the poor have low levels of education, are not unionized, and are not employed in large bureaucracies (if they are employed at all), they are not encouraged by their life circumstances or their work situations to adopt the modern values. And their family life, reflecting these material conditions, remains more traditional.

Many of the statistical indicators of personal and familial unhappiness are stronger in this segment of American society than in any other—the incidence, for example, of drug addiction, child abuse, murder, rape, incest, assault, desertion, and physical and mental illness.[12] The family unit is torn apart, primarily, by objective and unremitting economic stress. The effective dominance of the wife and mother is strongest in this class, despite the appearance of male dominance, because the husband is least able to legitimate his authority in the home by means of personal or economic assets. Unable to get adequate, secure employment, he is likely to escape the field and become part of the drifting American underclass of temporary employees in agriculture, in hotels, laundries, kitchens, basements, and nonunionized factories and hospitals.

Courtship and marriage are not romanticized and idealized in the lower working class. The decision to marry is often casual, the result of a fatalistic acceptance of the inevitable, particularly in the case of pre-marital pregnancy. Teenage marriages, precipitated by pregnancy, are common. A choice of partners within the same neighborhood is also common, because geographic mobility is relatively circumscribed in this class. The young cannot afford to travel and they do not go off to college.

Husband and wife are often emotionally estranged and isolated, separated by suffering and unfulfilled expectations. Sex is mutually exploitative, used more consciously and deliberately than in other classes, to support the economic needs of the female and the narcissistic ego needs of the male. Communication is halting and sporadic, reflecting cultural traditions and cumulative anger and frustration. Overt display of affection is rare in the absence of sentiment and optimism. The husband defines the marital relationship in terms of the gratification of his physical needs, and the wife accepts this, but longs for more. Since the husband-wife relationship tends to be characterized by emotional frustration and isolation, and since the wife has few outside interests, the lower working-class woman views her primary status in life as that of mother, rather than wife. The mother-child relationship is the strongest and most intimate family tie in this class as it tends to be, generally, in traditional societies.

Female-headed households, regardless of ethnic origin, are frequent in urban slum areas, since the husband is often an economic burden and the wife may be better able to obtain and hold a job. Welfare policies that specify the absence of an adult male in the home as a condition for obtaining government funds reinforce this pattern. The desire for love, companionship, children, and economic support, which cannot be gratified any other way, often leads the lower working-class woman into a fatalistic acceptance of a succession of temporary male partners, who provide a shadowy semblance of the cultural ideal.

A few social scientists, and many spokesmen for the poor, have defended this pattern as an appropriate and highly adaptive response to life circumstances. They have accused critics of arbitrarily imposing their own middle-class values on the poor, who do not share these values. More recent careful community research indicates, however, that these patterns are not preferred, and that overwhelming misery, despair, guilt, and frustration are common features of this kind of existence. The deserted mother and child and the seemingly irresponsible male represent a settling for less by people who are defeated in their initial efforts to live by values that are modern and urban and are middle class only incidentally because this class can achieve them more readily.

Childrearing practices among the poor also reflect life circumstances and the opportunity structure. The discipline of children is most harsh, most severe, and most inconsistent in this class, emphasizing strict situational obedience, and values such as neatness and cleanliness that are taken for granted in other classes. Where chaos is a real possibility, order and discipline will be emphasized more. Where basic physical deprivation is endemic, childrearing focuses on the physical. Slum mothers with large families and low levels of education have little time and limited verbal concepts for introspecting about their childrens' motivations, deeper feelings, and psychological development. As in traditional agricultural societies, physical survival is an overriding value.

Work experiences color family relationships. Engaged in occupations that are routine and under direct supervision, requiring few communication skills and with little possibility to exercise autonomy and independent judgment, the poor do not encourage these traits in their children. It is not that they do not want to; they are exposed to urban values, and they would act them out if they could. The slum mother nags her child to do well in school. The child perceives the undertone of hopelessness, however, and this undertone will remain until objective circumstances change and opportunity is available and is perceived as such by this class.

Poor families have been portrayed as perpetuating poverty because traditional values of the subculture of poverty—fatalism, particularly—are ill suited to the adoption of urban values in an urban environment. The controversy over which comes first, economic conditions or subcultural values, are like other dichotomies—heredity and environment, free will and determinism, for example —that have exercised intellectuals and academicians in the past. But this particular controversy is more amenable to empirical investigation and resolution.

Beginning in the late 1940s, David McClelland and his associates, first at Wesleyan University and later at Harvard, and many other social scientists since then, have been engaged in studies of the sources and consequences of achievement motivation in families and in societies.[13] We now know, after vast quantities of painstaking cross-cultural research, that high levels of achievement motivation in children in all societies are associated with particular parent-child relationships. Mothers of children with a strong need to achieve set high standards according to some criterion of excellence. They are deeply involved with their children and they use strong sanctions to encourage successful competitive performance. Fathers are not authoritarian; they encourage independent judgment and self-reliance in their children. While they pursue a hands-off policy with respect to dictating behavior, they are at the same time, however, also deeply involved in their childrens' accomplishments. Dominance, overprotection, and overindulgence, which subvert the resourcefulness and effort required for successful competition, and neglect and rejection, insofar as they lower self-confidence and aspirations, are associated with low levels of achievement motivation in children.

In an early work, McClelland elaborated a theory of social change in which he attributed differences in the level of technological development of various societies historically to the presence or absence of childrearing practices that promote achievement motivation. He discounted changing economic conditions as a factor affecting, if not determining, these childrearing practices: "It is difficult to argue. . . . that material advance came first and created a higher need for achievement." And "men with high achievement motives will find a way to economic achievement given fairly wide variations in opportunity and social structure."

To the biological and economic determinisms of the Social Darwinist and Marxist models of social change was added a new deterministic model: psychological determinism. McClelland advised social scientists to direct their attention to "psychological concerns that in the long run determine what happens in history."[14]

In a very recent study, McClelland and his associates, after attempting to instill achievement motivation in Indian businessmen, reversed their previous position and, in a courageous about-face, concluded that the social situation—the existence of objective opportunity in the environment—is the crucial factor in competitive accomplishment: "A man cannot convert increased motivation into increased activity unless he has a real opportunity to do so." [15] McClelland's original formulation of the importance of parental ideologies and childrearing methods in determining the course of world history ignored objective changes in opportunity as this affects parental values. Childrearing practices do not exist in a social vacuum.

McClelland, in his early work, claimed that the upper class does not typically produce children with strong achievement motivation because upper-class fathers are powerful and tend to dominate and control their sons. It could also be argued that since high status for upper-class sons is guaranteed, parents have less need to encourage competitive excellence in their children. The lower strata have this need, but they will not set high standards, with the necessary confidence and conviction, unless they perceive the possibility of success for their children as realistic and attainable. The argument, then, that the traditional values of poor families obstructs acculturation to urban values, particularly to achievement and an active, rational approach to the environment, ignores this all-important fact.

THE UPPER MIDDLE-CLASS FAMILY

The upper middle-class family in America is the epitome and the vanguard of much that is modern in contemporary family life.[16] Because it is close to the causes and consequences of social change, the emphasis in this stratum is on the new—the latest in ideas, in consumption patterns, and in human relationships.

Upper middle-class men and women are highly successful business executives, public servants, professionals, and entertainers, who are near but not at the top of various occupational and income hierarchies in government, business, the professions, and recreation. They have careers, not jobs, and, at least within the present middle-aged depression-born generation, they are highly invested in these careers and in the work ethic. They are not usually alienated at work, since they do not experience the blocked mobility that results from a lack of formal education. At the higher levels of the status game, many are called but few are chosen. Exceptional talent, hard work, and drive, however, can conceivably result in national recognition and achieved upper-class status, for at least some members of this social stratum. Upper middle-class employees also have a great deal of freedom on the job, since the higher the prestige of an occupation, the greater is the degree of autonomy at work.

The upper middle-class family is highly mobile, along all three of the dimensions of mobility that I have described—social, psychological, and geographic. The relatively isolated nuclear family is most likely to be found within this stratum, although it is probably not typical, even here. While husband-wife and parent-child relationships tend to be equalitarian, the husband's authority within the family stems more from achieved resources than from cultural definition, however. To describe the family as equalitarian does not mean that each partner has absolutely equal authority in all decisions about what to do, where to go, whom to see, and how to behave. If this were the case, decision-making would often be stalemated. A more accurate description of family authority patterns in what are described as equalitarian households is that power, influence, and authority are situational and vary according to what is being decided and who is more invested in the outcome. Since men, for example, are the major breadwinners in the majority of homes in American society, they generally make the decision as to where the family will live and whether they will move in response to a new job opportunity.

While the husband's authority is high, it is not unilateral. Many decisions are based on discussion and mutual accomodation, and if the wife has more skill, interest, or investment in a particular area of decision-making, her arguments are likely to prevail. If she does not work and has more of the resource of time at her disposal, she will perform the preliminary tasks that lead to a decision in such areas as selecting furniture, finding an apartment, selecting a house, and investigating travel possibilities, for example. But the husband participates in the final decision, even if it is not in an area that interests him most. His opinion carries more or less weight, depending upon his skills, preference, or interest in whatever is being decided.

The partner role relationship is quite frequent in the urban upper middle class, particularly among professionals. The sharing of home-making and childrearing obligations, however, is usually more limited than in the lower middle class, less because of cultural sex role definitions than because of the demands of the husband's career. The wife may delegate homemaking chores, in part, to paid help, although she usually continues to perform many of the traditional functions in the home and to regard her marital role as her primary status in life. Regardless of the prestige of the wife's occupation, and even if it is higher than the prestige of the husband's occupation, the wife will not become dominant in the household unless she outearns her husband.[17] This parallels the situation in the upper working class, where the wife may have a white-collar job, but does not outearn her husband and does not, therefore, become dominant.

Communication, in the absence of psychopathology, is free, intimate, and intensive between all members of the upper middle-class family. This is a highly educated stratum, typically, and as such, family members have the verbal tools and the intellectual orientation that promotes introspection and concern with personal development and individual freedom. For this reason and because of the greater personal freedom parents experience in their own lives, permissive childrearing practices are most prevalent in this class.

Rationalism is highly valued in the upper middle class but irrationalism is better understood and, therefore, more feared. Faith in the expert is almost supreme and the preoccupation with the latest discovery, the newest scientific technique, and the current formula for more effective childrearing, improved marital interaction, and better homes and gardens is endless.

Since many upper middle-class families have been socially mobile, the past is usually not venerated. This is exemplified by home furnishings which are typically avant garde and, income permitting, often of original design. Those members of this class who identify with the upper class will furnish their homes with antiques—family heirlooms that have lost their original home, purchased by those who long for an ancestral home and the venerable past they do not have.

Conspicuous consumption is usually high in mobile or marginal families who have the means to validate their ambiguous or changing status by material acquisitions. The upper middle class, particularly successful businessmen, are in the forefront of this kind of consumption behavior, limited only by their means or by the expedient necessity not to upstage their superiors, if they are employed in large organizations.[18] Professionals have their academic degrees to validate status and are, for that reason, somewhat less likely to be conspicuous consumers.

The artistic, creative, and intellectual segment of the upper middle class attempts to avoid placement within the class structure and obvious identification with class symbols, but they also have evolved a typical and identifiable life style. They may live in working-class neighborhoods or warehouse districts, but they furnish their homes in typical ways, at any particular time, and they place the strongest emphasis on the urban values in their ideal role conceptions and in their actual family relationships.

THE LOWER MIDDLE-CLASS FAMILY

Respectability, conformity, and petty striving have been the major descriptive labels used by social scientists, invidiously usually, in attempts to profile this particular stratum of American society. But this too is changing. Recent studies of the lower middle class tend to be more discriminating, less biased, and more sympathetic.[19] Respectability, for example, may still be a very basic value in this class, but from all evidence, the group sex movement, although small in numbers, has drawn many of its recruits from this stratum.[20] The upper middle class does not have the time to engage in organized group sex activities and in the constant pursuit of new partner couples that is required for successful participation in the movement, and the working class is still too traditional and repressed in the area of sexual behavior.

Even in this kind of breaking out of conventional practices, however, the traditional value of fidelity is preserved, and the modern value of equality between the sexes is proclaimed by lower middle-class swingers. In group sex activities, married couples participate together or not at all and elaborate precautions are taken to insure that relationships with new couples are segmented and limited strictly to sex, thus providing less threat to the stability of the marital relationship of participants.

In general, however, and despite glaring but infrequent exceptions, the standard of respectability is still quite binding for the great majority of families in this stratum. Lower level white-collar workers are the backbone of the nation, not only as members, but as active supporters of patriotic and religious organizations. Lower middle-class parents and children pack the churches, Boy Scout and Girl Scout organizations, the Kiwanis and Lions Clubs, and veterans organizations.

This class is in between the working class and the upper middle class in the adoption of certain modern values. The emphasis on instilling achievement motivation in their children is quite high, for example, boosted by more objective availability of opportunity than in the working class and not subverted by affluence and the tendency toward overindulgence that has been characteristic of many upper middle-class families, particularly since World War II. While childrearing practices are less authoritarian than in the working class, and physical punishment is not a frequently used technique for disciplining children, permissiveness is tempered by stricter limits and by more emphasis on the rights of the parent than is typical in the upper middle class.

Unlike the working class, whose models are usually within the same stratum, the lower middle class identifies upward and is somewhat more concerned with status validation and striving, but they are not usually conspicuous consumers. Thrift and saving are still highly valued despite the enticements of an installment-plan economy. And while they are prevented from rising in the class structure by virtue of limited education, they strive to help their children move into the upper middle class and will often make extreme sacrifices for this goal.

Many lower middle-class families now live in tract suburbs that are ethnically varied but relatively homogeneous with respect to age and income. And they are not usually as lonely or isolated as is the modern working class. Visiting as couples in the evening or coffee klatsching during the day, and the cooperative exchange of babysitting and other services, provide the functional equivalent of extended family activities and mutual aid for many residents of these burgeoning suburban communities.[21]

The amount of joint activity and sharing of obligations within the home is highest in this stratum. Traditional sex role definitions are less rigid than in the working class and the husband is usually more available than in the upper middle class to share in household and childrearing activities. The wife often maintains the fiction of male dominance (Wait 'till your father gets home!), but bilateral decisions and consultation with the husband on mundane decisions is more frequent here than in the working class.

While they are not in the forefront of change in family roles and values, and while traditional values such as ethnocentrism are more prevalent, the children of this stratum of American society are next in line to experience many of the innovations first institutionalized in the upper middle class. With a higher general level of education, greater upward social mobility, and greater economic resources, the differences in acculturation to modern values all but disappear. But these differences are significant, and they continue to divide the upper and lower levels of the largest and fastest growing segment of the American class structure in very real ways.

THE OLD UPPER-CLASS FAMILY

The two levels of the upper class in America, upper and lower, or old and new, are distinguished according to the age of family wealth. The old upper class has inherited its wealth from an elite who are no longer alive, and the new upper class is first-generation rich and famous.

Since upper-class individuals do not answer questionnaires, empirical studies of this stratum in the United States are very limited in number. Those that are available, furthermore, contain little information about upper-class family life.[22] Anecdotal, journalistic accounts are not necessarily representative of all upper-class families and are likely to be biased, since it is difficult for middle-class journalists or social scientists to write with detachment about a segment of society whose wealth and circumstances are often beyond imagining. Accounts of this class have also been written by those who are in it, insiders who are natural participant observers and who write about what they know. But these accounts also suffer from bias—the bias of the deeply involved, rather than the bias of the awed, the envious, or the critical.[23]

What, then, do we know about this class that social scientists, journalists, and member-spokesmen might agree about? Fortunately, we are concerned with family roles and relationships—a far less controversial topic than the political and economic behavior of the hereditary wealthy and a topic about which there is more consensus.

As with the working class, the old upper class divides into the traditional and the modern, in values, behavior, and world outlook, and this is largely associated with age and generation. The traditional old upper class has as its models Anglo-Saxon Protestant ancestors who established the family fortune—in land ownership before the Civil War and in business and fluid capital since then. In the traditional old upper class, the values of familism, patriarchalism, and ethnocentrism are the basic constituents of family roles. Other values, often identified with the Protestant ethic, are also widespread—values such as frugality, sobriety, emotional reserve, physical endurance, impulse control, and the constructive use of leisure time. The work ethic is strong, whether it is channeled into gainful employment or into community service.

The great emphasis that is placed on genealogy and family lineage is reflected in naming practices such as the use of surnames of earlier branches of the family, or of the mother's family, as given or middle names. Family solidarity is reinforced by frequent rituals and ceremonies—debutante balls, formal engagements, large weddings, baptisms, and Thanksgiving and Christmas gatherings of the clan. It is not unusual to see older adolescents traveling in Europe and elsewhere with their parents or other relatives, a phenomenon that is rare in the middle class, and not only for financial reasons. The extended family is a binding reality in this class, cemented by economic dependence and the control by the older generation of vast economic resources. Nepotism is a duty, not only to the individual, but to the family line. Those family members who control the family fortune feel strongly obligated to pass on the wealth intact at least, and enhanced if possible. The family black sheep and ne'er-do-well are not only tolerated, but family members will go to great lengths to protect them for the sake of the family reputation.

Ethnocentrism is strong, but it is the kind of ethnocentrism that is based not on fear or lack of information about out-groups, but on the desire to preserve the family from taint by the middle classes or by minority group members, an attitude with long historical precedence in economically stratified societies. To this end upper-class families isolate themselves and their children by developing their own exclusive clubs, resorts, and schools. The value of ethnocentrism has also been symbolized in the traditional upper class in the past by loyalty and deep involvement in local community affairs by families whose localism was grounded in land ownership in the South or business enterprises in the Northeast.

In the traditional hereditary upper class, marriages are no longer arranged but great pressure is exerted on the young, sometimes subtly, but often not so subtly, to marry within the group. Largely because of the slight tendency of upper-class males to marry down, and also because of the surplus of females in all classes, women in the upper class have a more difficult time obtaining marital partners. Their field of eligibles is highly restricted. For this reason and others, such as the greater difficulty in obtaining divorce freely because of more complicated family finances, the average age at marriage tends to be higher for the upper class generally.

The double standard is strong among traditional members of the upper class. Because marital alliances, particularly in the past, were undertaken often to fulfill familistic obligations, upper-class males frequently maintained mistresses to fulfill the erotic needs that may not have been gratified in their marriages.

Nuclear family relationships in the traditional upper class have been characterized by formality, ritual, and emotional reserve. The unilateral authority of the husband and father is not a façade, preserved as a sop to cultural dictate; it is an effective reality. Separateness, a symptom of extreme differences in authority within the family, has also been a characteristic of the traditional upper class, as indicated by the custom of maintaining separate bedrooms for husband and wife and by long separations from children, who are sent to boarding schools or who remain in the continuous care of servants whether the parents are at home or are traveling.

The husband and wife relationship is characterized by a clear and distinct separation in roles. The wife functions as hostess and companion, particularly on formal occasions and the husband typically engages in business or public service activities. A large number of upper-class males in the United States, incidentally, earn salaries in gainful employment, an indication of the persistence of the work ethic in this class.

Parent-child conflict is muted in the traditional upper class, as it is in the upper class generally, traditional or modern, old or new, by the presence of nurses, governesses, housekeepers, and other surrogates who are actually involved in the day-to-day custodial care and disciplining of the children. The mother, however, acts as the ultimate arbiter in conflicts between children and servants, if she happens to be present.

The traditional, hereditary upper class is changing, as are all classes in rapidly changing America, and the major reasons for change are pretty much the same. Technological advances affect all classes, however differently in detail, as does increased mobility, changing opportunity structures, and other social conditions that undermine remaining traditional values. When large corporations, requiring highly skilled managers, absorb the family businesses of the hereditary rich into national and international corporations, the scion of the old family may be retained in what was formerly the family business, if he is talented, or if his name on the corporation masthead promotes solidarity, as constitutional monarchs are retained in Europe as a symbol of solidarity or past glory. But this is not typical. Local community roots are weakened for this class, as for others, but for the upper class, geographic mobility, international in scope, becomes a more significant type of mobility than in other classes.

The rise of the meritocracy and the decline of nepotism infringe on the ability of the old upper class to maintain its social exclusiveness. Prestigious schools and colleges expand their recruitment under pressures of an equalitarianism stemming from a need of a wider base of talent to keep complex technologies and economies operating and from social movements that are ultimately responding to this need. The newly rich and the near-rich aristocracy of talent push on and into old upper class havens and retreats slowly but more effectively than in the past. The modern, more mobile hereditary upper class becomes cosmopolitan and international, more equalitarian and less ethnocentric.

The breaking of local geographic ties that occurs with the decline of family businesses has also been enhanced since World War II by the availability of high-speed jet transport. The dinner party network has become worldwide as has the entourage of friends, functionaries, and servants. And although familism persists, it is much modified by the circumstances of broader horizons and the greater opportunity for the children of the rich, also, to strike out on their own in nonfamily controlled occupations.

THE NEW UPPER-CLASS FAMILY

In the past, the new upper-class, self-made men who have climbed usually from middle-class origins to the very top positions in business, government, and the professions, would have continued to be defined as middle class. They would have served the upper class, but they would not have been granted the right to socialize and intermarry with the hereditary wealthy. In industrialized society, however, the criteria of overall prestige are weighted somewhat differently. While hereditary wealth and family lineage are important, skill and talent, particularly of the caliber that has resulted in national or international fame, become very highly valued. The new elite of talent in the United States, often of minority group origins, are international jet-setters and conspicuous consumers of an order that is qualitatively different from that of their former middle-class compatriots whom they have left behind.

They value achievement and hard work highly since this is the basis of their claim for recognition and acceptance. Gracious living, the way of life of the old upper class, is difficult for these successful men to emulate. Their wives are better able to adapt to the demands of the new status since the companion role is one they may have performed before their husbands achieved fame. Where the wife is unable to make this transition, a divorce may result. The mass media publicize divorces of celebrities from the women they married when they were very young, but the actual frequency of these divorces, however, is not very high outside of the entertainment field.

Family relationships in the new upper class reflect in part their middle-class origins and also the changed circumstances of the family. Marital relationships are more equalitarian, less formal and reserved, and somewhat less stable than those of the old upper class, but the two classes are merging in these respects, and also with respect to parent-child relationships, which are more spontaneous, more permissive, and more emotionally intense and involved.

A controversy that has exercised numerous observers is whether the new upper class is responsible for the changes which have been occuring within the younger, more modern, hereditary upper-class families, or whether the newly arrived families will, with time, acculturate to the traditional patterns of the old upper class. It seems most likely that both are responding to the changed conditions, material and ideological, of modern times and that the traditional values will continue their decline. The new elite of talent are not likely to embrace patterns that are dying out in the old upper class, and the latter are changing, not because they are emulating their new associates, but because their objective life circumstances have changed.

To the question, "Who killed Society?" (Society in this case meaning old money families), the answer is that Society is alive and well. The old upper class has not been corrupted by the new upper class. The core and the leaders of the Jet Set, formerly known as Cafe Society, are and have always been, members of the old upper class, a fact that has been carefully documented recently.[24] In modern times, as one investigator has observed, talented celebrities are invited to eat dinner with their "betters," whereas in former times, they entertained during or after dinner. And the sons and daughters of the new elite, born to wealth and educated in exclusive preparatory schools, often marry the sons and daughters of the old upper class. The circulation of elites, in the case of marriage, remains largely within the category of the very wealthy, old and new.

ROLE CONFLICT AND CLASS

In highly industrialized societies, family roles not only change in content very rapidly, but another phenomenon, role conflict, becomes constant, universal, and more intense.[25] In each of the major social classes, in contemporary America, families experience somewhat unique variations in the type and intensity of role conflict.

Roles, as I pointed out in chapter 1, are explicit or implicit guides or blueprints for thought, emotion, and behavior, that spell out what the individual can or cannot, should or should not, and must or must not do as an occupant of a particular status. In modern societies, the content of roles, particularly values, attitudes, beliefs, and norms, is constantly changing and the number of roles is constantly expanding.

Individuals experience role conflict—the feeling of being frustrated by unfulfilled expectations or contradictory, incongruous, or impossible demands—when they do not have the psychic or material resources to enact a role (the lower working-class male who cannot fulfill the breadwinner requirement of the husband role in our society, for example); when incompatible demands are simultaneously required within the same role (the requirement that middle-class wives restrict their activities and interests to the home and, at the same time, remain interesting, stimulating companions to their husbands); when individuals are torn by incompatible demands of various roles (the employed wife and mother, for example); or when role conceptions and expectations are not mutual (the husband who wants a full-time traditional wife but is married to a woman who wants a professional career, for example).

The culturally defined content of roles and even more importantly, the means of techniques for enacting roles, are constantly changing in highly industrialized societies. The rational, active mastery orientation of modern man is barely equal to the challenge of proliferating roles and role obligations and the multiple contradictions and incongruities of these changing roles.

Families in all classes experience the strain of role conflict for different reasons. In the working class, the major source of role conflict probably is the frequent lack of economic resources to fulfill role obligations. The survival of traditional values in circumstances where they are no longer appropriate is another serious problem in this class. The new values in marriage, companionship and intimate sharing of psychological experiences, for example, are incongruous with traditional sex role definitions, still strong in this class, that prescribe separateness of interests and activities of husband and wife.

In the middle class, economic problems are less pressing, family members are involved in many more and varied activities, are less unquestioningly accepting of traditional role definitions, and more experimental in their approach to fulfilling these role obligations. Here other reasons for role conflict are more prevalent. In the upper middle class, for example, motherhood is often experienced as a crisis. The college educated young woman, independent and accustomed to a great deal of freedom and varied experience, may find the demands of unrelieved motherhood and the restrictions of 24-hour-a-day total responsibility for another human being incompatible with her previous socialization experiences and values, and with her personality.

Among successful professionals, 60- to 80-hour work weeks are not uncommon. The overlapping demands of various roles is probably the most frequent source of role conflict in this segment of the population. The expressive requirements of the husband and father role are difficult to fulfill, not because of surviving traditional definitions of masculinity, but because the time and energy required in occupational roles leaves little time for fulfilling family obligations.

In the upper class, familism and the frequent, protracted economic dependence of adult sons and daughters, even into middle age and beyond, or until the death of the family patriarch or matriarch, is incompatible with the modern values of individualism and independence. In this stratum, as in the working class, the persistence of traditional values in the face of changed circumstances subverts the mutuality in role expectations that make for smooth family functioning.

The companion role, which is common for women in this class, requires that a woman remain an interesting and erotically stimulating companion throughout the life span. This may be difficult to achieve given the increased life span, the rather abrupt aging in women after menopause, and the lack of a gainful occupational base as a source of interest, involvment, and topics of conversation. Community service activities, which utilized personal skills of higher status women in the past, are increasingly taken over by professionals and by the welfare state in technologically developed societies. Middle-class women in the empty nest stage, with leisure time and no inclination to work, or with inadequate or outdated skills for obtaining employment appropriate to their status in life, face the same problem.

MERGING TRENDS IN FAMILY LIFE

Before turning to the question of the future of the American family, I would like to review very briefly the major and continuing overall trends in marital relationships and parent-child relationships, for all classes, all ethnic groups and for rural as well as urban families in the United States. These trends, it is important to remember, are emerging in all highly industrialized societies in the West, but are particularly characteristic of American society—for historical and ideological reasons, but also because the United States has the most advanced technology, by far, of any country in the world.

Societies with high levels of technological development change rapidly and require highly educated, psychologically flexible, and mobile populations. The higher levels of education and the breakdown of extended family and community controls characteristic of modern societies promote a greater tendency to think critically and to use rational means for achieving goals, a decrease in ethnocentrism and an increase in tolerance of human differences.

Childrearing practices become less authoritarian, reflecting the necessity to produce men and women who can adapt to rapid social change and to the possibilities of many more choices and alternatives in occupations and ways of life. Individualism, particularly in its components of self-discipline and self-direction, is more adaptive than the ability to take orders and to confrom unquestioningly to situational norms in modern societies. When norms are constantly changing, general principles as guides to behavior become more realistic and appropriate than specific rules and regulations.

Declining authoritarianism in childrearing by parents who have more flexibility and more choices and alternatives in their own lives produces children who are more tolerant of outgroups, more honest and psychologically introspective, less sexually repressed, and less hostile. At the same time, the greater availability of objective educational and occupational opportunity, the greater need for drive and talent, and the decline of nepotism tends to promote emphasis on achievement in childrearing in all classes, all ethnic groups, and in all regions and locales—urban, urbanizing, and rural.

Marital interaction also reflects these changed empirical conditions and values. Since married men and women have more options, they are guided less by ideals of duty, obligation, loyalty, self-sacrifice, and arbitrary cultural norms in their role conceptions, and more by standards such as companionship, free and open communication, mutual gratification—sexual and psychological—and mutual growth. These patterns are underwritten by the greater leisure and abundance experienced by most people in automating societies. While the trends in marital relationships, childrearing practices, and social character are most pronounced in the upper middle classes, the new values and role conceptions are diffusing upward and downward because all families, albeit in varying degrees, are exposed to the demands and the effects of modern technology and developments in scientific knowledge.

7

THE FUTURE OF THE
AMERICAN FAMILY

In America, social thinkers and social scientists are more apt to be remembered for their failures of prediction than for their contributions to knowledge and social thought. In an individualistic society, citizens take pride in proving the experts wrong. Man's indomitable will and his untrammeled independence are thereby confirmed.

Predictions are often based on the assumption of a continuation of ongoing trends, but even if the underlying reasons for these trends are well understood, predictions can be formulated only in the language of probability. The need to predict, however, despite the risks, is stronger than ever. When human survival is threatened as never before, social planning becomes an imperative of rational social change in an increasingly interdependent world community and in the increasingly complex societal units that comprise it. This is a major reason why the social sciences have become prominent in industrial societies; they provide the data and the understanding that are the bases, if not the inspiration, for social planning.

To predict, and to believe in one's predictions, endows the future with order, logic, and a modicum of security, but this kind of vision is almost impossible to maintain in modern times. World events are often irrational by any logic. History is a tug of war between confident expectations and unforeseen disasters. The unanticipated and the not readily controllable intervene to upset even the most limited predictions.

Government policy is another factor that cannot be readily predicted, particularly in the short run, and particularly in heterogeneous societies like the United States that are not governed by a single set of common, stable, and logically consistent ideological principles. Power, furthermore, is too rarely obtained by those who have the qualities of mind or character to transcend the immediate interests of self, family, community, or nation. The broader directions and ultimate imperatives of social life often elude political leaders.

One cannot predict with assurance, therefore, that enlightened policies of one era will continue into the next. The overall trend in technologically developed societies, however, has been in the direction of increasing equality in education, income, life styles, and life chances, whatever the disparities are that remain. This fact is relevant to the task of long-range prediction and eases that task somewhat.

In modern societies, governments are more potent in determining the direction of social change because of centralized and more efficient means of communication, coercion, and persuasion. While immediate government policies may at times seem retrogressive or worse as judged by humanitarian standards, the long-range trend in the conduct of political leaders in industrial societies, however, has been away from the unchecked and unqualified corruption and greed of familistic autocrats and oligarchs in agricultural societies.

As the general level of objective, material deprivation and suffering declines, and as the general level of education rises in modern societies, all institutions are affected, including the family. Rationalism becomes a valued orientation in human relationships, as do sentiment and humanism—at least among the more highly educated and comfortable. These standards are not necessary consequences of increases in material comfort and scientific knowledge, but they are more likely to prevail where the social and material environment is less brutalizing and mystifying.

The growth of knowledge and insight into human motivation that psychology and the other social sciences have gradually provided over the past century can be used rationally to prevent the recurrent tragedies of history and autobiography that have characterized human societies since their primordial beginnings. Witch hunts, for example, have historically been a frequent consequence of high levels of frustration in human populations, particularly of sudden rises in these levels of frustration due to defeat in war, plagues, droughts, and other natural or man-made catastrophes. As knowledge and understanding of the mechanisms of defense, particularly projecton and displacement, and of how and why they operate, becomes part of the cultural heritage in modern societies, we can predict at least the possibility of somewhat more control over these irrational responses.

The task of becoming aware of, understanding, and above all, admitting and communicating unconscious, repressed, or not easily acceptable motives and impulses, is a major challenge in human relationships in an era where total destruction and extinction of the human species is possible. It impinges upon (if it does not determine the survival of) nations, families, friendships, and all other human relationships. The spread of this kind of awareness and honesty can diminish unwarranted fears and anxieties and prevent inappropriate reactions of hostility and destructiveness. This educational task—the sensitizing of human beings to the role of unconscious motivations, unrealistic fears, and posturing and pretense in their relationships with each other—is the ultimate and possibly the final challenge to the behavioral sciences in the last third of the twentieth century.

This brings us to another major problem in making predictions and in evaluating predictions that are made about people, their institutions, and their material environments. Visions of the future are in large measure affected and often distorted by the personality traits of visionaries—by the optimism or pessimism, trust or suspicion, loves or hates that characterize particular scientists, philosophers, theologians, mystics, or just plain folks. The future is an ink blot test.

The possible discovery in the near future of a technique for artificial innovulation (the implanting of a fertilized ovum in the womb), for example, will be hailed by the optimist as a rational solution to the often tragic frustration of women who are sterile. The pessimist will focus on the possible negative consequences of the development of this technique: that women who are unwilling to undergo the physical ordeal of reproduction, for whatever reasons, will hire mercenaries to provide host wombs and to bear their children.[1]

Social critics sometimes project their unconscious impulses and needs onto the world at large. The impulse to destroy, for example, may be experienced as a fear of world destruction. Personal destiny may be confused with the destiny of nations, social institutions, and the human species. The problem then, is to disentangle fear from wish, myth from reality, and possibility from inevitability. And this is not an easy task when social reality is extremely complex, constantly changing, and beyond the capacity of any single individual to understand totally and in depth.

A final source of possible bias in making predictions stems from the distorting or limiting effect of social location on perception. Class membership, race, nationality, sex, religion, level of education, age and generation influence world views. Complete detachment from the anchors of time and place in viewing world history and world trends is often more an ideal than an actuality in social scientific research and theory.

What, then, can be said, with caution but with some assurance, about the structure and functioning of the family in American society in the future? How will cultural and subculturally defined family roles continue to change in response to developments in technology and scientific knowledge? What trends appear likely to continue? What problems will persist? What challenges will be met? What are the possible consequences of failures to meet these challenges?[2]

AN UNDERLYING ASSUMPTION

THE PERSISTENCE OF THE NUCLEAR FAMILY

A more basic question is whether the family as a recognized social group will continue to exist *at all*. In times of severe societal crisis, the moral deterioration of the family is commonly lamented and the demise of the family is a favorite prediction of sages and seers. The present era, in America, is a fruitful one for this kind of criticism and speculation.

That the contemporary American family is in deep trouble, in some respects, is indicated by the fact that many serious people, among them students, radicals, artists, academicians, and leaders of women's liberation groups, are currently raising the question of the continued necessity and desirability of a nuclear family, based as it is on an exclusive, enduring, heterosexual pairing relationship and an exclusive parent-child relationship.[3]

Nevertheless, the nuclear family will not only persist into the twenty-first century, but it will be stronger than ever. We live in a time of rising psychological as well as economic expectations. The family as an institution will not be abolished because people expect more of it and are more apt to express and act on their dissatisfactions. This is more likely to preserve than to destroy the institution of marriage, which is the basis of the nuclear family. Other forms— homosexual marriages, group marriages, single parent households, communes—will probably become more prevalent with the increased tolerance of individual choice and cultural pluralism in less ethnocentric, more educated, and more permissively reared citizens. But ultimately for biological reasons, and more immediately for psychological reasons, the pairing husband and wife relationship and the exclusive parent-child relationship will endure.

The fact of a continuous, nonseasonal sex drive and the prolonged period of physical and emotional dependence which are biologically distinctive to the human species underlies this prediction. No society has existed or can exist without norms regulating the continuous sex drive of human beings. Sexual conflict, rivalry, and jealousy must be at least minimally controlled in order to ensure the cooperation that becomes increasingly imperative in highly specialized and consequently increasingly interdependent technologically developed societies. The control of sexual behavior is the reason for socially sanctioned heterosexual pairing relationships that are required to endure, at least ideally, in human societies, and these relationships are essential for human and societal survival. Both past and present utopian communal experiments in which sexual behavior has not been exclusive or limited in some way break up more often over this issue than any other. The leaders exact sexual privileges that less powerful members, after a while, will no longer tolerate.

The history of the Oneida community provides an unusually clear illustration of this process. Sexual rivalry was the recognized and openly stated reason for the dissolution of the original utopian settlement in which enduring monogamous relationships were prohibited and leaders were given special privileges in the breeding of new members and in access to the community's nubile young women. The original community broke up over this issue as the second generation came of age and began to question the charismatic basis of the leaders' sexual privileges.

The biological sex drives are a constant potential source of disruption to human social organization. Socially sanctioned family relationships, however varied in form, represent an attempt (not always successful) to regulate these drives in the interest of human and societal survival.

The other basic biological traits and needs of human beings for prolonged physical and intellectual care and for emotional security can be delegated to nonfamily groups, in part. Certainly the physical and intellectual growth needs of infants, children, and adolescents could be effectively and efficiently provided for by substitute groups. In fact this has been the historical trend as societies have developed technologically. The shifting of responsibility for the health, education, and welfare of family members to the government has, however, stopped short at the complete allocation to it of the function of emotional gratification.

The inherent and inescapable problem here is that optimal emotional gratification requires a stable, dependable one-to-one relationship between human beings. This is certainly the implication of the vast numbers of research studies of emotional deprivation and the etiology of neurosis in children that have been reported in the social sciences, particularly in psychology, over the past fifty years. And this need for an enduring and secure source of emotional gratification is not limited to infants and children. It persists into and throughout adulthood and is a major reason why marital pairing relationships will persist in the highly automated America of the future, although for different reasons than in the past. These relationships will increasingly be sanctioned less by mutual economic necessity and conceptions of duty than by recognized psychological necessity.

That this necessity is recognized by young people is indicated by the results of a recent nationwide Gallup Poll of college students in which a large majority felt that there was too little emphasis on family life currently in the United States.[4] Students were more concerned about the maintenance and strengthening of family life than they were about economic reform, personal autonomy, technocracy, and other issues that are currently defined as social problems.

It is quite possible to dull the human need for continuous love and affection, to deny or repress this need, to channel it into sublimated forms, or to convert it into opposite kinds of needs, such as hate and sadism, for example, but this is accomplished at great psychic cost to the individual, if not to the society. The cost may take the form of anxiety, guilt, and depression, or a compulsive need for achievement, power, and recognition. The latter may promote creativity and productivity, but it can also result in brutality, murder, and carnage.

The satisfaction of emotional needs, furthermore, underlies and, to an important extent, affects the physical and intellectual growth of infants and children. Studies of the damaging effects on ill or orphaned children of separation from parents—the slowing of growth, the retardation of intelligence, and even premature death—date back to the 1920s. This is not to argue against day care centers, but it is an argument against the elimination of stable love objects for infants and children which can only be guaranteed by the preservation of the institution of the family. No society has ever been able to delegate completely the task of providing for the emotional needs of infants and children to substitute nonfamilial groups, because it is not possible to do so.

The basic difficulty in attempting to allocate the satisfaction of emotional needs on a large scale to specialized groups outside of the family and household in populous societies is that this would have to be carried out in bureaucratic settings. And bureaucracy is inimical to the emotions. The family is the only area of life in industrial society that is not bureaucratized. All other major institutions—the government, the economy, religion, and recreation—have been transformed by the creeping and inexorable proliferation of bureaucracy. Most people in our society, with the exception of the very old, the very young, a shrinking category of self-employed and a diminishing number of unemployed housewives, spend a major portion of their lives in bureaucratic settings.

The highest values in bureaucratically managed organizations are efficiency and predictability; the basic orientation in social relationships is impersonal. Human emotional needs are irrelevant and detrimental to good bureaucratic procedure, since emotions do not further the ends of efficiency or predictability. It is doubtful that the basic function of the family in providing for the emotional needs of infants and children could be adequately carried out by meritocratically recruited teachers and nurses. These individuals might be very committed and service-oriented, but they would be likely to change jobs in a mobile society and they would limit their emotional involvement with their clients, by definition of themselves as professionals.

Social science has come up with some answers to the problem of how to provide more adequately for the emotional needs of children in institutional settings. It is now known that children fare better in hospitals and nurseries if one nurse is assigned to a specific number of children than if all nurses are assigned indiscriminately to care for all of the children. While this practice approaches the exclusive, one-to-one parent-child relationship, it does not duplicate it and it cannot replace it.

Marriage and the nuclear family will continue as basic institutions in human societies, functioning imperfectly and inefficiently, and sometimes malevolently, but persevering because it is not possible to come up with anything more workable to provide for the basic emotional needs of human beings—young or old.

CURRENT STRESSES

The troubles of the nuclear family in industrial societies, generally, and in American society, particularly, stem largely from the inability of this type of family structure to provide certain of the services performed in the past by the extended family. Adequate health, education, and welfare provision, particularly for the two nonproductive generations in modern societies, the young and the old, is increasingly an insurmountable problem for the nuclear family. The unrelieved and sometimes unbearably intense parent-child relationship, where childrearing is not shared at least in part by others, and the loneliness of nuclear family units, increasingly turned in on themselves in contracted and relatively isolated settings, is another major problem.

Role conflicts stemming from discontinuities between previous social-ization experiences and the marital and parental expectations of men and women and, on the other hand, the actual demands, realities, and obligations of family life are a third major problem.

The first set of problems could easily be resolved, and will very likely be resolved by an extension of the welfare state to provide free medical care for all, free higher education, student stipends, complete support for the aged, family allowances for the support of children, and federally subsidized child care facilities, beginning at birth, for those who need or want these facilities.

These contemplated economic reforms are not a naive vision, but simply an extension of the trend toward increased humanism and ra-tionalism (despite grotesque setbacks, at times) that have historically accompanied scientific and technological developments in human so-cieties. These policies already exist in some countries where the re-sponsibility of government for the dignity, comfort, and health of citi-zens is more readily accepted than in America.

The loneliness and the overly intense relationships of the nuclear family can also be offset by government action to subsidize collective living arrangements—a course already pursued by private builders and planners of New Towns in America and, on a more altruistic basis, by philosophical, religious, and political utopians. The latter, however, cannot provide a mass solution to the problems of family life in our society since their movements represent a withdrawal. Ideologically, they face that age-old problem of utopian communities, the problem of holding on to the second generation, and practically, their technology and economy are too primitive to sustain them. If they industrialize, they may survive, but they lose their utopian qual-ity.[5]

Margaret Mead, who has a talent for anticipating social forms be-fore they come into existence, in an Epilogue to the President's Re-port on the Status of Women in 1965, called for more cooperative types of living, with homes closer to places of work, nurseries for ba-bies, communal restaurants, full summer care for all school-age chil-dren, and more nursery school and after-school groups.[6] Her recom-mendation that children be cared for, in part, and to a greater extent than at present, by trained, well-paid, and committed professionals, is a solution to the increasing unavailability of the now liberated grandmother, the working mother, and the disappearing servant class for the task of full-time childrearing.

We are beginning to approach these ideals with the new living arrangements that are coming into existence and with the proposed federally subsidized child development centers, although it will probably be some time before we have the idyllic situation envisioned by Dr. Mead. The spread of planned total communities, publicly or privately sponsored and voluntarily recruited, where family members can live, work, and play with the cooperative sharing of some responsibilities previously performed by the extended family, will provide a solution to some of the stresses of contemporary family life, particularly for those with strong needs for sociability and affiliation.

The planned New Towns and other structures such as urban cooperatives and collectives, which are not isolated, geographically or economically, and whose residents are often recruited on the basis of similar occupational interests, do not have the disadvantage of overarching social controls that utopian communities require in order to survive. These controls are often informal, but they are always present even in communes that profess to be anarchic. Rigid social controls are inconsistent with the extreme individualism relative to other modern nations that characterizes the American people, an individualism that is likely to increase given trends toward increased mobility, higher general levels of education, and declining authoritarianism in childrearing practices. For this reason also utopian communes are not likely to become a mass phenomenon in America.

The third major source of difficulty in contemporary family life, role conflicts that arise from inadequate preparation or unrealistic expectations, can also be expected to decline with time. The growing rationalism and declining fatalism that characterize more highly educated citizens will be a prime factor here. Family-life education courses, sex education courses, and more informal means of spreading scientific knowledge will help, as will new techniques such as effective planned parenthood, genetic counseling, artificial innovulation, and the predetermining of the sex of offspring—techniques that diminish or prevent needless and easily remediable suffering, frustration, or conflict in family life.

The redefinition of sex roles that is currently taking place in America will also strengthen the nuclear family ultimately, because it will reinforce the modern values of individualism, rationalism, and equalitarianism that are an accompaniment of the demands and the rewards of modern science and technology. It is the cultural lag of persisting traditional role definitions, not the modern redefinitions of sex roles, that are mainly responsible for the role conflicts in family life in contemporary America.

The possible danger to the preservation of the nuclear family as a social unit arises not from more flexible and less stereotyped husband and wife roles which, after all, reflect the modern standards of psychological gratification and mutual fulfillment in marital relationships, but from the attempt to force the liberated partner role arbitrarily on all women, regardless of their values, temperaments, abilities, skills, and interests. It would be just as destructive to impose this new role on all married women as it is to impose the traditional wife and mother role on all married women regardless of their unique physical, emotional, and intellectual needs and resources.

FUTURE CHANGE

In making specific predictions about the future of the family, I shall refer only to the American family. These predictions are optimistic, because I am making certain assumptions about government policy and world events. I am assuming government aid to the nuclear family will approach that of a total welfare state, and I am also assuming that the enormous gap in the standard of living between this country and most of the rest of the world, a gap that is increasingly dangerous, will not result in the destruction of the United States as an independent nation.

COURTSHIP AND LOVE

We can confidently expect that marital choices in the future will more than ever be based on nonexpedient personal preference. As nepotism continues its decline in determining the economic fate of young people, family pressures and influence in the area of marital choice will also continue to decline. As women achieve increasing independence, by developing their potential in whatever way they choose (occupationally, recreationally, creatively), they will have greater freedom from economic considerations and from the need to fulfill ambitions vicariously in making marital choices. Personality, values, and interests of potential mates will become uppermost in the decision of whether and whom to marry. Class, religion, and ethnic origin (including racial origins) will become less significant in affecting marital choices as young men and women continue to be more highly educated, more mobile, and less ethnocentric. The romantic love ideal will ultimately become reality rather than myth as a basis for marriage in our society.

Premarital sexual intercourse will be virtually universal for all classes and both sexes, underwritten by developments in medical science and technology that will almost completely eliminate the danger of unwanted pregnancy. Promiscuity, however, defined as sex for sex' sake, without particular regard for the object, is not likely to become typical, certainly not as a life-long pattern. Promiscuity requires a casual, nonsentimental, and completely hedonistic orientation toward sexual behavior which most human beings, and women in particular, do not have. This kind of behavior, in fact, has been found to be associated with severe psychological problems and feelings of depression and emotional isolation. The view of others as sexual objects and no more, furthermore, is antithetical to the historical trend in man-woman relationships in industrial societies—which has been moving toward stronger affectional ties and increasing recognition of individual differences, dignity, and worth.

The double standard, which permits sexual freedom to males but not to females, will continue its decline during certain stages in the life cycle, but it will not disappear entirely until there is a dramatic revision of sex role definitions so that males and females have completely equal status and equal responsibility for childrearing and family support. At the present time, the double standard is least evident in those classes and in the stage of the life cycle (before marriage) when women are most independent and sex role stereotype and segregation is least pronounced. As women become more independent of men with respect to economic and social status, their sexual behavior loses its character as a commodity to be traded or witheld for extrinsic rewards. Sexual activity becomes freer and more intrinsically gratifying for women, as it is and has been for men.

The living together pattern, as a prelude to marriage, will diffuse from the upper middle class to other strata and probably become universal in our society. We have no data on the fate of these relationships with respect to eventual marriage. Couples who live together without the sanction of marriage are difficult to locate since they do not register anywhere. At present, however, it appears that most of these relationships do result in marriage. Whether this will continue will depend on how necessary future generations will feel is the formal ritual of marriage, as a sanction for promoting security in the pairing relationship. The need for security will persist, but ceremonial and legal supports for this need may not.

Public ritual as a means of social control has declined generally in developed societies, as internal controls have increasingly guided human relationships and human behavior. The marriage ritual may become vestigial as have initiation rites, fertility rites and, increasingly, funeral rites.

The feeling of love involves a strong identification and concern with the needs of another human being. This will become more prevalent as a basis for the man-woman relationship (and for its continuation) as individuals are less dwarfed by extreme economic deprivation and the psychological suffering it intensifies. Economists have estimated that the actual purchasing power of the average family in the United States will at least double and possibly triple by the year 2000.[7] Children who grow up in families where there is less economic stress and competition and more security, leisure, companionship, affection, and support will be better able to give and to receive love as adults.

MARITAL INTERACTION

Nuclear family relationships will become even more important than they presently are as work becomes less time-consuming and less crucial to human existence in automated America. As the work ethic declines, there will be more complete sharing by family members of activities, tasks, and interests. As materialism declines, the basic orientation in family relationships in all classes will shift increasingly from economic security toward psychological fulfillment.

The question of power and authority and who has it within the family will become obsolete. The head of the household, as concept and as fact, will disappear. Parents will defer to and learn from children, if the occasion suggests, as they will defer to and learn from each other. There will be more experimentation, more choice, and more tolerance of individual, subcultural, and cultural differences in family role conceptions and behavior.

The divorce rate will level off from its present all-time high, in part because of increased abundance, which is associated with lower divorce rates, at least within social classes, and in part because expectations in marriage will be more realistic. The current high divorce rates reflect higher and often unattainable standards rather than an actual deterioration in the quality of marital life, relative to the past. Marriage will persist because it can compensate in the security of deep and lasting emotional response for what it lacks in perpetual excitement. But this has yet to be recognized by many people who are experiencing the first flush of exhilaration that stems from release from traditional role prescriptions.

The extravagant vistas promulgated by the mass media and fed by runaway fantasy need correcting along more realistic lines. And this too will come as behavioral science continues to provide the data and the techniques of more honest appraisals of self, others, and society. People will increasingly use behavioral science technology—self- and family-directed techniques for reducing family conflict—that will become common knowledge. These techniques will be brought into the home increasingly through television demonstrations, books, magazines, and word of mouth. Face-to-face professional help will be more frequently supplemented in this way, because the felt need will be overwhelming and beyond the capacity of professionals to handle directly, and because ours is a self-help culture.

The current epidemic of divorces among men and women who have been married more than ten years will decrease as the differential rates of intellectual and psychological growth of mature men and women decline. As women continue to seek self-development (in esthetic and creative activities as well as in gainful occupations) they can be expected to achieve the increased self-respect that is basic to an equalitarian and mutually gratifying relationship.

The waning of the work ethic from its present high levels, an inevitable accompaniment of vastly increased productivity, and the decline of materialism, when abundance is taken for granted, will also reinforce higher self-esteem for the housewife who is not gainfully employed. As materialism diminishes so will the tendency to evaluate human beings in terms of their earnings or other economic criteria.

Sexual problems in marriage will decrease with the rising status of women, the increased emphasis on impulse gratification, the decline in psychological inhibitions about sex, and the spread of scientific knowledge about the sexual act. The latter will not lead to a mechanization of sexual behavior as is sometimes feared. A growing humanism will deflect perfunctory perversions of the new knowledge and this knowledge will be very helpful in the not-infrequent instances where a simple lack of information is at the root of sexual difficulties.

The sexual act will be increasingly valued as a natural and mutually gratifying experience, devoid of arbitrary implications for the verification of masculinity or femininity. We can also anticipate much broader and more flexible definitions of proper sexual techniques and outlets. Practices that are now regarded as immature or perverted, including masturbation where other outlets are unavailable or inadequate, will be defined as acceptable and proper.

Extramarital sexual behavior will probably continue to increase, particularly on the part of those who are dissatisfied with their marriages and who need a crutch or a bridge to freedom. A countervailing force, however, will be the rising status of women which will diminish the incidence of sexual liaisons that are temporary and exploitatively motivated and which will promote more gratifying intra-marital sex.

PARENTS AND CHILDREN

Parent-child relationships in the future can be expected to continue to be warmer, more permissive, and oriented primarily toward mutual psychological gratification. As the burden of economic support of children and the aged is assumed by the government to a greater extent, children will cease to be viewed as an investment to be repaid by support of the parents in their old age. The permissive ideal, misunderstood and misapplied in the form of overprotection and overindulgence in many upper middle-class families in recent years, will be increasingly tempered by limits and strictness in childrearing. This will be underwritten by the growth of the person-centered world view which grants rights to parents (particularly mothers) as well as to children.

The problem of the too intense parent-child relationship in the nuclear family can be expected to diminish somewhat with the spread of universal, government subsidized day care centers for infants and young children that will probably be utilized by many middle- and working-class parents in the future, on a voluntary basis. The great importance of the first three years of life to future intellectual development has now been established by social scientists, as has the strong relationship between adequate nutrition and health care and emotional and intellectual growth. The government has a strong interest in promoting intellectual competence in its populace, not to mention the need to reduce welfare rolls—a more compelling reason, currently, for the establishment of government subsidized child development centers.

Whatever specific forms day care centers will take eventually, particularly with respect to the qualifications and the quality of the personnel who staff them, the family's responsibility for socializing its young is likely to be narrowed still more in the future. This change will be simply a further extension of a long-range trend that has paralleled technological and scientific advances in human societies and that has placed in the hands of trained experts more effective techniques than are available to the family for fulfilling many of its age-old functions.

The family will still be left with the function of providing for the basic emotional needs of its children—but for many families this will take place after hours. After hours, however, will be a large part of the day or the week, if we consider that the estimated average work week in the year 2000, if the trend since the turn of the century continues, will be fifteen hours.[8]

American society in the future will not need vast numbers of workers to produce goods, but it will need many more people to work with human beings, given the much higher standard of skills required by advanced technology and the increased knowledge of how much effort is involved in the effective development of human potential.

Women can be expected to fill many of the new positions that will be created in the fields of health, education, and welfare should the government extend its role in this area dramatically. If this happens, the trend toward gainful employment for women throughout the life cycle will continue, and pre-school day care for infants and children on a voluntary basis will become widespread.

Conflict between middle-aged adults, their adolescent children, and their aged parents will also decline. The probable extension of the government's responsibility for economic support of the young and the old will reduce the independence-dependence conflicts that these two generations suffer because they are not economically productive. This will diminish the resentment and guilt in intergenerational relationships that stems from economic responsibilities that are too burdensome for the small nuclear family to carry.[9]

Value conflicts between middle-aged adults and their aged parents can also be expected to decline as both generations are increasingly urban and American born and as class differences in values and material circumstances diminish. The continued urbanization of America will weaken the traditional values of familism and authoritarianism, particularly, and the intergenerational conflict that this promotes. The continued limitation of immigration to this country, the spread of higher levels of education for all citizens, and the adoption of similar values and similar life styles by all classes and ethnic groups will reduce intergenerational conflicts that are not of idiosyncratic psychological origin.

The decline in the extent of sexual repression in older people, as the current middle aged and young, less sexually inhibited generations age, may also be a factor here. Some anthropologists and other social scientists feel that envy and hostility toward the young by the older generation in a particular society is closely related to the extent of its sexual frustration. Bruno Bettelheim, for example, feels that envy of the young was probably less severe in nonliterate societies where older people experienced sexual gratification and continued to experience this gratification as long as they were physically able.[10]

All of these factors—greater affluence for all, more government support for the young and the old, fewer discrepancies in cultural conditioning and attained educational levels, less sexual repression, and the leveling of class differences in values and ways of life—plus continued advances in the fields of communication and transportation should promote intergenerational family cohesion and buffer the centrifugal effects of rapid social change and increased mobility.   —

A CAUTIONARY POSTSCRIPT

The house of cards that I have erected in the preceding pages is a fragile vision of future familial and individual contentment that rests largely on an as-if foundation of rational, humanitarian and timely action on the part of the U.S. government. The survival of the nuclear family remains a question, not because it is intrinsically and inevitably doomed, but because it needs massive help that only a basic reallocation of national resources can provide.

In many respects, the nuclear family, even at present, provides gratifications that were rare, unheard of, and unhoped for in traditional societies. In other respects, its members suffer frustrations equally foreign to the life conditions and mutual expectations of family members in traditional societies. The troubles of the contemporary nuclear family are largely soluble, however, given rational social and family planning, and the means that science, technology, and growing humanitarianism make possible.

Much of the misery in contemporary family life is a mixture of objective deprivation and rising expectations. Changing expectations promote feelings of discontent, but they can also encourage constructive change in societies, families, and individuals. The standard for constructive change is the realization of the eternal human need for the fulfilled life—however this is defined. Government will have to render much more help to the American nuclear family for the realization of this goal and it will have to do so soon. It will either plan more effectively, or both the nation and the family will perish —because their ultimate fates are inseparable.

NOTES

I. THE SOCIOLOGICAL MANDATE

1. William H. Masters and Virginia E. Johnson, *Human Sexual Response* (Boston: Little, Brown, 1966).

2. Lee Rainwater, *And The Poor Get Children* (Chicago: Quadrangle Books, 1960).

3. Robert O. Blood Jr. and Donald M. Wolfe, *Husbands and Wives: The Dynamics of Married Living* (New York: Free Press, 1960).

4. F. Ivan Nye and Lois Wladis Hoffman, *The Employed Mother in America* (Chicago: Rand McNally, 1963).

5. A good recent source for papers on experimental studies of family interaction is William D. Winter and Antonio J. Ferreira, eds., *Research in Family Interaction* (Palo Alto: Science and Behavior Books, 1969).

6. Richard Hofstadter in *Social Darwinism and American Thought* (Boston: Beacon Press, 1955) discusses the historical role of this model in the ideological battles between proponents of the welfare state and rugged individualism.

7. See Frederick Engels, *The Origin of the Family, Private Property, and the State* (Chicago: Charles H. Kerr, 1902). *The Woman Question* (New York: International Publishers, 1951) contains excerpts from the writings on the family by Karl Marx, Frederick Engels, V. I. Lenin, and Joseph Stalin.

8. Robert K. Merton has provided one of the clearest statements of this model in *Social Theory and Social Structure* (Glencoe, Ill.: Free Press, 1957), pp. 19–84.

9. A comprehensive review of various conceptual frameworks, both descriptive and explanatory, that have been used in the analysis of the family can be found in F. Ivan Nye and Felix M. Berardo, *Emerging Conceptual Frameworks in Family Analysis* (New York: Macmillan, 1966).

10. Arthur R. Jensen, "How Much Can We Boost I.Q. and Scholastic Achievement?" *Harvard Educational Review,* 39 (Winter, 1969), 1–123.

11. Quoted in "Jensenism, N. The Theory that I.Q. is Largely Determined by the Genes," by Lee Edson, *New York Times Sunday Magazine,* August 31, 1969, pp. 10–11.

12. See Arthur R. Jensen, "Reducing the Heredity-Environment Uncertainty," *Harvard Educational Review Reprint Series,* 2 (1969), 212.

13. Gerhard Lenski, for example, utilizes the evolutionary model as an organizing principle in his analysis of societies and social change in *Human Societies* (New York: McGraw Hill, 1970).

14. Robert W. Winch, *The Modern Family* (3d ed.; New York: Holt, Rinehart and Winston, 1971), p. 29.

15. Kingsley Davis and Wilbert E. Moore, "Some Principles of Stratification," *American Sociological Review,* 10 (1945), 243; see also Talcott Parsons, "A Revised Analytical Approach to the Theory of Social Stratification," in *Essays in Sociological Theory* (Glencoe, Ill.: Free Press, 1954), pp. 386–439.

16. William Goode, *The Family* (Englewood Cliffs, N.J.: Prentice-Hall, 1964), p. 21.

17. *Ibid.,* p. 24.

18. A notable exception is in the work of Emile Durkheim, a nineteenth-century founder of modern functionalism. See Emile Durkheim (1893), *The Division of Labor in Society,* trans. by George Simpson (New York: Macmillan, 1933).

19. See Talcott Parsons, argument in *Societies: Evolutionary and Comparative Perspectives* (Englewood Cliffs, N.J., Prentice-Hall, 1966).

20. Suzanne Keller attempts to correct for the omission of power in the functionalist model in *Beyond the Ruling Class* (New York: Random House, 1963).

21. See Kingsley Davis, "The Myth of Functional Analysis in Sociology and Anthropology," *American Sociological Review,* 24 (1950), 757–72, for an elaboration of this point.

22. Two recent efforts in this direction are Gerhard Lenski *Power and Privilege* (New York: McGraw-Hill, 1966); and Pierre L. Van Den Berghe, "Dialectic and Functionalism: Toward a Theoretical Synthesis," *American Sociological Review,* 28 (1964), 695–705.

23. Herbert Spencer (1873), *The Study of Sociology* (Ann Arbor: University of Michigan Press, 1961), pp. 341–42.

24. Jesse R. Pitts, "The Structural-Functional Approach," in Harold T.

Christensen, *Handbook of Marriage and the Family* (Chicago: Rand McNally, 1964), p. 76.

25. Engels, *The Origin of the Family,* pp. 60, 89.

26. *Ibid.,* pp. 70, 71.

27. *Ibid.,* pp. 98–100.

28. See William J. Goode, *World Revolution and Family Patterns* (New York: Free Press, 1963).

29. Blood and Wolfe, *Husbands and Wives,* pp. 40–41.

30. For a review of research on family authority patterns over the past ten years, see Constantina Safilios-Rothschild, "The Study of Family Power Structure: A Review 1960–1969," *Journal of Marriage and the Family,* 32 (1970), 539–52; see also Hyman Rodman, "Marital Power in France, Greece, Yugoslavia, and the United States: A Cross-National Discussion," *Journal of Marriage and the Family,* 29 (1967), 320–24.

31. Merton, *Social Theory and Social Structure,* pp. 5–6.

32. A pioneering approach to this level of analysis can be found in a paper by Gerald Handel, "Psychological Study of Whole Families," *Psychological Bulletin,* 63 (1965), 19–41. See also Gerald Handel, ed., *The Psychosocial Interior of the Family* (Chicago: Aldine, 1967; rev. ed., 1972).

33. Emile Durkheim (1897), *Suicide,* trans. by John A. Spaulding and George Simpson (Glencoe, Ill.: Free Press, 1951).

34. See Alex Inkeles, "Industrial Man: The Relation of Status to Experience, Perception and Value," *American Journal of Sociology,* 66 (1960), 1–31; also, Melvin L. Kohn, *Class and Conformity* (Homewood, Ill.: Dorsey Press, 1969); and Edward C. Devereaux, Urie Bronfenbrenner, and Robert R. Rodgers, "Child-Rearing in England and the United States: A Cross-National Comparison," *Journal of Marriage and the Family,* 31 (1969), 257–70.

35. Lee Rainwater, "Work and Identity in the Lower Class," in Sam Bass Warner Jr., ed., *Planning for a Nation of Cities* (Cambridge: M.I.T. Press, 1968), pp. 105–23; also Elliot Liebow, *Talley's Corner* (Boston: Little, Brown, 1967).

36. Herbert Barry III, Margaret K. Bacon, and Irvin L. Child, "A Cross-Cultural Survey of Some Sex Differences in Socialization," *Journal of Abnormal and Social Psychology,* 55 (1957), 327–32; also Eleanor E. Maccoby, ed., *The Development of Sex Differences* (Stanford: Stanford University Press, 1966).

37. This description is based in part on a role analysis originally formulated by Clifford Kirkpatrick. See *The Family* (New York: Ronald Press, 1963), pp. 168–69.

38. Lee Rainwater, "Marital Sexuality in Four Cultures of Poverty," *Journal of Marriage and the Family,* 26 (1964), 457–66; Alfred C. Kinsey, Wardell B. Pomeroy, Clyde E. Martin, and Paul H. Gebhard, *Sexual*

Behavior in the Human Female (Philadelphia: W. B. Saunders, 1953), pp. 378–81.

39. David L. Gutmann, "An Exploration of Ego Configurations in Middle and Later Life," in Bernice L. Neugarten et al., *Personality in Middle and Late Life* (New York: Atherton Press, 1964), pp. 105–13; see also Bernice L. Neugarten, ed., *Middle Age and Aging* (Chicago: University of Chicago Press, 1968).

40. For an elaboration of this idea, see Elaine Cumming and William H. Henry, *Growing Old: The Process of Disengagement* (New York: Basic Books, 1961).

41. Ethel Shanas and Gordon F. Streib, eds., *Social Structure and the Family: Generational Relations* (Englewood Cliffs, N.J.: Prentice-Hall, 1965), particularly the paper by Robert A. LeVine, "Intergenerational Tensions and Extended Family Structures in Africa," pp. 188–204.

42. See David Sudnow, *Passing On: The Social Organization of Dying* (Englewood Cliffs, N.J.: Prentice-Hall, 1967).

2. THE BIOLOGICAL BASE

1. Melford E. Spiro discusses this problem in "Is the Family Universal?: The Israeli Case," *American Anthropologist*, 16 (1954), 839–46. A reprinted and updated version of this paper appears in Norman W. Bell and Ezra F. Vogel, eds., *A Modern Introduction to the Family* (New York: Free Press, 1968), pp. 68–79.

2. The work of Harry F. Harlow and his associates has provided dramatic evidence of the effect of isolation and maternal deprivation on instinctual behavior in monkeys. See Harry F. Harlow and Margaret K. Harlow, "Social Deprivation in Monkeys," *Scientific American*, 5 (1962), 136–46; also Jack P. Hailman, "How an Instinct is Learned," *Scientific American*, 12 (1969), 98–106, which describes similar findings in experiments with sea gull chicks.

3. Reported in the New York *Times*, December 5, 1969, p. 21.

4. For a summary of recent research on this topic, see Judith M. Bardwick, *Psychology of Women* (New York, Harper and Row, 1971), ch. 2.

5. Margaret Mead reported on one such society, the Mundugumor, in *Sex and Temperament in Three Primitive Societies* (New York: William Morrow, 1935), pp. 129–71.

6. Kingsley Davis, "Extreme Social Isolation of a Child," *American Journal of Sociology*, 45 (1940), 554–65; and Kingsley Davis, "Final Note on a Case of Extreme Isolation," *American Journal of Sociology*, 52 (1947), 432–37.

7. See David L. Gutmann, "Aging Among Highland Maya: A Compara-

tive Study," in Bernice L. Neugarten, ed., *Middle Age and Aging* (Chicago: University of Chicago Press, 1968), pp. 444–52.

8. Philippe Aries, *Centuries of Childhood* (New York: Vintage Books, 1962).

9. Herbert Goldhamer and Albert Marshall, *Psychosis and Civilization* (Glencoe, Ill.: Free Press, 1953).

10. Leo Srole et al., *Mental Health in the Metropolis* (New York: McGraw-Hill, 1962).

11. The classic and pioneering study in this field is August Hollingshead and Frederick C. Redlich, *Social Class and Mental Illness* (New York: Wiley, 1958).

12. Srole et al., *Mental Health in the Metropolis,* p. 215.

13. Studies reporting positive consequences of kibbutz childrearing are Mordecai Kaffman, "Evaluation of Emotional Disturbance in 403 Israeli Kibbutz Children," *American Journal of Psychiatry,* 117 (1961), 732–38; and Albert J. Rabin, "Infants and Children Under Conditions of 'Intermittent' Mothering in the Kibbutz," *American Journal of Orthopsychiatry,* 28 (1958), 577–86. Two studies emphasizing negative aspects of personality development are Schmuel Golan, "Collective Education in the Kibbutz," *Psychiatry,* 22 (1957), 167–77; and Helen Faigin, "Social Behavior of Young Children in the Kibbutz," *Journal of Abnormal and Social Psychology,* 56 (1958), 117–29. *Children of the Kibbutz* (Cambridge: Harvard University Press, 1958) by Melford Spiro, and *Children of the Dream* (New York: Macmillan, 1969) by Bruno Bettelheim present a mixed picture.

14. Spiro, *Children of the Kibbutz,* p. 423.

15. For a discussion of recent changes in kibbutz settlements see Yonina Talmon-Garber, "The Family in a Revolutionary Movement: The Case of the Kibbutz in Israel," in Meyer Nimkoff, ed., *Comparative Family Systems* (Boston: Houghton Mifflin, 1965), pp. 259–86; also A.I. Rabin, "The Sexes: Ideology and Reality in the Israeli Kibbutz," in Georgene H. Seward and Robert C. Williamson, eds., *Sex Roles in Changing Society* (New York: Random House, 1970), pp. 285–307.

16. See George D. Spindler, *Education and Culture* (New York: Holt, Rinehart and Winston, 1963).

17. *Social Class, Race and Psychological Development* edited by Martin Deutch, Irwin Katz and Arthur R. Jensen (New York: Holt, Rinehart and Winston, 1968). Part II, contains a summary of research on intellectual and language development of young children in the lower working class.

18. For a recent and comprehensive survey of research on early cognitive development see Raymond H. Starr Jr., "Cognitive Development in Infancy: Assessment, Acceleration, and Actualization," *Merrill-Palmer*

Quarterly, 17 (1971), 153–86: also Jerome Kagan, "Do Infants Think?" *Scientific American*, 226 (1972), 74–83.

19. See J. P. Scott, "Critical Periods in Behavior Development," *Science*, 13 (1962), 949–58.

20. See J. McVickers Hunt, *Intelligence and Experience* (New York: Ronald Press, 1961); also Benjamin S. Bloom, *Stability and Change in Human Characteristics* (New York: Wiley, 1964).

21. For a general overview of sociological and anthropological approaches to the topic of adolescence, see Hans Sebald, *Adolescence: A Sociological Analysis* (New York: Appleton-Century-Crofts, 1968); and Yehudi Cohen, *The Transition from Childhood to Adolescence* (Chicago: Aldine, 1964).

22. On the biological changes at puberty, a good reference work is J. M. Tanner, *Growth at Adolescence* (Springfield, Ill.: Charles C. Thomas, 1965).

23. Sebald, *Adolescence,* pp. 118–25, reviews the evidence from a number of studies on the relationship between nutrition, growth, and the average age of onset of puberty. These studies use menstruation as an index of puberty since it can be timed exactly, unlike the gradual changes that occur in males at puberty.

24. Margaret Mead, *Coming of Age in Samoa* (New York: William Morrow, 1928).

25. William J. Goode, "The Theoretical Importance of Love," *American Sociological Review,* 24 (1959), 38–47.

26. See Hugo G. Beigel, "Romantic Love," *American Sociological Review,* 16 (1951), 326–34; also Morton M. Hunt, *The Natural History of Love* (New York: Knopf, 1959).

27. See Robert R. Bell, *Premarital Sex in a Changing Society* (Englewood Cliffs, N.J.: Prentice-Hall, 1966), which contains a good summary of the social scientific data on the topic of premarital sexual attitudes and behavior in the United States.

28. See Constantina Safilios-Rothschild, "Attitudes of Greek Spouses Toward Marital Infidelity," in Gerhard Neubeck, ed., *Extramarital Relations* (Englewood Cliffs, N.J.: Prentice-Hall, 1969), pp. 77–93.

29. Richard Von Krafft-Ebbing (1882), *Psychopathia Sexualis* (New York: Putnam, 1965); Havelock Ellis (1897), *Studies in the Psychology of Sex* (6 vols.; Philadelphia: F. A. Davis, 1905–1915; Sigmund Freud (1905), "Three Essays on the Theory of Sexuality," in *The Standard Edition of the Complete Psychological Works of Sigmund Freud,* trans. and ed. by James Strachey (24 vols.; London: Hogarth, 1953–66), VII, 125–243.

30. Ira L. Reiss, "America's Sex Standards," in John H. Gagnon and William Simon, eds., *The Sexual Scene* (Chicago: Aldine Press, 1970), pp. 43–58.

31. See E. James Anthony, "The Reactions of Parents to Adolescents and Their Behavior," in E. James Anthony and Terese Benedek, eds., *Parenthood* (Boston: Little, Brown, 1970), pp. 307–24.

32. See Joseph Adelson, "What Generation Gap?" in the *New York Times Magazine,* January 18, 1970, p. 9.

33. Ira L. Reiss, *The Social Context of Premarital Permissiveness* (New York: Holt, Rinehart and Winston, 1967), p. 172.

34. A good summary of biological, psychological, and sociological studies of the aging process, although written in disconcertingly abrupt style, is Marvin R. Koller's *Social Gerontology* (New York: Random House, 1968). An excellent book, but limited largely to psychological studies, is James E. Birren's *The Psychology of Aging* (Englewood Cliffs, N.J.: Prentice-Hall, 1964). Other good sources are Clark Tibbitts ed., *Handbook of Social Gerontology* (Chicago: University of Chicago Press, 1960); Bernice L. Neugarten, ed., *Middle Age and Aging* (Chicago: University of Chicago Press, 1968); and Matilda White Riley and Ann Foner, eds., *Aging and Society* (New York: Russell Sage, 1968).

35. The classic and still unsurpassed study of the aged in nonliterate societies is Leo W. Simmons, *The Role of the Aged in Primitive Society* (New Haven: Yale University Press, 1945).

36. A number of studies have reached this conclusion. For recent evidence on this point see Thomas Tissue, "Downward Mobility in Old Age," *Social Problems,* 18 (1970), 577–86.

37. Pauline Bart, *Depression in Middle-Aged Women* (Boston: Schenkman, in press).

38. See James Leslie McCary, *Human Sexuality* (Princeton: D. Van Nostrand, 1967), ch. 16; also Leon Salzman, "Recently Exploded Sexual Myths," in Donald L. Taylor, ed., *Human Sexual Development* (Philadelphia: F. A. Davis, 1970), pp. 194–204.

39. Ashley Montagu refers to this genetic difference in the title of his book, *The Natural Superiority of Women* (New York: Macmillan, 1968).

40. See Eleanor E. Maccoby, "Sex Differences in Intellectual Functioning," in Eleanor E. Maccoby, ed., *The Development of Sex Differences* (Stanford, Calif.: Stanford University Press, 1966), pp. 25–55.

41. Konrad Lorenz, *On Aggression* (New York: Harcourt, Brace and World, 1966; Robert Ardrey, *African Genesis* (New York: Atheneum, 1961) and *The Territorial Imperative* (New York: Atheneum, 1966).

42. For a review of the evidence on the genetic basis of human aggression by a variety of experts from different fields, see M. F. Ashley Montagu, ed., *Man and Aggression* (New York: Oxford University Press, 1968).

43. See the classic and original work on this topic by John Dollard and his associates, *Frustration and Aggression* (New Haven: Yale University Press, 1935).

3: TYPES OF HUMAN SOCIETIES

1. The work of V. Gordon Childe on technological development in human societies underlies much of this discussion. See *Man Makes Himself* New York: Mentor, 1951) and *What Happened in History* (Baltimore: Penguin, 1964). Another valuable source is Gideon Sjoberg, *The Preindustrial City: Past and Present* (Glencoe, Ill.: Free Press, 1960). See also the previously mentioned sociology text employing the technological evolution model by Gerhard Lenski, *Human Societies* (New York: McGraw-Hill, 1970).

2. See Emile Durkheim (1902), *The Elementary Forms of the Religious Life*, trans. by J.W. Swain (Glencoe, Ill.: Free Press, 1947); also Bronislaw Malinowski, *Magic, Science and Religion* (Glencoe, Ill.: Free Press, 1948).

3. Guy E. Swanson, *The Birth of the Gods: The Origin of Primitive Beliefs* (Ann Arbor: University of Michigan Press, 1960), ch. 3.

4. See Max Weber (1922), *The Sociology of Religion,* trans. and ed. by Ephraim Fischoff (Boston: Beacon Press, 1963), ch. 2.

5. See Robert Redfield, *Peasant Societies and Culture* (Chicago: University of Chicago, 1956).

6. See Gerhard Lenski, *Power and Privilege* (New York: McGraw-Hill, 1966), pp. 267–70.

7. See Robert Heilbroner, *The Making of Economic Society* (Englewood Cliffs, N.J.: Prentice-Hall, 1962).

8. For a brilliant analysis of the relationship between the theoretical contributions of the founders of sociology and the dominant ideologies, interests, and problems of the societies in which they lived, see Lewis Coser, *Masters of Sociological Thought* (New York: Harcourt, Brace and Jovanovich, 1971).

9. See Max Weber (1904), *The Protestant Ethic and the Spirit of Capitalism,* trans. by Talcott Parsons (New York: Scribner, 1958) for a classic statement of this thesis; also R. H. Tawney, *Religion and the Rise of Capitalism* (New York: Mentor, 1947) for a somewhat different interpretation.

10. Two classic social scientific statements of the changing nature of social relationships in urban, industrial societies are: Ferdinand Toennies (1887), *Community and Society,* trans. and ed. by Charles P. Loomis (East Lansing: Michigan State University Press, 1957); and Georg Simmel (1900), "The Metropolis and Mental Life," in *The Sociology of Georg Simmel,* trans. and ed. by Kurt H. Wolff (Glencoe, Ill.: Free Press, 1950), pp. 409–24.

4. VARIETIES OF FAMILY LIFE

1. William J. Goode, *World Revolution and Family Patterns* (New York: Free Press, 1963), p. 25.

2. Meyer F. Nimkoff and Russell Middleton, "Types of Family and Types of Economy," *American Journal of Sociology,* 66 (1960), 215–25; also M. F. Nimkoff, ed., *Comparative Family Systems* (Boston: Houghton Mifflin), ch. 3.

3. See William N. Stephens, *The Family in Cross-Cultural Perspective* (New York, Holt, Rinehart and Winston, 1963); also Stewart A. Queen and Robert W. Habenstein, *The Family in Various Cultures* (3d ed.; Philadelphia: Lippincott, 1967).

4. George Peter Murdock, *Social Structure* (Glencoe, Ill.: Free Press, 1949), pp. 36–37; also Dwight B. Heath, "Sexual Division of Labor and Cross-Cultural Research," *Social Forces,* 37 (1958), 77–79.

5. Goode, *World Revolution and Family Patterns,* ch. 3.

6. See Neil Smelser, *Social Change in the Industrial Revolution* (Chicago: University of Chicago Press, 1959).

7. For a superb account of transitional patterns in an industrializing society, see Oscar Lewis, *Five Families* (New York: Basic Books, (1959).

8. See Michael Young and Peter Willmott, *Family and Kinship in East London* (Baltimore: Penguin Books, 1962).

9. Herbert Gans, in *The Urban Villagers* (New York: Free Press, 1962), describes the effects of urban renewal on Italian extended families in the West End of Boston.

10. On the question of the modified extended family in the contemporary United States, see Marvin B. Sussman and Lee Burchinal, "Kin Family Network: Unheralded Structure in Current Conceptualization in Family Functioning," *Marriage and Family Living,* 24 (1962), 231–40; and Alfred M. Mirande, "The Isolated Nuclear Family Hypothesis: A Reanalysis, in John N. Edwards, ed., *The Family and Change* (New York: Knopf, 1969), pp. 153–63.

11. See Lee Rainwater, Richard P. Coleman, and Gerald Handel, *Workingman's Wife* (New York: MacFadden, 1962); also Michael Young and Peter Willmott, *Family and Kinship in East London,* Part II; and Irving Tallman, "Working-Class Wives in Surburbia: Fulfillment or Crisis," *Journal of Marriage and the Family,* 31 (1969), 65–72.

12. Frank E. Furstenberg, "Industrialization and the American Family: A Look Backward," *American Sociological Review,* 31 (1966), 326–37.

13. Sidney M. Greenfield, "Industrialization and the Family in Sociological Theory," *American Journal of Sociology,* 67 (1961), pp. 312–22.

14. See Sarah Davidson, "Open Land: Getting Back to the Communal Garden," *Harper's Magazine* (June, 1970), pp. 92–102.

15. See Robert F. Winch, "Permanence and Change in the History of the American Family and Some Speculation as to Its Future," *Journal of Marriage and the Family*, 32 (1970), pp. 6–15.

16. For an early formulation of the concept of functional prerequisites, see John W. Bennett and Melvin M. Tumin, *Social Life: Structure and Function* (New York: Knopf, 1948), ch. 4; also Talcott Parsons, *The Social System* (Glencoe, Ill.: Free Press, 1951).

17. Betty Yorburg, *Utopia and Reality: A Collective Portrait of American Socialists* (New York: Columbia University Press, 1969).

18. F. Ivan Nye and Lois W. Hoffman, *The Employed Mother in America* (Chicago: Rand McNally, 1963), ch. 24.

19. Arthur W. Calhoun, *A Social History of the American Family* (Glendale, California: Arthur H. Clark, 1917), I, 120.

20. Sigmund Freud (1921), "Group Psychology and the Analysis of the Ego," in *The Standard Edition of the Complete Psychological Works of Sigmund Freud,* trans. and ed. by James Strachey (24 vols.; London: Hogarth, 1953–66), XVIII, 69–143.

21. See Pamela H. Todd, "An Exploratory Study of Negro-White Intermarriage in Indiana," *Marriage and Family Living*, 26 (1964), 209–19.

22. Sigmund Freud (1914), "On Narcissism: An Introduction," in *The Standard Edition of the Complete . . . Works,* XIV, 87.

23. See Robert F. Winch, *The Modern Family* (New York: Holt, Rinehart and Winston, 1971).

24. George Peter Murdock, "Comparative Data on the Division of Labor by Sex," *Social Forces,* 15 (1937), 553.

25. See Talcott Parsons and Robert F. Bales, eds., *Family, Socialization and Interaction Process* (Glencoes, Ill.: Free Press, 1955), particularly the paper by Morris Zelditch Jr., "Role Differentiation in the Nuclear Family: A Comparative Study," pp. 307–59.

26. Alan C. Kerckoff, "Husband-Wife Expectations and Reactions to Retirement," *Journal of Gerontology,* 19 (1964), 510–16.

27. See Helena Z. Lopata, "The Life Cycle of the Social Role of Housewife," *Sociology and Social Research,* 51 (1966), 5–22; also Irwin Deutscher, "The Quality of Postparental Life" *Journal of Marriage and the Family,* 26 (1964), 52–60; and Harold Feldman, "Parenthood and Marriage: Myths and Realities," paper presented at Merrill Palmer Conference on the family, 1969.

28. Lee Rainwater, *Family Design: Marital Sexuality, Family Size, and Contraception* (Chicago: Aldine, 1965).

29. George P Murdock, "Family Stability in Non-European Cultures,"

Annals of the American Academy of Political and Social Science, 272 (1950), 197.

30. Paul Jacobson, *American Marriage and Divorce* (New York: Holt, 1959).

31. William J. Goode, "Family Disorganization," in Robert K. Merton and Robert Nisbet, eds., *Contemporary Social Problems* (3d ed., New York: Harcourt, Brace, and Jovanovich, 1971), p. 482.

32. Two good sources on the consequences of divorce are William J. Goode, *After Divorce* (Glencoe, Ill.: Free Press, 1956); and Paul Bohannon, ed., *Divorce and After* (New York: Doubleday, 1970).

33. For a recent summary of research on this topic and a comprehensive bibliography, see John P. Kirscht and Ronald C. Dillehay, *Dimensions of Authoritarianism: A Review of Theory and Research* (Lexington: University of Kentucky Press, 1967).

34. See, for example, Wesley Becker, "Consequences of Different Kinds of Parental Discipline," in Martin L. Hoffman and Lois W. Hoffman, eds., *Child Development Research* (New York: Russel Sage, 1964), pp. 169–208.

35. See Diana Baumrind, "Effects of Authoritative Parental Control of Child Behavior," *Child Development,* 37 (1966), 888–907; also Stanley Coopersmith, *The Antecedents of Self-Esteem* (San Francisco: Freeman, 1967); and William A. Westley and Nathan B. Epstein, *The Silent Majority* (San Francisco: Jossey-Bass, 1969).

36. See E. T. Prothro, *Childrearing in the Lebanon* (Cambridge: Harvard University Press, 1961); also Alex Inkeles, "The Modernization of Man," in Myron Weiner, ed., *Modernization* (New York: Basic Books, 1966), pp. 138–50; and Robert A. Le Vine, Nancy H. Klein, and Constance F. Owne, "Modernization and Father-Child Relationships in Nigeria," in Norman W. Bell and Ezra F. Vogel, eds., *A Modern Introduction to the Family* (New York: Free Press, 1968), pp. 558–74.

37. Margaret Mead, *Culture and Commitment* (New York: Natural History Press, 1970).

38. Frank F. Furstenberg Jr., "Industrialization and the American Family: A Look Backward," *American Sociological Review,* 31 (1966), 326–37; also Seymour Martin Lipset, "A Changing American Character?", in Michael McGiffert, ed., *The Character of Americans* (Homewood, Ill.: Dorsey Press, 1964), pp. 302–30.

5. AMERICAN VARIATIONS: ETHNIC CONTRASTS

1. See, for example, Robin F. Williams, *American Society* (2d ed.; New York: Knopf, 1965).

2. See Gerhard Lenski, *The Religious Factor* (New York: Doubleday Anchor, 1963).

3. David McClelland, *The Achieving Society* (New York: Van Nostrand, 1961), pp. 356–73; see also David L. Featherman, "The Socioeconomic Achievement of White Religio-Ethnic Sub Groups: Social and Psychological Explanations," *American Sociological Review*, 36 (1971), 207–22; and Howard Schuman, "The Religious Factor in Detroit: Review, Replication, and Reanalysis," *American Sociological Review*, 36 (1971), 30–48.

4. For a review of data from eighteen national surveys conducted from 1943 to 1965 on the relative economic, educational, and occupational status of Protestants and Catholics in the United States, see Norval D. Glenn and Ruth Hyland, "Religious Preference and Wordly Success: Some Evidence from National Surveys," *American Sociological Review*, 32 (1967), 73–85.

5. Research on the black middle-class family is scant and fragmented. See Thomas F. Pettigrew, *A Profile of the Negro American* (Princeton, N.J.: Van Nostrand, 1964), pp. 32–34; also Andrew Billingsley, *Black Families in White America* (Englewood Cliffs, N.J.: Prentice-Hall, 1968), pp. 131–37; E. Franklin Frazier, *Black Bourgeousie* (New York: Crowell-Collier, 1962); and John H. Scanzoni, *The Black Family in Modern Society* (Boston: Allyn and Bacon, 1971).

6. On this topic, see S. M. Miller and Pamela A. Roby, *The Future of Inequality* (New York: Basic Books, 1970), particularly ch. 1.

7. For a somewhat different definition of the concept and a more complex view of the process of assimilation, see Milton M. Gordon, *Assimilation in American Life: The Role of Race, Religion, and National Origin* (New York: Oxford, 1964).

8. This finding is from a 1971 survey reported in the New York *Times,* October 18, 1971, p. 1.

9. See *The Social and Economic Status of Negroes in the United States, 1970,* No. 38 (Washington, D.C.: Government Printing Office, 1970), p. 23.

10. Richard Centers, Bertram H. Raven, and Aroldo Rodrigues, "Conjugal Power Structure: A Re-examination," *American Sociological Review,* 36 (1971), 264–77.

11. Andrew Billingsley, *Black Families in White America,* p. 25.

12. George F. Boyd, "The Levels of Aspiration of White and Negro Children in a Non-Segregated Elementary School," *Journal of Social Psychology,* 48 (1952), 191–96; also Bernard C. Rosen, "Race, Ethnicity, and the Achievement Syndrome," in B. C. Rosen, H. J. Crockett, and C. Z. Nunn, eds., *Achievement in American Society* (Boston: Schenkman, 1969), pp. 131–53.

13. Hylan Lewis, "Culture, Class and Family Life Among Low-Income

Urban Negroes," in Arnold M. Rose and Herbert Hill, eds., *Employment, Race and Poverty* (New York: Harcourt, Brace and World, 1967).

14. See Scanzoni, *The Black Family in Modern Society,* ch. 5.

15. John Steinbeck, *Travels With Charley* (New York: Bantam Books, 1962). For a more balanced profile and one that belies nostalgic conceptions about the Mexican peasant heritage, see Oscar Lewis, *Five Families* (New York: Mentor Books, 1959), pp. 33–64; and *Life in a Mexican Village: Tepoztlán Restudied* (Urbana: University of Illinois Press, 1951).

16. A recent and monumental study of this largest Spanish-speaking minority in the United States, with an extensive bibliography, is Leo Grebler, Joan W. Moore, and Ralph C. Guzman, *The Mexican-American People* (New York: Free Press, 1970); see also Joan W. Moore with Alfredo Cuellar, *Mexican Americans* (Englewood Cliffs, N.J.: Prentice-Hall, 1970); and Arthur J. Rubel, *Mexican-Americans in a Texas City* (Austin: University of Texas Press, 1966).

17. Grebler et. al., *The Mexican-American People,* Part IV.

18. See Harry H. L. Kitano, *Japanese Americans* (Englewood Cliffs, N.J.: Prentice-Hall, 1969), pp. 77–78.

19. See William Goode, *World Revolution and Family Patterns* (New York: Free Press, 1963), pp. 328–33.

20. Ruth Benedict, *The Chrysanthemum and the Sword* (Boston: Houghton Mifflin, 1946); also Robert J. Smith and Richard K. Beardsley, eds., *Japanese Culture: Its Development and Characteristics* (Chicago: Aldine, 1962).

21. Harry H. L. Kitano, "Differential Child-Rearing Attitudes Between First and Second Generation Japanese in the United States," *Journal of Social Psychology,* 57 (1961), 13–16; also William Caudill and Helen Weinstein, "Maternal Care and Infant Behavior in Japanese and American Urban Middle-Class Families," in Rene Koenig and Reuben Hill, eds., *Yearbook of the International Sociological Association* (Switzerland: Broz, 1966.

22. Centers, Raven, and Rodrigues, "Conjugal Power Structure," *American Sociological Review,* 36 (1971), 264–77.

23. Gerald Meredith and Connie Meredith, "Acculturation and Personality Among Japanese American College Students in Hawaii," *Journal of Social Psychology,* 62 (1966), 175–82.

24. For a superb account of shtetl culture, see Mark Zborowski and Elizabeth Herzog, *Life Is With People* (New York: International Universities Press, 1951).

25. See, for example, Paul H. Williams, *South Italian Folkways in Europe and America* (New Haven: Yale University Press, 1938).

26. Two interesting case studies of this process as it took place, with some variation, in Minneapolis and in Providence, Rhode Island are Judith R. Kramer and Seymour Leventman, *Children of the Gilded Ghetto*

(New Haven: Yale University Press, 1961); and Sidney Goldstein and Calvin Goldschneider, *Jewish Americans: Three Generations in a Jewish Community* (Englewood Cliffs, N.J.: Prentice Hall, 1968).

27. See, for example, Fred L. Strodtbeck, "Family Interaction, Values and Achievement," in Marshall Sklare, ed., *The Jews: Social Patterns of an American Group* (New York: Free Press, 1958), pp. 147–65.

28. Milton Gordon, *Assimilation in American Life* (New York: Oxford University Press, 1964), chs. 7 and 8.

29. Robert F. Winch, Scott Greer, and Rae Lesser Blumberg, "Ethnicity and Extended Familism in an Upper Middle-Class Suburb," *American Sociological Review* 32 (1967), 265–72.

6. AMERICAN VARIATIONS: CLASS DIFFERENCES

1. A good sociological text on the general topic of social stratification in America is Harold M. Hodges Jr., *Social Stratification: Class in America* (Cambridge, Mass.: Schenkman Books, 1964). For a provocative and controversial analysis of post-World War II changes within the American middle class, see Joseph Bensman and Arthur J. Vidich, *The New American Society* (Chicago: Quadrangle Press, 1971).

2. Friends who are most highly valued tend to be of slightly higher status, in fact. See Edward O. Laumann, *Prestige and Association in an Urban Community* (Indianapolis: Bobbs-Merrill, 1966). In this connection, see also Edward Shils, "Deference," pp. 104–32 in John A. Jackson, ed., *Social Stratification: Sociological Studies* (Cambridge: Cambridge University Press, 1968).

3. A good anthology of papers on many aspects of working-class life is Arthur B. Shostak and William Gomberg, eds., *Blue-Collar World* (Englewood Cliffs, N.J.: Prentice-Hall, 1964). Two excellent interview reports on upper working-class family life are: Mirra Komarovsky, *Blue-Collar Marriage* (New York: Random House, 1964); and Lee Rainwater, Richard P. Coleman, and Gerald Handel, *Working Man's Wife* (Chicago: Oceana, 1959). A recent single-author synthesis of research on the white upper working class, with particular emphasis on the job situation, is Arthur B. Shostak's *Blue-Collar Life* (New York: Random House, 1969).

4. For data on the relationship between educational and economic resources and parental authority, see Thomas Ewin Smith, "Foundations of Parental Influence Upon Adolescence: An Application of Social Power Theory," *American Sociological Review*, 35 (1970), 860–73.

5. Thorstein Veblen (1899, 1912), *The Theory of the Leisure Class* (New York: Mentor, 1953), p. 42.

6. This applies also to the poor. See David Caplovitz, *The Poor Pay More* (New York: Free Press, 1963), p. 110.

7. For a clear and concise discussion of these two segments of the working class, see Gerald Handel and Lee Rainwater, "Persistence and Change in Working-Class Life Style," in Arthur B. Shostak and William Gomberg, eds., *Blue-Collar World,* pp. 36–41.

8. Lee Rainwater, *Family Design: Marital Sexuality, Family Size and Contraception* (Chicago: Aldine, 1965).

9. Michael Young and Peter Willmott, *Family and Kinship in East London* (Baltimore: Penguin Books, 1957); see also Hanna Gavron, *The Captive Wife: Conflicts of House-Bound Mothers* (New York: Humanities Press, 1966).

10. I am not including in this category large numbers of the aged and young people (graduate students, for example) who are classified as poor according to official government standards, but whose status is a function of stage in the life cycle rather than total life history.

11. Melvin L. Kohn, "Bureaucratic Man: A Portrait and an Interpretation," *American Sociological Review,* 36 (1971), 461–74.

12. Literally hundreds of statistical studies of the American poor have appeared within the past decade. Among the most perceptive qualitative studies that attempt to portray the life of the poor in depth, in various settings, are: Oscar Lewis, *Five Families* (New York: Basic Books, 1959); Harry M. Caudill, *Night Comes to the Cumberland* (Boston: Atlantic-Little Brown, 1963); Elliot Liebow, *Talley's Corner* (Boston: Beacon, 1967); Gerald D. Suttles, *The Social Order of the Slum* (Chicago: University of Chicago Press, 1968); and Ulf Hannerz, *Soulside* (New York: Columbia University Press, 1969).

13. For an excellent and up-to-date review of some of the research in this area, see Bernard C. Rosen, Harry J. Crockett Jr., and Clyde Z. Nunn, eds., *Achievement in American Society* (Cambridge, Mass.: Schenkman, 1969); see also Rose Laub Coser, ed., *Life Cycle and Achievement in America* (New York: Harper and Row, 1969).

14. David C. McClelland, *The Achieving Society* (New York: Van Nostrand, 1961), pp. 93, 105.

15. David C. McClelland and David G. Winter, *Motivating Economic Achievement* (New York: Free Press, 1969), p. 311.

16. This account is based on a variety of sources, few of which are concerned exclusively with the upper middle class. Two exceptions, one an excellent community study and one an interview study, are John R. Seeley, R. Alexander Sim, and Elizabeth W. Loosley, *Crestwood Heights* (New York: Basic Books, 1956); and John F. Cuber with Peggy B. Haroff, *The Significant Americans* (New York: Appleton-Century-Crofts, 1966).

17. T. Neal Garland, "The Better Half? The Male in the Dual Profession Family," paper presented at the annual meeting of the American Sociological Association, Washington, D.C., 1970; also Margaret M. Poloma and T. Neal Garland, "The Married, Professional Woman: A Study in Tolerance of Domestication," *Journal of Marriage and the Family*, 33 (1971), 531–40; and Lynda L. Holmstrom, *The Two-Career Family* (Boston: Schenkman, 1972).

18. William H. Whyte Jr., *The Organization Man* (New York: Doubleday Anchor, 1959).

19. See, for example, Herbert Gans, *The Levittowners* (New York: Pantheon Books, 1967).

20. Mary L. Walshok, "The Emergence of Middle-Class Deviant Sub-Cultures: The Case of Swingers," *Social Problems*, 18 (1971), 488–95; see also Gilbert Bartell, "Group Sex Among the Mid-Americans," *Journal of Sex Research*, 6 (1970), 113–30.

21. William H. Whyte Jr., *The Organization Man*, Part II.

22. E. Digby Baltzell, *The Philadelphia Gentlemen: The Making of a National Upper Class* (Glencoe, Ill: Free Press, 1958); *The Protestant Establishment* (New York: Knopf, 1964); and G. William Domhoff, *The Higher Circles* (New York: Vintage, 1970) are examples of attempts by social scientists to present documented profiles of this class.

23. A well-known example is Cleveland Amory. See *The Proper Bostonians* (New York: Dutton, 1947) and *Who Killed Society?* (New York: Pocketbooks, 1960); also Lanfranco Rasponi, *The International Nomads* (New York: Putnam, 1966).

24. G. William Domhoff, *The Higher Circles*, ch. 3.

25. See William J. Goode, "A Theory of Role Strain," *American Sociological Review*, 25 (1960), 483–96. A brief and useful general discussion of role theory, followed by a collection of papers on the family, illustrating the interactional type of role analysis, can be found in Jerold Heiss, ed., *Family Roles and Interaction: An Anthology* (Chicago: Rand McNally, 1968). Other sources that focus primarily on interactional data, with stronger emphasis on psychological dimensions, are Robert D. Hess and Gerald Handel, *Family Worlds* (Chicago: University of Chicago Press, 1959); and Gerald Handel, ed., *The Psycho-Social Interior of the Family* (Chicago: Aldine, 1967).

7. THE FUTURE OF THE AMERICAN FAMILY

1. The two views, and which is pessimistic and which optimistic, can be inferred from the titles of two recent books on the topic of advances in biological science and the possible effects of these advances on the family.

See Robert T. Francoeur, *Utopian Motherhood* (Garden City, N.Y.: Doubleday, 1970); also Paul Ramsey, *Fabricated Man* (New Haven: Yale University Press, 1970).

2. Several recent anthologies devoted entirely or in part to the topic of the future of the family are Herbert A. Otto, ed., *The Family in Search of a Future* (New York: Appleton-Century-Crofts, 1970); Richard E. Farson, Philip M. Hauser, Herbert Stroup, and Anthony J. Wiener, eds., *The Future of the Family* (New York: Family Service Association of America, 1969); Arlene S. Skolnick and Jerome H. Skolnick, eds., *Family in Transition* (Boston: Little, Brown, 1971); John N. Edwards, ed., *The Family and Change* (New York: Knopf, 1969).

3. Among the more impassioned pleas for the abolition of the nuclear family are: Barrington Moore Jr., "Thoughts on the Future of the Family," in Barrington Moore, *Political Power and Social Theory* (Cambridge: Harvard University Press, 1958), pp. 160–78; David Cooper, *The Death of the Family* (New York: Vintage, 1971); and Germaine Greer, *The Female Eunuch* (New York: McGraw-Hill, 1971).

4. Reported in *Newsweek,* February 22, 1971, pp. 61–63.

5. See Maren Lockwood Carden, *Oneida: Utopian Community to Modern Corporation* (Baltimore: Johns Hopkins Press, 1969), for a case study illustration of this process.

6. Margaret Mead and Frances Bagley Kaplan, eds., *American Women: The Report of the President's Commission on the Status of Women and Other Publications of the Commission* (New York: Scribners, 1965), p. 187.

7. See, for example, Herbert Simon, *The Shape of Automation* (New York: Harper and Row, 1965); also Herman Kahn and Anthony J. Wiener, *The Year 2000: A Framework For Speculation on the Next Thirty-Three Years* (New York: Macmillan, 1967).

8. Delbert C. Miller and William H. Form, *Industrial Sociology* (New York: Harper and Row, 1967), p. 815.

9. For evidence on this point, see Peter Townsend, *The Family Life of Old People* (Glencoe, Ill.: Free Press, 1957); also Yonina Talman-Garber, "Aging in Israel, A Planned Society," in Bernice T. Neugarten, ed., *Middle Age and Aging* (Chicago: University of Chicago Press, 1968), pp. 461–68; and Ethel Shanas and Gordon F. Streib, *Social Structure and the Family: Generational Relations* (Englewood Cliffs, N.J.: Prentice-Hall, 1965), Part V, particularly.

10. Bruno Bettelheim, *Symbolic Wounds* (rev. ed.; New York: Collier Books, 1962), p. 145.

INDEX

THE CHANGING FAMILY
Betty Yorburg

This concise but comprehensive introduction to the basic social institution of the family discusses what sociologists' diverse investigations tell us about its historical role and its probable future one in response to the pressure of rapid social change.

Dr. Yorburg begins by explaining the perspectives by which sociologists have sought to understand the family. She outlines the biological base of family life as it has been found in the study of both animal and human society, the human life cycle, and in sex differences. She then goes on to examine family roles with emphasis on the basic values underlying husband-wife and parent-child relationships throughout history as well as in different cultures, giving a sense that today's family is a product of long development and historical forces. The contemporary American family is viewed in its fascinating ethnic and class variety.

Using the findings of social science as a foundation, Dr. Yorburg assesses the behavior changes of young and old that are variously hailed or decried today. Such newly prevalent phenomena as the living together of unmarried middle-class young men and women, homosexual marriage, and communes assume a new meaning in the context the author provides. The last chapter addresses the future of the American family with specific predictions about courtship and love, the status of women, divorce, the generation gap, sexual behavior, child rearing practices, and other topics that are current causes of concern, confusion, despair, or optimism in American society today.

" . . . comprehensive without attempting to be encyclopedic, it is well written, it has logical organization. . . . " Jessie Bernard, author of *The Future of Marriage*

" . . . clear, thoughtful, and coherent. . . . This is an interesting and useful work, ably done." Gerald Handel, The City College and the Graduate School, The City University of New York

Dr. Betty Yorburg is Assistant Professor of Sociology at The City College of The City University of New York. She is the author of *Utopia and Reality: A Collective Portrait of American Socialists,* published by Columbia University Press in 1969.

COLUMBIA UNIVERSITY PRESS
NEW YORK AND LONDON